Dinner Table Debates

Harry Beeching

CONTENTS

Introduction
Parents and Populism

Growing up with two party loyalists for parents helps keep you informed; having them both come from opposite ends of the political spectrum keeps it interesting.

Mornings were spent listening to the early morning news over marmite on toast - nothing less controversial and polarising would do in our family! - The success of New Labour, The Iraq War, The Credit Crunch, the rise of austerity; everything was discussed in our household. Of course, this barrage of external and domestic opinion often came in the form of argument, and it didn't differ much from those we regularly hear across a family dinner table, even if you were spared the regularity of such discussions that mark out my family. Classic lines like "How are we going to pay for this?", "This would never have happened if Thatcher was still around!" and predictably, "This country really is going to the dogs," would regularly make an appearance over breakfast.

An unfortunate side-effect of this was my certainty that this level of debate was acceptable everywhere. Teachers in my final years of schooling would regularly have to deal with unfiltered opinions and very little tact when discussing even the most sensitive and personal issues. The shocked stares and gasps from my peers only spurred me to come up with ever more outrageous statements, from abolishing the NHS to banning all immigration. Fortunately, a mixture of my classmates getting bored of my attention-seeking and the occasional smack-down from my rather better-informed teachers resulted in a (slightly) more balanced approach to forming opinions, rather than the crucible of fire I was used to at home. In fact, I quickly realised that having my views challenged, either in person or in the occasional book I managed to struggle through, was not only essential for improving my arguments but also developing my views.

Being proved wrong is never a pleasant experience. I have dug enough holes trying to escape admitting such mistakes to know plenty about this, but fortunately there is occasionally a nugget of gold at the bottom. As with everything there is far more gain in learning from errors than repeating the same mistakes. In fact, one of the early motivations for writing this book was to test my ideas and my arguments. Sure enough, several times my research on a particular chapter had me questioning and reworking my thoughts and views on a particular issue. Aside from reminding me of how little we know about things we love to argue about, it also proved that allowing challenge to our views and incorporating new ideas is a great exercise, especially if you are able to defeat your own arguments before being proved wrong in public later!

Another motivation, in direct opposition to the first, was the growing lack of understanding and acceptance of opposing views that appears to be growing around the world today. Many commentators have argued that the world has become more polarised and angrier in recent years, as a few of these headlines prove:

On Brexit:

"If you believe in Britain vote leave"

- *The Daily Mail*

> *"The opportunities for people living here in the UK, will be more secure, will be better, if we're inside the European Union."*
>
> - *Theresa May*

"I'd vote to stay in the single market. I'm in favour of the single market."

> - *Boris Johnson, 2013*

On abiding to the Coronavirus lockdown, Spring 2020:

"Cummings is taking us for fools. He must resign."

– *The Daily Mail*

"Cummings should stay, he just acted as any good father would."

– *The Express*

On BLM protests:

"Marxist-chic BLM is a disturbing threat to racial progress."

– *The Telegraph*

"Premier League's Black Lives Matter support cannot be fleeting."

– *Eni Aluko, Sky Sports*

Slightly more detailed analysis was also conducted by Kings College London, proving that Brexit identity in particular had become more extreme and less accepting of the other side, even three years after the vote took place:

Despite the EU referendum taking place back in 2016, the proportion of people who very strongly identified with how they voted in the referendum increased between 2018 and the election year of 2019, from 44% to 55%. This far outweighed the proportion who felt very strong in their support of their political party, only 22%.

When asked to rate how they felt about the different sides of the debate out of 100, both sides are also equally negative about the other side. Leave supporters rated remain supporters at 23/100, just above Labour supporters at 21/100 and well above other leave supporters at 71/100.

Remain supporters had an even more negative rating for the other side, just 19/100, second only in coldness to Boris Johnson at 14/100 and well below 71/100 for other remain supporters.

The same is true in the US, where attitudes on everything from the size of the state to the environment have grown further apart in the last decade. Particularly noticeable in the past ten years has been the disappearance of the neutral. While there is a positive side to this, we can hope that this means a greater political involvement, with more people making a firm decision on their political allegiance, it also suggests an inability for either side to backdown from their opinions and thereby for compromises to be made. The delays to a second US support package for the Covid-19 crisis in 2020 is evidence of this, as is the seemingly never-ending 'negotiations' between the UK government and the EU. (Since I wrote this the UK government and EU commission have agreed a Brexit deal, however the need for regulatory standards to remain aligned in future mean there will be no sudden end to negotiations if we want to strike out and decide our own laws that diverge too far from those of the EU; strap in folks, there's plenty still to come!)

This lack of middle ground and the combative scenes on our televisions between ardent supporters of the different sides of Brexit, BLM and even debates over masks has led to growing talk of the infamous US 'culture wars' arriving on UK shores. Quickly a country with over 65 million inhabitants has been boiled down to just two caricatures, 'snowflake' millennial liberals and old 'boomer' racists. A deeper look reveals this is far from the truth, however, as the NATCEN Social Research Institute finds. Attitudes on the roles of women, homosexuality and even immigration have begun to converge since the turn of the century and has continued even with the advent of Brexit.

As an example, ask yourself what % of Conservative voters believe that the NHS is vital to the UK and should be protected, as opposed to Labour supporters?

The difference is under 5%, with 90% of Conservatives vs. 94% of Labour supporters agreeing with the statement. Even if we assume a degree of guilt-caused dishonesty, these results are remarkably close compared to the average media column or Question Time audience member.

Feelings on traditional gender roles continue to converge too. Since 2017, over 70% of people disagree with the view that men should be sole breadwinners and women should look after the home and family, up from under 40% in the 1980s.

Despite us being closer to each other's opinions than ever, I cannot be alone in having experienced dinner table debates on everything from the state of the economy to the acceptable quantity of mushrooms to be added to a meat pie, (for the record the answer is none according to my brother). With predictable regularity it seems many families, whether it's Christmas or seeing the in-laws, are predisposed to finding flashpoints of disagreement in everyday conversation.

I can happily report, however, that my immediate and extended family do still talk to each other, regardless of the level of disagreement around the breakfast, lunch and dinner table. For the most part, I think this holds for everyone else. Even topics that seem to create permanent divides between politicians and whole swathes of the nation such as race, immigration and the benefits system are generally forgiven between friends and family... eventually.

Unfortunately, this ability to empathise and accept other people's opinions doesn't seem to hold when we lose sight of the other side. Whether its walking into a voting booth, preaching to our own team, or arguing anonymously online, we are understandably more ready to personally attack or label each other unfeeling or stupid for holding the views we do.

I believe the crucial difference is that when we disagree with people we know; we accept this uncomfortable period due to the past agreements and shared positive experiences we have together. For example, I forgive my brother for his eating habits and he forgives my unhealthy interest in reading out the latest addition of The Economist to anyone who will listen because we'll both be playing hockey together tomorrow, (even if different rivalries emerge there; he is a skilful forward while my technique as a defender has been likened to a brick wall).

This level of mutual understanding has retreated in recent years, as populists across the world have harnessed strong feelings on a particular subject to win over supporters, and supercharging this to the extent that their supporters will allow them to do anything else as they are 'on my team'. Much like I continue to support Paul Pogba despite his repeated disappearances in big games as he is 'my player', supporters of such populism will forgive anything as long as the original argument is strong enough.

"I could stand in the middle of Fifth Avenue and shoot somebody, and I wouldn't lose any voters,"

- *Donald Trump*

But What is Populism?

It can be summed up with one of its most used caricatures, the Establishment. Populists rail against the Establishment, they promote the idea that those in power do not serve the people and so the people, as the ultimate power and soul of a nation, must push for change against their democratically elected overlords. That last phrase may sound like an oxymoron, how can a democracy elect an overlord? Populists would argue that hidden interests and foreign powers drive these people to renege on their promises to the electorate. Many, particularly on the wrong side of the 2016 US presidential campaign and the 2016 EU Referendum would accuse populists of doing the same.

Regardless of the motives of these groups, the populists and the Establishment, the way people vote tells us much about how society is working, or not working. The success of populism across the western world suggests a deep-rooted unhappiness with how things are currently run.

It is reasonable to assume populism has always been with us. From as early as the 19th century, members of the Russian middle-class organised movements that had begun to politicise the agrarian peasantry into pushing for reform against the governing elite. While the early 20th century saw the rise of Marxism and Fascism, which is characterised by a strong ruling elite and so not by definition populist, their methods for gaining control, particularly in the latter case by galvanising nationalistic feelings within Germany and setting the people against what was claimed as an elite manipulated and controlled by the Jews, is not dissimilar. This particularly horrible form of scapegoating populism is not unlike how some populist governments have claimed George Soros is at the heart of a Jewish conspiracy to flood Europe with immigrants and destroy countries:

Recep Tayyip Erdoğan, the Prime Minister of Turkey, has claimed Soros of being at the centre of a Jewish conspiracy to "divide and shatter" Turkey.

Meanwhile, in his home country of Hungary where he has spent hundreds of millions of dollars on free school meals, human rights and education, Soros was subjected to the following anti-Semitic stereotypes by the Hungarian Prime Minister of the time.

"We are fighting an enemy that is different from us. Not open but hiding. Not straightforward but crafty. Not honest but unprincipled. Not national but international. Does not believe in working but speculates with money. Does not have its own homeland but feels it owns the whole world," he said.

-       *Viktor Orban*

I am not suggesting we are staring down the barrel of another fascist uprising, nor a war in Europe. I think these actions merely point out that the tactics used today are no different from those of populists in previous eras, and to that end they are likely to create similar divides and require equally fierce challenge to avoid spreading further.

A part of the world that has seen more populism in the last century than anywhere is, arguably, Latin America. From as early as the Great Depression in 1929, countries across the continent were elected on populist mandates. For example, Getulio Vargas in Brazil, who maintained an image as a bulwark to the rise of communism in the country, but also Peron in Argentina and Ibarra in Ecuador.

Recent literature has suggested that this prevalence of populism is due to the mix of democratic elections, mixed with huge inequality across the region, making such calls for the people to rise up against the elites both effective in driving support from the masses but also having the institutions in place to take advantage of such popularity.

Populism in Europe has only recently made a comeback, following a period of calm after World War 2 where such attempts were regarded as dangerous to the hard-won peace in the region. Recent populist arguments have become far more impactful, largely those over self-determination in a world beyond our control. Brexit is an obvious example, where decades of blame from politicians on not having power over Brussels meant that taking back control became more important than whatever the latest scandal over a UKIP MEP was.

I vividly remember attending an EU referendum debate in which one of the pro-leave members was slated as a populist repeatedly by the pro-remain members. Whatever the argument, whether it be over immigration, jobs or Europe, the UKIP member would put up a wide variety of reasons for leaving, even suggesting to the Pro-remain members of the audience that they would put him out of the job if they sided with him. Meanwhile few positive stories came from the remain side, mostly stories of financial ruin and assertions that only racists would vote to leave. Whatever I felt of the pro-leave arguments and the accuracy of the pro-remain comments on economic damage, I remember saying to a friend in the bar afterwards that if the country had voted on the basis of that debate alone, we'd be leaving the EU tonight.

Super-Populism

The form of populism outlined above seems credible, but why has it grown from one specific topic (Brexit in the UK, Trump in the US) to cover almost all decisions in society?

As we saw from the statistics above, views on race and other social disputes are converging, yet we have seen the 'us vs. them' attitude seep into almost any public dispute:

"Remoaners are a miserable lot – they even moaned about England's World Cup winning streak."

- The Telegraph

"Whiny Bristol remoaners complain about their street being used in Theresa May's Brexit video."

- The Sun

In many ways this is understandable, as long as the cause you are supporting will achieve your aims, it makes sense to focus less on side issues that are less important to you. I don't worry about the possibility of being run over by a car walking to work as earning a living is more important than the fractional possibility of an accident. When you arrive at the metaphorical lights, however, the tables turn and the risk shoots up as the cars start rushing past. The danger for those in pursuit of a wider goal is that they become blind to a rising risk of the side issues outweighing the main goal.

This explains why the attempts by the opposition to the rise of populism (which after all, simply claims to just be doing what people want) has often fallen on deaf ears, as instead of understanding the position and finding a set of common ground, as we may do with an obstinate aunt or uncle, they have lazily held their own views as simply being morally superior and so above such discussions.

"Working class leavers were derided as turkeys voting for Christmas, but it is the middle-class Remainers who have been running around like headless chickens."

- *Dr Lisa McKenzie, Middlesex University*

But why care? Why don't we just discard these people, never visit the grandparents again, refuse to sit down with that friend who won't shut up about immigration or fishing?

One issue can be summed up with a simple but regular issue for couples; the 'I don't mind' minefield. In the same way that my girlfriend will insist she doesn't mind where we go for lunch and then looks at me sourly when I attempt to enter an outlet she doesn't like, if we do not engage with others on areas we disagree, we could find ourselves forced into a position we would have avoided if we had taken the chance (And a lack of engagement of national issues can result in far more long-lasting issues). Unlike my girlfriend you cannot go back into the voting booth and declare you've changed your mind and 'WE ARE NOT GOING TO THAT SAME COFFEE SHOP AGAIN, HARRY!'

A second and growing issue that has been brought into sharp relief by the Covid-19 Crisis is that if we allow our decisions to be guided on one major point of contention, we often limit the pool of available talent on other decisions and roles that should be decided on independently of the original argument. It also means that less time will be devoted to considering other potential risks and future challenges and dampens the power of those seen as the opposition on the first argument, to challenge and contribute to future discussions. Three out of the top four ministerial positions in Britain are currently held by Brexiteers, while previous Chancellors and decade-long loyalists to the party have been expelled. In the US, advisers supported Donald Trump's anti-mask campaign, the organising of the Tulsa election rally during a pandemic and even his debunked claim that his inauguration day crowd was larger than Obama's. This may be because the president saw 91% of his executive team leave (not including cabinet secretaries or times when multiple people in the same role left office), a higher turnover than any of his five predecessors. This requirement to be supportive of the singular issue of the day dilutes the talent pool and restricts constructive criticism. We must encourage understanding of different viewpoints, summed up well with the title of Doris Kearns Goodwin's book:

Team of Rivals: The political genius of Abraham Lincoln.

Looking at the impacts of the pandemic on different countries', we can see how allowing someone's view on one thing to taint our vision of them is damaging, worse if this is based on a characteristic they cannot impact, such as race. This has led to one dimensional leadership in many countries, and these are the places we see Covid has hit hardest.

For example, in the UK the budgetary response to the Coronavirus has been second only to Canada in the G7, yet, as of Spring 2021, the UK is set to see the highest contraction of its economy and the highest number of Coronavirus-linked deaths per 100,000. This has been blamed on a mixture of reasons but whether it is the slowness to lockdown, the poor rollout of the track and trace system, and the repeatedly last minutes decisions on restriction guidelines, much of this boils down to the divisions in the country paralysing Westminster from acting quickly and with confidence, terrified of igniting the divisions that have grown throughout the country.

"policymaking in the UK is still stuck in the old world in which the two subjects [health and wealth] are kept apart" …

"The government started out reluctant to lock down the economy, misperceiving what is in reality a short-term investment in the benefits of a virus free economy as a 'cost' to be traded off against lives lost."

- Tony Yates, Former Head of Monetary Policy Strategy, The Bank of England

Meanwhile in the US, the previous president refused to wear a mask and was encouraging people to discard the advice of international, 'establishment' authorities such as the WTO and WHO long before the rise of the Coronavirus. In Brazil, President Jair Bolsonaro joined anti-lockdown protests in the capital, while government medical advisers were sacked. The failure of these populist leaders to encourage their populations (if they tried at all) to believe in the institutions and experts they had been criticising for months shows the danger of allowing such scale of division to take root in a country.

While the global economy has started to recover and vaccines continue to be rolled out across the world, we are yet to see the full impact of this crisis. The end of job retention schemes, sustained supply chain issues and the bite of higher taxation are still to be fully realised. We must act now to change this pattern of emotion over information and enact policies based on merit and not their adherence to common political or cultural lines.

Tackling Tribalism

A good place to start, as with any argument, is to find the source of disagreement, rather than focussing on the symptoms. For example, many household tiffs can start over something simple, such as who took the bins out last, or who forgot to turn the oven off, but arguing over a single action avoids facing the cause of these disputes, that often both sides feel they do more around the house and the other should muck in more.

The EU Referendum was held in 2016, but anti-EU sentiment has lasted as long as the institution itself. Margaret Thatcher is often remembered sporting an uncharacteristically flamboyant, pro-EU jumper but had previously held views on the block that makes the garment look as out of place in her belief system as it must have done with her famously austere wardrobe. She and many in her party argued against the reunification of Germany and then the greater integration of Europe. Even when the party accepted defeat and agreed to the Maastricht Treaty in 1993, anti-EU sentiment remained in a young Conservative MP who left the party to join one more aligned with his Eurosceptic beliefs; Nigel Farage.

So, if anti-EU sentiment is nothing new, why did such populism rise to dominance in 2016?

The answer I believe has more in common with our dining rooms than with any foreign parliament.

He's Got More Than Me!

My father can often be late to the dinner table. He claims it is because he is working, even if he was spotted minutes before in front of the television. He will then spend a further 5 minutes scrutinising the portion size of each member of the group before declaring that someone has been given more than him. It's all fun and games until someone attempts a redistribution of resources, namely by nicking the nearest Yorkshire pudding or roast potato.

The thought of losing out and seeing someone scoffing more of your favourites than you is a powerful emotion. Many social experiments have seen how people react more strongly to inequality than most emotional stimuli. Even apes have been seen to express anger at receiving an unfair amount compared to their peers.

Inequality has not just been a cause of arguments in my household, but across the country, and since inequality rose in the 80s and 90s, populism and anger have risen with it. UK election statistics from the House of Commons Library show that the percentage of vote share going to parties outside of Labour, Conservative and Liberal Democrats had been rising in England from 1987, peaking in 2015, just before the Referendum. This dissatisfaction with the Establishment can be seen in Scotland too, with the rise of the SNP over the same period.

Meanwhile data from the ONS and World Health and Income Databases show that income inequality has been on the rise in many parts of the English-speaking world. This matches closely with the rise of populism. For instance, the UK and the US in particular have seen inequality rise as well as Trump and Brexit appearing from seemingly nowhere, while in continental Europe inequality has flatlined, and populist parties like those of Marine Le Pen and Catalonia have been defeated or at least hamstrung by more liberal partners, as was the case in Italy over the same time period.

This does much to explain the unrelenting support for populist projects like Brexit and Trump. It is not that the EU, immigration or China have suddenly become any more of a problem than they were already, but that our societies have become more unequal. These extreme political decisions were seen, and still are today, as a means to correct issues, sparked in the previous century.

Before we jump too quickly to pronounce policy makers of the late 70s and 80s the architects of division today, it is worth noting that while inequality increased during this period, so did economic growth in many of these countries.

The policies of Margaret Thatcher and Ronald Reagan, while controversial at the time and remain so today, were succeeded by almost a decade of growth, reaching post-war records by end of the period.

The policies of deregulation, privatisation and greater competition coincided with the UK moving from being consistently below the euro area in terms of economic growth throughout the 60s and 70s to, not only outperforming the area as a whole, but even overtaking many of the stronger economies of the time that we like to envy today, such as Germany.

This displays two characteristics of market-based systems that often appear to come hand in hand. Inequality and economic growth have been rising in parallel since the industrial revolution. Some of this is obvious and more palatable, such as moving from purely agrarian economies, where 90% of the population are farmers and earn roughly the same, to manufacturing, leading to wealthier urban workers and a growing number of business leaders. However, inequality and growth can spiral in a less acceptable way.

If government spending on things like social security is reduced to pay for reducing taxes, incomes at the top can rise without a loss of productivity at the bottom. This is because an unemployed worker is not productive and so in a purely numbers (and very cold, heartless) sense, removing benefits from the unemployed to spend elsewhere will increase output. This is not popular in most modern societies and rightly so. As a result, we must make sure that inequality and growth rise in a controlled way, allowing for meritocratic and technological inequality, rather than by pumping up our overall output at the expense of those at the bottom.

While a compromise might be possible, as displayed by the Nordic countries, with Norway, Sweden and Denmark regularly making their way into the top ten for GDP per capita and bottom ten for income inequality, this sadly was not the course set by the new Labour government in 1997, whose election was arguably the first tangible sign that the status-quo was under fire. Inequality continued to rise until 2010, where the global financial crisis paused this increase by helpfully making everyone poorer. And recent evidence by the ONS shows that inequality has continued to fall since:

"FYE 2011 and FYE 2020, original income inequality fell by 1.7 percentage points to 49.7%. This release shows that the proportion of low-paid hourly jobs fell from 21.3% in 2010 to 16.2% in 2019. Furthermore, while the pay differential between the 5th and 95th percentile of full-time employees was 4.7 in 2019, this has fallen from 5.4 since 2010."

– Income Inequality in the UK, ONS, 2020

So has Brexit done what I believe in reality it set out to achieve? Have we seen not a demand for racism to make a return as many have lazily coined this, but a reallocation of income to further reduce the crony capitalism we unleashed in the 80s, to be replaced not by another system, but a more meritocratic society where only the hard working become rich and push the country's narrative?

While the data on this is far from complete, there is little evidence that Brexit has so far had a marked change on overall income inequality, for better or worse. What has changed is that since 2016 incomes have grown in the areas that the average man or woman in the street are unlikely to be impressed by.

Arguably the inequality that is hardest to stomach, wealth, the inequality that comes not from someone's work today but from their or their family's work in the past, is rising. This old money is far less productive than the new. It is conservative, less likely to invest in new technology and prefers to look for ways to influence politicians to protect its position than allow challenge, leading to the popular image of zombie firms. These are companies that earn enough to stay afloat and repay loan interest, but require public support to pay back their debts and become truly profitable.

An example of this political lobbying would be the dispute between black cab drivers and Ride-hailing apps in London. The previous ban of a particularly famous brand was based upon alleged malpractice by the Company, and yet it has not been banned elsewhere. Surely if the Company is failing to protect its customers' safety and employees' wages, surely it should be banned across the country? This highlights the impact of political influence. In a place like London where there are enough cabbies to influence policy makers, ride-hailing apps are banned. In Leamington Spa where I often used both forms of transport to get home from the pub, there were far fewer cabs and no such ban. Some may argue that these companies' loss making anti-competitive business model is a good excuse to ban them from such areas, but if so, why was this not the reason given by London, and not the reason to roll out a country-wide ban?

The recent GameStop saga sheds more light on the shady practice of lobbying government for protection, rather than working for profits. As of January 30th, 2021, shares in the bricks and mortar gaming shop were up 1,587%, meaning that it was then worth $150, up from $4 a year before. Even more surprising is that the surge had nothing to do with the success of GameStop. Hedge funds had bet heavily that the company's share price would fall, and so when an army of retail investors (code for normal people who have a go at investing casually on the weekends) started piling into the stock, these funds started losing billions. The managers of these funds started to buy stocks to cover their losses, further inflating the price. Within days the CEOs of US stock exchanges and Hedge Funds were calling for something you'd never thought you'd hear from Wall Street executives, regulation. They claimed that the activity of these retail investors was market manipulation that needed to be limited. The fact that it is now over ten years since market manipulation led to a crash and the biggest bailout of the financial sector in history should not stop us from seeing the irony in these claims. Managers claiming now that such actions are dangerous were making similar moves earlier in the year. Claims by billionaire investors about the hotel industry crashing during the pandemic, were followed by those same investors buying hotel stock at the bottom of the market, before racking up billions as the hysteria they had created abated.

Another common problem of established interest and old money is when it is funnelled by mutual funds and other money managers into making short-term returns at the expense of the wider country's interests, such as Phoenix's take-over of Rover. By cutting costs in the short term the company was able to sell Rover a profit but ultimately doomed the car maker by reducing its ability to produce the quality of cars to rival the likes of German and Japanese carmakers.

The worst symptom of wealth inequality by far to anyone who has worked a day in their lives (my father might like to say otherwise but I think most of us would fall into this bracket) is of course, the rich kids.

We've all been there when they turn up late, don't bother getting involved in the class, seminar, or meeting, and swan off again. Normally you console yourself by thinking that these people won't benefit from this, they won't get the grades, the promotion, etc. But then you find out that she's being groomed to take over the family business, or that he's gone on a 5-year holiday to the far east to 'find himself'.

There are few things that grate more than someone who benefits through no work on their part, but this is the kind of inequality we have faced in the West since the 1980s. Since Thomas Piketty wrote "Capital in the Twenty-First Century" in 2013, we may have seen income inequality plateau in the UK, suggesting an end to over 30 years of increasing unfairness driving anger, but we have also seen the growth rate of wealth outstripping earnings (think the value of houses versus pay rises). The amount of 'unearned income' more than doubled during the period of austerity, meaning the top 10% saw their overall earnings (outside of worked income) double from an average of £19,000 to £38,000, while average incomes stagnated at £25,000.

All the while as the total size of the pie rises, the difference in slice size becomes more obvious, even if the ratio of the cuts have stayed the same. For example, even if relative wealth inequality has stayed still, the gap in absolute terms between richest and poorest households' deciles has widened dramatically, from £1.9m to £2.5m, over the past decade.

This growing inequality is therefore not just more obvious, but more distressing to those left behind. No wonder then that areas from Birkenhead near Liverpool to Havant on the south coast, areas with particular spatial inequality, where you can throw a stone from a council house and hit a mansion, voted leave so emphatically in 2016.

And what of those more well-to-do, white-washed areas that voted Brexit? The top 10% of the country leaves a lot of people in the 90%, and for those not blessed with unearned income streams, 2007/8 marked a huge drop in living standards. While still relatively well-off compared to the vast majority of the country, the remaining middle classes, largely white, male, approaching or at pension age, are seeing their characteristics attacked. Whether it's Britain's got talent showcasing BLM activists or Sky axing Matt LeTissier, all around them they see their group attacked. As their earnings have stagnated, they see those beneath them obtaining greater representation. While they are far from being overtaken, that mix of jealousy from the top 10 pulling away, while seeing those at the bottom get the opportunity to grab more of the pie, they have sent a message to the government that they have been left behind too, even if in an absolute sense they are better off.

As a result, I believe this flow of populism is only set to increase as the worst types of inequality in our society increases further, and this must be remedied before another wave of change is brought about that is not directly linked to its symptoms.

The real failure in my eyes is not the rise of populism, as this is just a symptom of unhappiness with the current governance model, but the inability of those in power to hear the complaints of the people, engage with the issues and plan a response before having change thrust upon them. Whether you supported Brexit or not, few would argue the way it has panned out has been a shambles. Had the issues with our membership been identified sooner, corrections or even a more orderly exit could have been organised, avoiding the bad blood that has built up between the two sides. Even more importantly, had we used this energy to oppose unfair inequality in our society, rather than picking fights with innocent bystanders, then maybe we would be solving the real issues of inequality in a productive way, rather than indirectly through EU-Exit.

1

Making a Circle of a Horseshoe

Even the most ardent adversaries often have more in common than anyone might guess. 'Opposites attract' is a corny phrase, but one that is regularly the case and, despite what might come across on the TV screen, is often truer in public discourse than in private.

A very close friend of mine is in the unfortunate position of supporting Manchester City, or at least it was unfortunate until it was bought by a multi-billionaire in 2008, which made the football club effectively owned and backed by the nation state of Abu Dhabi. Since then, the fortunes of the two Mancunian clubs have changed somewhat with City winning ten major honours in the last ten years and United not having won a Premier League title since the 12/13 season. Yet this change in success rate has not altered how often we discuss the sport, regularly picking over the bones of City's latest victim or United's most recent disappointing result. As a United fan, I regularly criticise the City team, fight tooth and nail to include more United players whenever we try to form a fantasy team from both Mancunian sides and, of course, claim City were just lucky whenever they win anything! [At the time of writing United seem to be closing the gap, but I won't touch on their recent form for fear of jinxing anything!]

The ability a particular winger for Man City, is a good example of our intense level of disagreement. My friend will often rave about his ability on the ball, his speed and his goalscoring record, to which I will immediately retort that anyone in that team could have a good goal scoring record if he stood near the goal long enough. Then I go on to claim that the player's less prolific international career is testament to his achievements being linked to his team. This has led to a level of commitment from both sides to highlight every piece of brilliant skill and every howler the player produces, to the point where I can be happily watching a game on television at home and receive a text from said friend to inform me that the man's last goal was amazing and that I don't know anything about football. A common response is usually a short compilation of all of the winger's dives in the last 12 months. This back and forth has continued even across continents, with his messages coming in from as far away as America to continue the feud.

One must wonder at this point why we are still talking to each other. Supporting opposing teams, brutally picking out each other's team's flaws, sending text barrages every time a goal that has nothing to do with our individual efforts goes in; this can't be fun for either party!

The truth is, however, that there is a rather obvious link between us that is far stronger than the differing allegiances to our clubs that divide us; our love of football, and apparently a good argument about which team is better.

The same holds for political parties, both here in the UK and further afield.

The Problem with the political compass

A regular occurrence on Facebook, alongside the questionnaires which find out which type of doughnut you are, is the political compass test. The premise is that proponents of the extremes of left and right, authoritarian and liberal, are further away from each other than from those in the centre.

The compass places the left and right of politics on opposing sides, suggesting the two will be the last to agree on any subject. However, history teaches us that this line is really more of a horseshoe than anything else and, like football supporters, while we may disagree strongly over the details, the overall message is often mutually shared between sides.

I first noticed this when reading Ha-Joon Chang's book on how the roots of the fundamental economic governance theories, capitalism and socialism, began. Before the Industrial Revolution, production was isolated in cottage industries, with low levels of productivity and basic concepts such as specialisation and economies of scale not in use. These terms sound complicated but, for those of us lucky enough to live in the 21st century, these concepts are very familiar. Just ask any pizza chain employee.

Walking into your average pizza place, usually in my case to get the discount for collection, you'll see no single employee completes a whole pizza by themselves. One member starts with the dough, rolling it out to the desired thickness. The next adds the toppings, before passing it on to the member of staff running the oven. Finally, the finished product is boxed up by a final employee who passes it to the customer. This division of jobs means each individual becomes better at their stage of production and improves the quality of each step of the process, ending with a better pizza, made in a shorter time. It also makes training quicker as you only need to teach one step for an employee to become useful. This example can be extended further, as these employees didn't grow the wheat to make the dough, or pick the tomatoes for the sauce, or mine, refine and mould the metal to make the oven. All these skills are split up to make the process more efficient.

While some of this existed before the Industrial Revolution it was still very possible for workers, particularly in rural areas, to grow all their own food, chop their firewood for heat, maintain their houses and produce any additional products they needed, such as clothing. This all changed in Britain but why and when exactly is still uncertain.

While the spark of revolution is debated, it is my belief that events that led to the UK's dominance were set in motion almost a century earlier, during the English Civil War. The end of the absolute power of the Throne resulted in the ability of, while not all the people, but a larger set of the population, to grow wealth independently, without interference from the divine right of kings. This led to there being greater value in innovation and return on investing in projects to stimulate wealth.

The first place this can be seen is in agriculture. Before the Industrial Revolution, land was worked and shared by individual families who depended on the common land for their survival. This resulted in inefficient working processes and overuse of the same parcels of land. Thinking back to pizzas, this is the equivalent of asking each employee to set up their own pizza stand within a common area and produce their own pizzas from start to finish. Even with ovens and produce supplied, having to learn every part of the process before being able to make a single pizza is a slow way to produce, and having several pizza stands in the same area is excessive. Customers will have to guess where to go from the multitude of options, and given a single producer will quickly be overwhelmed with orders, customers will have to try several stands at busy times, before finding a smaller queue, or simply not bother looking in which case there will be a long queue at one stand and nobody at another. Before the Industrial Revolution this led to what has been coined 'the Tragedy of the Commons', where multiple families would work common land but act as individuals rather than as a single organisation. This meant they couldn't afford to leave sections of the land for a season to allow the soil to recover from use, and because output was not shared, instead of everyone working on the best land to produce crops and leaving barren land for other uses, such as manufacturing, everyone was forced to use whatever land they could, with the best land quickly becoming overused and people being forced to use progressively substandard land as populations grew.

Greater freedoms following the Civil War gave rise to more opportunities for wealth creation over hoarding income (known as Mercantilism). This incentivised those with wealth to purchase land through the Enclosure Acts. This was a process where lots of small holdings owned by the King and the nobility, but run by subsistence farmers, were bought up and restructured so that families no longer lived on and worked one patch of land but instead were part of a larger workforce that maintained one big section of land. Now, instead of lots of small ownerships, large farms were created. Once a farmer was not dependent on all his land producing food to sustain himself, as enough could be produced from a piece of the larger farm he had bought, he could afford to use crop rotation, had the money for fertiliser, could invest in new farming technologies; the list continues. This eradication of the Tragedy of the Commons resulted in increased agricultural capacity that meant urbanisation could occur without starvation as fewer farmers were needed for the same output. This defeated the Malthusian prediction that any increase in wealth would lead to a growing population that would outstrip food output. This coincided with greater technological advancement, catalysed by the same greater level of freedom to innovate without fear of losing any returns to the British Monarchy. Spinning jennies and the cotton gin allowed workers to produce more in smaller spaces, creating demand for workers in cities just as enclosure provided a greater supply of cheap labour. These improvements lead to greater worker productivity, allowing wages to rise across the Country. A worker that produces ten times the products for the owner to sell can be paid ten times more, assuming benevolence on the owner's part or collectivisation of workers of course. As wages rose, so did consumption, coupled with greater amounts of produce to trade. This led to a spiral of increased output and incomes that pushed the first Industrial Revolution.

This is a child-friendly depiction of enclosure. The reality is that many of the new landowners lobbied the UK Parliament and used their existing wealth to gain land, often unfairly, while many people who had worked the land for generations were displaced to work in factories. The process of enclosure was far from a perfect picture of employer-employee relations, but it did spur productivity in agriculture to levels never before seen and was essential in providing the spare capacity needed to fill the factories and drive the growth that mark this crucial part of economic history.

Therefore, the image of coal and steam driving the Industrial Revolution is arguably overplayed, with greater worker mobilisation contributing more to the beginning of the Revolution. In many ways, the Revolution was less about new technology and more about managing the existing resources, land and labour, in a more efficient and productive way, which allowed for investment and the research into new technologies to thrive. For instance, being able to produce more manufactured goods would have been no use without the available workers to run the machines. Without enclosure increasing productivity in agriculture, the technological advancements of the time would not have been utilised as the men and women required to work the machines could not have been spared from the fields without a resulting famine.

Mercantilist Mochas

The Industrial Revolution led to what was, at the time, an unprecedented level of growth, that changed the landscape of Britain from a green and pleasant land to one of dark satanic mills. This widening gap between Britain in the 18th century and the rest of Europe was as a result of greater political and economic freedom than on the Continent, where new ideas were slower to take root, even in economies moving faster to modernise their agriculture than the UK. The fundamental change following the emergence of specialisation and the end of the Tragedy of the Commons was the move from

Mercantilism to a greater emphasis on free trade. Mercantilism has had a renaissance in recent years but is still a relatively uncommon term. It can be summed up by three coffee shops. (You can tell where I've been while writing this – nothing but coffee and fast-food analogies!)

All three shops are profit driven, but one takes an aspect of this to the extreme by refusing to buy anything from local suppliers and relying only on home grown ingredients. In this (granted imaginary and weird coffee shop) the owners have the space to grow enough coffee beans and collect enough water to make black coffee. While this would go down well with me, I imagine the vast majority of you are probably wondering about milk, sugar or perhaps (in my partner's case) a nice slice of cake or two on the side. However, the shop's refusal to bring in goods from outside means black coffee is all you're getting! Understandably, this firm's success is limited by the number of caffeine addicts like me, but also the land available to grow more coffee beans. Given the quality of the coffee cannot be improved, quantity is all the owners can go for and even this will eventually be limited by the space the owners have available.

In the second shop, the owners are a little more relaxed on costs. They buy in milk and sugar, and even some other drinks and snacks to offer Joe Public. They own roughly the same land and can only grow coffee beans, but the second shop has traded some income for ways of improving its offering, such as a supply of milk or sugar. As a result, a greater range of tastes will enter shop number two. I think in most cases people would probably be happy to pay more for coffee with some milk or indeed anything but bitter black coffee. As a result, even with higher costs, the higher price and number of coffees sold, profits will probably be higher at shop two.

One issue remains, however, in that the second shop is still run by cash hoarders. All the profits, after deductions for basics like milk and other coffee producing expenses, are kept back like shop one. As a result, it doesn't expand, and it doesn't pay for extra roasters, grinders and new espresso machines. Therefore, while it has a greater range of coffee and other goods available, over time it will fall behind in terms of delivery speed and grade of the coffee it can produce compared to, say, shop three which invests in better quality and more coffee producing goods.

My possible lack of knowledge of coffee making aside, this simplified example illustrates the three economic models that existed at the cradle of the Industrial Revolution. Shop One is the likes of France at the time, heavily Mercantilist, led by a monarch who had absolute power and demanded that gold (or wealth as he saw it) be hoarded within the country. He viewed trade as a zero sum game with imports (like milk and sugar) should be minimised while exports (coffee) should be maximised. This was heavily limited by the range of exports available to France and others like it, as well as the additional problem that if you simply hoard your income, your living standards don't improve. I might save up some money at the end of each month, but until I spend it on a bigger house, better healthcare or a rainy-day deposit at a local bank in case I am made unemployed (all of which involve purchasing a service from someone else) I do not materially gain in any way.

Shop Two is the Netherlands, arguably the favourite for an Industrial Revolution at the start of the 18th century. It had a less severe view of mercantilism, trade was okay, even imports. But crucially, this was only accepted on the basis that the imports supported the growth of better-quality exports and thus more profits which were then hoarded. As a result, the investment in new technologies and better management of resources (like factories over individual workers) did not occur.

Meanwhile in the UK, due to its more liberal political system and openness to new ideas and businesses, investment was much higher during this period. This led to the discovery of new technology and, which together with the greater freedom of trade led in turn to the First Industrial Revolution.

Far from a socialist paradise, the nobility in Britain did own three quarters of the wealth, however, in France this was just a third and in Russia nobles held almost no power, with the monarch still all but omnipotent. In England, aristocratic status was within reach of anyone with enough money or who had served his (as opposed to her at the time sadly) country sufficiently, particular examples including General John Churchill, ancestor of Winston, and Horatio Walpole, father of Robert Walpole, Britain's first Prime Minister, both of whom rose from humble beginnings to enter the nobility. This relatively higher level of social mobility (and relatively does a lot of lifting here) gave the middle classes in the UK the incentive to invent new ideas and products. At the same time the venture capitalists of the nobility provided the funding to make use of these inventions to push growth and drive the Industrial Revolution. Their compatriots in Continental Europe, meanwhile, were losing their status for entering into working pursuits. This led to a supremely high level of inequality and a correspondingly low level of social mobility which contributed to growing resentment in the rest of the population, rising to a crescendo during the French Revolution.

Back to Horseshoes

So why have I been rattling on about the Industrial Revolution? About pizza and coffee?

One reason is that I am a nerd for the former and an addict for the latter. However, what makes this interesting for others (hopefully!) is that collectivisation under the Soviet Union, the dawn of socialist and ultimately communist planned economies, the antithesis to the market economies I described above, achieved the same results as the capitalists in Britain. The forced movement of agricultural workers into cities as the communist party took control of their lands, forced industrialisation in the same way as had been incentivised by the capitalists before them.

The birth of what appear to be the opposite ends of the economic compass are remarkably similar. What had started with economics quickly shifted to include political views, coming to a head during the Cold War. Both sides had seen massive growth as a result of greater centralisation of land and labour, allowing for specialisation and urbanisation, but whereas one group believed in entrepreneur-led pizza places, the other believed in government-run pizzas stands.

This historical competition was potentially destructive, to the point of nuclear war then, while today's issues thankfully have not reached this level of risk, it has proved very effective at dividing people. While previously the battle with opposing politics in a foreign country caused only minor disagreement between the populace, today, families are split over economic and political left and right. As we saw in the last chapter, disagreements previously seen in the US are on the rise in the UK and has led to ever more extreme positions being taken, leading to dangerous rhetoric and horrific acts such as the murder of an elected MP from the UK in 2016.

Despite this, we can still see the similarities that drive these vastly differing opinions. Traditional members of the left and right in the UK campaigned for Brexit on the basis of protecting British jobs from immigration and foreign companies.

More recently both sides have come together to campaign for businesses to reopen following the first wave of Coronavirus in order to protect low pay workers. Traditional right-leaning commentators have been accused of campaigning for businesses to be allowed to open, not to protect worker's pay, but to disguise their true motive of protecting business rents. However, this further proves the point that while the motives may differ, the underlining view that economic damage should also be considered, not just the immediate health of the population, is similar even between traditional opponents.

One need only look at both side's view of the BBC and the 'mainstream media' to see how extreme opposites often hold similar views, especially against the centre.

"It's the BBC's rightwing bias that is the threat to democracy and journalism"

-       *The Guardian*

"BBC is a platform for left-wing and Remainers"

-       *The Express*

And data from The UK in a Changing Europe show that the general population is even closer on economic values than the politicians!

We can see from these examples, whether it's the development of entire nations, or the latest viral argument on LBC, that the reality is that the ordinary people on the street hold views much closer to each other than first appears. Therefore, our current division is instead a result of over-hyping the minority of differences that exist between us.

By stepping back from the headlines and focussing on what unites us we are more likely to discuss where we differ in a productive way rather than shouting at each other over the extremes. We should enjoy speaking about football, but not get over invested in Manchester City's performances! This will help us ignore the extremes put forward by the press and help us see the real differences between people on our side and others, we may even start to question our own side and develop our own opinion. Hopefully this will enable us to work together to control issues that affect us all, such as the Pandemic, rather than delaying any progress by arguing over masks.

Much like my family meals, where usually we are only one joke away from putting our differences aside, I believe with the right push in the right place, some understanding of others' troubles and not looking to score points at every opportunity, the same can be achieved on a national level. With this realisation that our differences and division are shallower than might first appear, In the following chapters I will propose a number of considerations for how we might pierce this veil and meet each other in the middle.

Failing to do so will result in us failing to meet the challenges of tomorrow, and suffering the consequences together, even if we remain divided.

2
Washing Up, Going to the Gym and Other Things I'll Do Tomorrow

After the meal, whether we have argued or not, one constant is, of course, the washing up - arguably my least favourite of daily chores. I will often convince myself that what the dishes really need is a good soak overnight before tackling them the next day. Even if the pots and pans show no sign of having any remaining food baked on, they'll go straight in the sink. I can persuade myself that a chopping board will need soaking if I try hard enough! This internal argument is of course just a thinly veiled excuse to get me out of the work I don't want to do. My partner, in opposition, would rather wash up and have the food go cold than leave dishes overnight - outrageous! Sadly, my full-proof soaking plan has one minor side-effect. I am in no more a mood for cleaning dishes first thing in the morning than I am at night.

I have cursed my past-self multiple times while looking for a clean piece of cutlery to eat my breakfast with. The truth is that while a small voice inside me knows when I abandon the washing up that it would be better just to face up to it, a much

33

larger voice is shouting that I should put my feet up and watch Netflix. As if by magic therefore this requirement for even the smallest of messes to soak comes to the forefront of this argument every time.

Daniel Kahneman described this phenomenon as a battle between the slow and fast parts of the brain. The slow part is the section that thinks logically and considers the long term, it knows washing up in the morning is no more pleasurable than straight away and suggests I might as well get on with it. Meanwhile the fast side of the brain appeals for instant gratification, preferring to put a painful or costing action off in pursuit of a quick win, such as sitting in front of the TV rather than doing the dishes, or writing this book for instance!

So why does the fast brain win?

Human beings tend to care more about the present than the future. If I offer you £100 today or £110 tomorrow, most would see a 10% increase for an extra day as a great return. Repeated studies have found, however, that in fact when given the choice the majority take the immediate benefit over the larger pay-out in the future. This discounting of the future may seem illogical at first, but you only have to imagine being offered this in the street by someone you have never met, claiming they will be back tomorrow with £110, to realise there is value in certainty. However, we are equally likely to do this with something less likely to be gone tomorrow, such as watching TV rather than doing chores. As we saw with my dishes, they will not vanish overnight and yet we still discount the benefits of the future, and therefore let the immediate cost convince us to put off an action till later.

When we look to form our opinions on the world and the ongoing discourse between different sides, we are often guilty of doing the same. People pick politicians because they sound good or stick to a party because it puts out soundbites they like:

"The problem with socialism is that you eventually run out of other people's money"

– Margaret Thatcher

"My fellow Americans, ask not what your country can do for you, ask what you can do for your country"

- John F. Kennedy

"If you're not a liberal at twenty you have no heart. If you are not a conservative at forty, you have no brain."

- Winston Churchill, John Adams, and several others apparently

Paying Not to Go to the Gym

How many people do you know who have signed up for a gym membership or news subscription that they never use?

A paper in 2006 tried to answer the former with predictable results. 7,752 people who took up a gym habit had their gym activity tracked for 3 years. The type of membership they used was also measured across the period. Three types of membership, annual purchase, pay as you go and the infamous automatic monthly renew were all included in this study.

Of the monthly fee payers, their average monthly spend was $70 and their average attendance was 4.3 times a month, resulting in a payment per visit of $17. That sounds steep for attendance at one of my least favourite places but downright nonsensical when you consider that the cost of a pay as you go membership averaged at $10 per visit. By simply switching to the more flexible option, gym goers could on average save $600 annually.

On average 2.31 months elapsed between the last visit and when participants cancelled their contract, meaning quitters paid on average $187 before admitting that they were never going again.

And it's not just gym memberships. Writing this now I am remembering a regular payment for a discount card on eating out in my local area. Lockdown and the threat of Coronavirus in my area has meant the value of this card has reduced massively, but I am still yet to cancel the card - maybe I'll start using it next month!

It's hard enough to motivate ourselves to do something in the present when the benefits are so far in the future, like going to the gym. It is even harder when the benefits are obscure, like whether following a particular news outlet or political party will benefit us. As a result, it is even easier to accept the easy answer that gives us a short-term benefit, like accepting a headline without reading further or repeating a slogan without researching the evidence behind it.

The average Trump rally provides a wealth of examples on this, given the former President's fondness for soundbites over details. In fairness, this approach helped build the straight and direct persona that won him so many admirers in the 2016 election. While many on the left could learn from the way complex issues are boiled down by the President to a single tweet, this can be harmful to the unaware voter. Quotes like "Lock her up," and "Send them back," not only struck a chord with the disenfranchised, hit by growing inequality in America, but it was easy to understand, to relay and of course to chant. However, the truth is that the arguments behind these statements were anything but. The crime for which Hillary Clinton should supposedly be locked up varies, but early in 2020 the Justice Department closed a 2-year probe into her business dealings. There had been an allegation from Trump that a Uranium deal was agreed with Russia, following a large donation to the Clinton Foundation. Neither Hillary, Bill nor anyone involved with the Foundation has been convicted. Meanwhile, the enquiry into Russian interference in the 2016 election has resulted in the leader of the enquiry, Robert Mueller, concluding that not only had Trump been helped by this interference but had also engaged in behaviours that might be viewed as obstructive. That may sound like typical lawyer talk, but the investigation has led to 199 criminal counts, and six people being imprisoned for their involvement, including top advisers to the President. However, this hasn't stopped the chants at Trump rallies. Another example of facts failing to get in the way of a good chant is that three of the four Democrat lawmakers that Trump tweeted should 'go back to other countries,' were born in the United States.

This acceptance of easy slogans over detail can also be seen in similar soundbites in the UK. The strapline for Vote Leave (Take back control!) brilliantly appeals to those on the hard end of deindustrialisation in the UK (think industries like shipbuilding or mining) and those left behind by soaring inequality since the 80s. A closer look, however, and one can quickly see that the pains of these supporters, while far better understood by the Leave campaign than the Remain, would not be solved simply by the Brexit vote. Pro-Remain radio shows managed to silence many of even the most ardent Leave voters with the simple question: "which laws from Brussels would they change once control had been taken back?" I vividly remember one caller ringing into LBC to argue they had voted leave to maintain the ability to use 3-pin plugs. When the host pointed out that the EU had permitted the use of 3-pin plugs and there were no plans for this to change, the caller fell silent, before reverting to the issue of bendy bananas. Another example was Boris Johnson's complaints that Brussels was constraining UK fisheries by demanding kippers be transported with ice packs to maintain freshness. Closer inspection revealed that this was in fact a health and safety law put in place by the United Kingdom.

We must battle our inner short-termism and not be drawn in by soundbites and throwaway lines we find appealing. Drinking six pints of beer in the evening might make you feel better at the time, but you will regret it by the morning. In this vein, we must find ways of picking a healthier diet of news and opinions, together with a significant dose of healthy scepticism. In this way more of us will avoid placing our well-founded frustration and votes with a group that may sound like they represent us, but in fact take us somewhere completely different.

In Defence of the Quick Answer

This short-term approach is not a totally illogical part of human nature. It is grounded and ultimately makes sense in evolutionary terms, as sometimes we must make quick decisions to avoid danger, and this served us particularly well in the past. Our ancestors didn't have time to consider the long-term impacts of climbing a tree to escape a predator; they needed to start climbing as soon as the first signs of danger appeared. Moreover, the world is more complex now than ever before. Anyone who has stood behind me while I make a choice at the ice cream counter will understand that sometimes we are ill-equipped to make a considered decision using the slow part of our brain without everyone behind us in the queue starting to bore holes in the back of our heads. Consequently, we use our quick judgement to make rules for ourselves and save time for other things. This is good for the people standing behind me in the queue when I decide I only like chocolate and immediately discard all other options, but terrible if we all start voting the same way in perpetuity based on how we have voted before. Thinking back to those statistics from King's College in chapter 1, it is evident that the way we vote and how we are judged today is heavily reliant on how we voted in 2016, whether it be Brexit or Trump, and that should be grounds to worry, regardless of which box you crossed.

Returning to my unfinished dishes (briefly I promise!) we are also likely to make a decision when the answer proposed is easy. It is easier to make up an excuse like soaking the dishes than it is to wash them up. It is also easy to blame outside forces for our mistakes, rather than face up to them. When defending our opinions, we are often likely to look for easy answers too, rather than questioning or adjusting our own beliefs. Accusing all politicians of lying, declaring something to be fake news, or claiming that a new idea wouldn't work here are good examples of this, but most often it can simply be that we are too busy to face whatever task or decision comes our way.

While a survey in 2014 found that the main reason people gave for not completing surveys was they were too busy, Jonathan Gershuny of Oxford University found that the total amount of time people spend working, paid or otherwise, has not increased in the US and Western Europe in past decades. Despite this, a combination of busyness becoming an indicator of success, and social media constantly pushing us to do more, be more and buy more has meant that the majority of the population now feel they have less time than ever before. I recently accepted a friend request from an old teammate who has dropped the hockey stick to take up running. Now I can't sit and browse for 2 seconds before seeing his latest story about completing another 10k and feeling guilty about not doing more exercise in my free time!

I believe that our busier lives (or at least the perception of such) have given us less time for personal reflection on our beliefs. We are asked too often what we think rather than why we think it. As a result, advocates of ideas both on the right and left of politics have been slow or simply immobile in the softening of their positions in recent years, even in the face of evidence or unintended consequences of these ideas - like me never learning to just do the dishes.

The coming chapters will outline the many methods others will employ to limit your ability to see the weaknesses of their argument and force you to take the easy option. However, I have found that winning the argument with myself, making the effort to engage the slow part of my brain, and taking time to assess my own and others' beliefs regularly is often the most important step in avoiding falling into the trap of outdated views and letting the costs of not facing up to change begin to pile up, like so many dirty plates.

Playing the Long Game

What are the steps we can take to avoid devaluing the future?

Congratulations are in order as the first step to managing our future discounting behaviour is being aware of it, so assuming you have not simply skipped to this page, your new or possibly reinforced awareness of discounting will help you make better decisions. For example, when I am deciding whether to go to the gym or not, I know that if I put it off until tomorrow, I will likely feel just as against the idea once tomorrow comes, then the next and the next, until suddenly I have wasted yet another week's worth of gym membership. Therefore, by understanding that my own short-termism will not be any less powerful tomorrow, I am able to make a more accurate decision on when the best time to go is. Understand that this does not vanquish our future discounting, but rather internalises it into our decision making, rather than pretending it does not exist and that somehow by magic we will be more inclined to visit the gym tomorrow.

Another way of discounting the future less is by creating short-term incentives to work towards long-term goals. If you reward yourself for doing something that you regularly put off because the benefits come too slowly, you are more likely to keep up the habit. Just make sure they are proportionate, rewarding yourself with a burger every time you break into a run for the bus is not going to help you achieve your fitness goals!

One method, used by a flatmate of mine at university, is to create commitment factors. He told us at the start of term that he had given up drinking for January. This was a bold move given that the flat had taken to using Tesco delivery only the term before just to avoid carrying the several crates of beer that would usually last us a fortnight at most. However, by telling us early on, he not only ensured a sizeable amount of banter for such a ridiculous idea, but suddenly also had several pairs of sceptical eyes watching what he bought from the shops and on a night out, keen to catch him out. By committing to not drinking he had ensured a severe and immediate cost (in more verbal abuse) if he gave up. This would ultimately help him avoid alcohol all the way through January, after which he vowed never to do such a thing ever again and immediately headed for the campus bar.

The final method is automating our choices, a method already widely used by governments, and in a slightly perverse way by companies, to have you sign up for things. Many studies have found that when people are automatically signed up for something, whether it's a donor card or a savings account, we are more likely to accept it than to change to that option if we are left to make the decision ourselves. Companies do something similar by having the 'I would like to hear about future offers' section automatically ticked, making us more likely to accept the spam that comes with a one-off purchase. As we will often discount the future costs of spam or whatever else we have signed up to, to the point that we can't even be bothered to untick a box, this is a sure-fire way of guaranteeing we do something. If we can automate decisions, we are likely to allow the fast side of the brain to dominate, then we are much more likely to avoid missing out on long-term benefits. For example, setting up a standing order which transfers a percentage of your monthly pay into a separate savings account at the start of the month, preventing you overspending during the month and failing to save for a rainy day.

I May be Left-handed, But I'm Always Right!

Realising you have come out with something demonstrably untrue or done something obviously incorrect in front of others is always painful, even in front of close friends and family. I regularly find myself in this position on the sports pitch. Not blessed with speed I found that centre-back became my natural position very quickly, and fortunately while passing, shooting and particularly dribbling were not my strong suits, tackling was. As a result, I can be relied upon, at my exceedingly amateur level, to put up a suitable standard of defence against opposition strikers, particularly favouring the diving tackle to make up for my lack of speed. This does not mean I am without error of course, for every brilliantly timed challenge there is at least one, if not more, horror show which leaves the opponent lying on the floor with the ball nowhere in sight and me facing a yellow card. Despite this regularity, however, if anyone ever attempts to inform me that I did something wrong the usual response is for me to blame the player, the pitch, the referee - pretty much anything to avoid blame. This mental block can be seen in most players, to the point that people who attempt to umpire games deserve a medal for dealing with the never-ending calls of "what are you thinking?" and "are you blind?"

"In economics the majority is always wrong."

- *John Kenneth Galbraith*

"When the facts change, I change my mind. What do you do, Sir?"

- *John Maynard Keynes... Probably*

Whether Keynes actually uttered these words is up for debate, less so is that admitting failure is painful, whether it be an inability to compute simple Mathematics, struggling to speak in public, or holding an opinion that is broken down immediately by someone else. Unlike my exploits on the hockey pitch, I am marginally better with taking intellectual criticism, just! My usual form when someone points out something I have said is unequivocally wrong is to mutter something along the lines of 'I'm not sure' or 'it doesn't matter', before changing the subject. If especially aggrieved, I will be obstinately quiet for the evening but the advantage, or perhaps curse of close friends, teammates or family, is that you can't avoid them forever. The period of moodiness usually results in me accepting the new idea, or if I am very fortunate realising something not previously considered. Either way my opinion is changed by the event and so as a group we have, hopefully, all developed slightly without serious offence or injury caused. With this same openness, and greater awareness of some of the countermeasures to falling into the trap of accepting the easy, often faulty argument, we can break out of the current tribalism that is reportedly growing across the country, or at least avoid the next time we are embarrassed by someone a little more clued up on the detail.

That's my Mug!

So why is it so hard to admit fault?

It is such a strong feeling for so many, that even to question this can seem odd, and yet explaining it can also be baffling. It is easier perhaps to think of admitting being wrong as losing something physical, rather than the less tangible example of losing an argument. In that vein, I shall now recount a famous (at least in behavioural economics circles, so probably not that famous) experiment involving mugs:

A simple experiment on a class of university students gave half a university-branded mug, while the other half were given $6, the normal retail price of the mug. Classical economics would predict that the students would begin to trade with each other. As the mugs were distributed randomly, theory would say that some students would prefer mugs and others, money. Those who had been allocated their preferred good would keep it and those who had not would trade. This is meant to be the basis for how a price is created, by finding out how many people would prefer the good over money. The result however was that hardly any students traded. Almost all those given mugs kept them, asking for an average price above $6, while those without offered on average only £2.50. This is known as the endowment effect and results in us putting a higher value on things we might lose than things we stand to gain. For example, goods at auction receive a higher price than the same thing in the shops, as people become attached to a good they are winning and then overpay to avoid losing it to someone else. In an argument, weirdly, this means we are more against losing than we are in favour of winning.

The Place Where Lost Things Go

A close friend of mine is an avid Duolingo user, currently coming up to over 365 uninterrupted days of at least 10 minutes learning. Her greatest fear is of course losing that streak, to the point that she has purchased many in-game lifelines to maintain her streak even though there are no tangible benefits of having one. Of course, there is a benefit, if an intangible one. It is simply that she can boast that her streak remains a good 60 days ahead of mine! By creating the threat of losing something, she has managed to harness loss aversion to work for her, forcing action by reminding her of an immediate cost for inaction.

Supermarkets and other retailers have become expert at harnessing this fear of loss. Limited time offers are a tried and tested method of harnessing our loss aversion. According to Business2Community, emails that promoted products 'conveying a sense of urgency', resulted in not only more sales but also faster sales because customers took less time to examine the offer before buying!

We've all been in this situation. We finish shopping, check our basket and then head for checkout and find we are just short of an arbitrary level after which we are offered free shipping. Notice however that it is not sold as a reduction to the overall cost of your basket, but rather a way to avoid paying the £5 or so which has already been added to your basket. This focus on you losing money for no return of goods brings up far stronger emotions than say, if we'd been offered the chance of receiving a discount of the same amount if we spent the extra. Loss aversion again is the answer, with plenty of people prepared to spend more than the saving on shipping just to avoid the feeling that they have paid for nothing.

On a personal level, these all pale in comparison to a method used by supermarkets and coffee shops, a points-based system. No – not the kind that puts extra barriers up for foreign people entering their shops; instead, for each purchase we receive points which (eventually) add up to a free coffee. For supermarkets this is often in the form of cashback. While on the face of it this might seem a friendly way of enticing you into the store, as there seems no costs to the system, just the warm glow we get from receiving a free coffee every now and again (especially if, like me, you stack up points buying espressos and then use them to buy a mega, chocolate-cream deluxe that would have cost far more than the coffees I used to get the free one in the first place). The truth sadly is that there is a darker side to this practice, which becomes apparent if you think about switching supermarket or coffee shop. If you have built up points and are closing in on a free good or sizeable saving on your next shop, if you then move to another chain or outlet, those points will be lost, unless you return to the original seller. In this way there is now a cost of switching to a rival and loss aversion starts to work against us. As a result, we can often be drawn in by such schemes, but often find they simply tie us down to visiting the same places again and again.

These feelings of potential loss often push us to undergo more pain in the hope we might escape the original feeling of failure. This even has a name in finance, the disposition effect, where investors will hold assets that have lost value for longer than those with assets that have gained in value, due to the fear of admitting to a loss on the one hand, and suffering a future loss on the as-yet unrealised gains on the other. For the average person, who is not a stock picker (whatever the Facebook ads might tell you) this can explain why so many of us dig a hole trying to escape making an error or being proved wrong.

Invest in the Long Term, and Don't be Afraid to Drop Falling Opinions

Whether it is our tendency to discount the future, or to overvalue what we already have, the first step to overcoming these cognitive biases is to admit they exist. Whether it's over an argument, a decision that has cost you or your business money, or the political flagpole you have nailed yourself to, understand that changing tack will feel worse than the reality of the positives and negatives of such a decision.

Our busy lives notwithstanding, I think people would benefit from taking more time to consider other opinions, give the slow part of the brain a chance to take over, and either prove their argument or produce another, influenced by the ideas of others. Being prepared to fight for our beliefs, but also understanding that changing our mind often feels more painful than the results of doing so. In changing our outlook in this way, we will understand others' points of view, improve on our own opinions and be in a better place to defend our case to others without falling out permanently. We might even accept we are wrong once in a while!

Time can often be found to think about both sides of an argument and bridge the gaps between people. I try to do both, by taking time off from watching Netflix to think about my position on things, by either reading other opinions or formalising my own. That way I still have an excuse to avoid doing the washing up!

3

Lies, Damn Lies and Misread Statistics

At this point, you may not find it surprising that I was part of my school's debating team. There we argued about everything from who should run the country to who would win the Champions League next year. Regardless of the argument however, the constant was always the need for evidence, for examples, for statistics.

It seems that another casualty of the rise of political tribalism is the importance, or at least confidence in statistics, evidence and experts. Up and down the country we have heard politicians, newspapers and others question even long-standing facts and attempt to reject the contribution of those who have dedicated their careers to the matter under discussion. This has sown confusion for many on what and who to believe. This in turn has given us further opportunity to accept the easy answer over considering all the pros and cons of difficult decisions.

However, the idea that accurate statistics are not a single truth but can be adjusted to suit the user's argument is not new. In 2021 Tim Harford released 'How to Make the World Add Up', on how to avoid misreading statistics and use them correctly, but over 60 years before Darrell Huff released a similar, if rather more bluntly-titled book, 'How to Lie With Statistics'. Both books are well worth reading, as they show how statistics can easily be used to mislead and affirm our pre-existing biases. More importantly, they prove that this does not make statistics obsolete.

In the 1940s and 50s statistics led to one of the greatest killers of the Century being unmasked - smoking. As late as 1900 the numbers of people suffering from lung cancer were so low, that it was often misdiagnosed as pneumonia or other lung illness. However, in the early part of the 20th century, evidence started growing of a sharp rise in people affected by this cancer, identified formally by Isaac Adler in Germany in 1912. From here the evidence snowballed, from studies showing that lung cancer was much more likely in smokers than non-smokers, to examining the impacts on rats of tobacco juice, to the discovery of carcinogenic chemicals in cigarette smoke. This culminated in the landmark 1964 US Surgeon General's report, which accepted the evidence that smoking did cause lung cancer in men.

Interestingly however, consensus on this point already existed before the end of the 1950s. So why the gap between academic and official support? The answer was a huge amount of lobbying from tobacco companies.

In the 1930s, different cigarette manufacturers competed to claim their products offered the best "throat protection against irritation and coughs."

American Tobacco was the first to start using physicians in their adverts to enhance their claims that smoking was healthy but were quickly followed by the rest of the Industry. In the same way, we see dentists promote certain toothpastes today.

In the face of a growing consensus that smoking was a cause of lung cancer, the Industry hit back, arguing the classic line that correlation does not prove causation, and that the evidence was not yet conclusive. Even after the 1964 report, tobacco companies continued to fund a research committee that claimed there was still controversy over the Report's conclusion. Harford notes that in 1965, Darrell Huff himself was brought in front of a US Senate Committee by big tobacco, arguing that the evidence of correlation between smoking and cancer was still to be proven as causal.

'Authors have shown that there is an association but they've differed in their interpretation. Some have considered that the only reasonable explanation is that smoking is a factor in producing disease. Others have not been prepared to deduce causation and have left the association unexplained.'

- Defence Attorney for Philip Morris International, Tobacco Litigation Case,1993

We look at this story now and laugh, how could people be fooled by such blatant spin and outright falsehoods?

Sadly, our abilities to tell the difference between the good, the bad and the ugly of statistics may have improved, but the PR firms and advertising agencies across politics and industry have been using these weapons for a lot longer and have marched ahead in recent years. You only have to walk down a local supermarket aisle to see the extent of their influence in our daily lives.

No added sugar is legally placed on products that are packed with the stuff, for example apple juice, with many brands holding more sugar per 100ml than Coca-Cola. Bread labelled as wholegrain espouses healthy attributes, but often only contains a small percentage of wholegrains, as there is no lower limit on the proportion of the loaf containing this type of cereal before the disingenuous labelling can be displayed on packaging. In fact, just picking up a box from my cupboard I can see that my wholegrain (and therefore supposedly healthy) cereal in fact contains more calories per 100g than the Starbursts in the cupboard next door. Many reduced-sugar chocolate bars have recently become available which in fact contain more calories than the original bar. This is because that missing sugar is replaced by fat, which holds more calories per gram than the sugar that was there in the first place! I have even picked up bottles of olive oil with 'light' in large lettering on the front, only to find in a much smaller font underneath that it is talking about the flavour or colour of the oil rather than the calories.

Things can remain shady, even when the government legislates on the minimum standards for food. In America, the US Department for Agriculture defines free range chicken as simply when the birds are "allowed to access the outside", suggesting that battery farming would be free range if the roof was removed periodically.

Despite this complexity, there are still many examples of some truly awful spin attempts that are easy to spot. For example, one toothpaste company that claimed to be recommended by 80% of dentists failed to mention that the survey allowed dentists to recommend multiple brands and so did not mean that this toothpaste should be preferred to all others. Similar adverts that say 9 out 10 cats prefer a particular brand of pet food, neglect to mention if the cats preferred this to anything else or whether in fact the animals were simply given the option of this brand or starve!

While these illustrations appear amusing, the truth is that we have become dangerously poor at understanding statistics. Research from Ipsos Mori in 2019 tested 2000 people's statistical ability and found that just 20% reached the level of a GCSE C grade.

This is unlikely to change anytime soon, as the general public value numeracy far less than reading and writing. 50% said they would be most proud of their children if they were very good at reading and writing vs only 21% for being very good at numbers. As for the parents themselves, 58% would feel embarrassed to say they were no good with reading or writing while only 47% would say the same for maths. Even more worrying is that we are hardly making up for this shortfall with our reading ability. A study in 2019 found that the average reading age of the UK population is just nine years old. As a result, our ability to understand even the simple statistics required to pick out blatant falsehoods is questionable.

Fortunately, there are many simple ways of improving our understanding of statistics and avoiding others pulling the wool over our eyes with confusing figures and misleading visuals. The aforementioned Harford and Huff cover this topic in more detail than I ever could in a single chapter, (and of course they beat me to it by releasing their books first) so I happily recommend both. However, as you've invested in this one, I'll put in some of what I view as the most important issues we face when judging statistics. Hopefully, these short examples will be sufficiently memorable to help you battle the bad statistics, and dare I say, fake news, that currently fills our news feeds!

The Trouble with Sample Size

A book centred around family arguments would be remiss not to mention Monopoly, the spark of many a family fireworks display. We've all been there, you own half the board, hotels everywhere, you can't possibly lose! And then your sibling, child, or parent skips past all of them, lands on free parking and you manage to roll the only combination that puts you straight on Mayfair with four houses and there goes the whole game. I more fondly remember a time when the boot was on the other foot. My brother was bawling that it shouldn't be possible to have rolled double two three times in a row. This incredible repetition of numbers, just when you don't want them, can be seen all over the place. Receiving endless black cards when you need a red in Solitaire and never managing to roll the required number to finish the game in Trivial Pursuit to name just two. But why does this happen with seemingly fair dice or a balanced deck of cards?

If we simplify Monopoly for a moment to just one die, we can see this more clearly. If we roll a six the first time, does this mean rolling again is less likely to result in another 6? The answer, regardless of how much my brother might complain, is no. Assuming that each roll does not physically alter the die in anyway, each throw has a one in six chance of producing each number. You are just as likely to roll a six the second time as the first. Therefore, while my brother might complain about getting double 2 repeatedly, the reality is that each roll is independent, and he will just have to deal with my laughter as he lands on my property for third time in a row!

The same is true for any experiment. Just because a few random cases give you the answer you want, this does not mean your argument is right. For example, three individuals selected at random who have brown hair, does not mean we are living in a solely brunette society. Each time you pick someone to sample, the probabilities reset. As a result, having three people in a row with brown hair is far from extraordinary. 48% of us in the UK are brunettes, but by sampling only 3 at random, you could easily get the impression that 100% of us have brown hair. This propensity for small sample sizes to create misleading results can be tested easily, even with a relatively small group of people. If you ask the group to guess a number, either one or two and eliminate all those who choose one of the options, you will find roughly half still in the game. Repeating this, completely at random, five or six times, you might be surprised to see many still standing and in fact in a room of just 100 people, the possibility of someone guessing correctly 6 times in a row is a near certainty.

So how do we conclude anything if unrepresentative conclusions are so common?

The answer is not to give up on experiments and surveys but to do more of them!

Each die roll or person surveyed may be random, but if we take a large enough sample of these random events, they gravitate towards an accurate proportion. For example, if we surveyed every person in the UK, we would find 48% have brown hair. If we surveyed say all but one, we will be marginally off. As the sample size is reduced, the size of possible error increases, as we are missing more of the picture. In the same way, if we roll a die enough times, the average number of sixes will tend towards 1 in every 6 throws. So, the first and most obvious lesson is that for any claim to be accurate, a sample size that reduces the size of error is essential. The right size largely depends on what claim you are making. If you make a sweeping statement about society, the sample size needs to be large. If you are making one about your school or workplace, the sample size will obviously be smaller. It is also worth noting that the more diverse the subject of the comment, the larger the sample size should be. For example, saying all Starbucks branches sell coffee is not one that requires a large sample as each shop is very similar. Saying all chain shops sell coffee however will require a larger sample size, given the greater diversity implied by the statement.

Who Framed the Question?

How statistics are presented is also important. Imagine two grim scenarios from my university textbook (not known for their light-heartedness):

Scenario 1 -

Option 1: Save 200 lives

Option 2: A 33% chance of saving 600 people, 66% probability that all 600 will die.

Which option would you pick?

Now consider another scenario:

Scenario 2 -

Option 1: 400 people will die

Option 2: A 33% chance that no people will die, 66% probability that all 600 will die.

Which option now?

Those who have heard something similar before may have noticed that the two scenarios are exactly the same, with the two possible outcomes identical for both scenario 1 and 2. Despite this, when given the option of being in either of the two scenarios, 72% of people pick the first, while only 28% pick the second. Since both offer the same expected results, statistically those questioned should feel indifferent to the question, splitting evenly fifty-fifty between scenarios.

The way a statement is framed can have a large impact on how someone reacts. A more relaxed and relevant example is the rule of 100 in retail. The concept is that any saving under £100 is best represented as a %, while anything over as an absolute figure. For example, £100 off the latest smart phone sounds a lot more than 10% (the implication being that modern smartphones are very expensive!). Meanwhile, 10% off a cup of coffee sounds a lot better than 20p off.

This is really important when we read stats in support of one argument or another.

Back to the supermarket briefly, and you may have noticed cereal has become a bodybuilder's mate in recent years, or at least that's how it's framed. Every other brand seems to have released an extra-protein version of their regular box, prompting many to think this is a better alternative and a good reason to have an extra spoonful every morning. The packaging is accurate in that the amount of protein in the good has increased, but while this has been put front and centre of the new branding, other, far less healthy additions, have also increased and so have understandably been kept in the small print on the back of the box. Happening to be sat in the coffee shop attached to my local supermarket at the time of writing, I was quickly able to pick on one cereal box in particular by having a look down the aisle (yes, I know, I need to get out more). With extra protein splashed across the front, it was easy to discover that there was 20% more of the macronutrient than in the original brand. In keeping with the rule of 100 described earlier, the absolute increase per 100 grams of cereal was well under 100 (it was in fact just a 2g increase!) Meanwhile the sugar count for the same amount of cereal was 6 grams higher (a 46% increase) and 5.8 grams higher in fat (a whopping 220% increase!). Similarly, buying food often comes with points on your supermarket card. The exchange rate on points to £s of savings, is as bad as the rate on the average Zimbabwe Dollar of recent history. This is because receiving 250 points sounds a lot better than saving under £1.25.

This shows us that in order to get an accurate picture of what matters, we must be clear on all the details. While the supermarket may want us to focus on the positive side, we must see all impacts of a new product choice or other decision, as well as the relevant size of all the changes.

Feuding with the Truth

Surveys, no matter the sample size can also be ruined if the individuals questioned are not honest.

Family Fortunes (or the far more amusing, in my opinion, US Family Feuds), is a game show with a simple premise. 100 people are asked a question before the show, and then the contestants must guess the most common answer given. The questions are often picked on their comedic quality and potential for euphemism, using the awkwardness of contestants to generate laughs. Silly answers are also popular, here are a few examples:

"Name something you do when your spouse/partner is angry."

"Name a fruit that reminds you of a part of the human body."

"Name something that you probably shouldn't send in an email."

Another example, a contestant was asked what they might light up. His response predictably, was marijuana. The number of people who gave this answer was very low, and the presenter suggested that few people were prepared to answer when questioned in public, that they would light up an illegal drug. Such issues are trivial here, but dishonesty can be a major issue from studies on new food products, where people offered free food are unlikely to say it was awful, to people polled for elections, especially when the polling is done by a particular party, or in a group of one section of voters. In this situation an individual is far more likely to go with the crowd or agree with the pollster just to get them to go away. Results from surveys at the ONS often show incorrect responses from people looking to make a joke or who simply can't be bothered to report things accurately. As a result, many responses state their income to be infinite, while others claim to have a negative income. Rounded numbers are also far more prevalent in surveys than in real life, given it is quicker to give a rough estimate of weekly earnings than to work it out properly. Therefore, when looking at any statistics we must be ready to question what possible pressure the individuals asked were under, and whether this might hide a 'silent majority' in the figures.

Dodgy Diagrams:

Diagrams should be used to make information easier to follow. When faced with a wall of writing or numbers our eyes often give up and look for the pictures. However, frequently charts and other data visualisation can be misleading, either by accident, or something more malevolent.

One chart produced by the Senate Budget Committee in 2011 gave the impression that the number of people receiving benefits had shot up between 2009 and 2011, (almost three times from the starting amount). However, a closer look showed that the count did not start at 0, but 94,000,000. As a result, while it might have looked like the numbers had increased massively, in fact they had only increased by 9% in over two years. This is not quite the same as the trebling it appeared to suggest in the first instance. This also emphasises the importance of scale. A big number might be quite small, relatively speaking, when compared across time or other countries, in the same way that a tall jockey looks small in a group of basketball players.

Another report in 2011 from a famous right-wing media platform in the states used a bar chart to show that more people in the US were on welfare than in full-time jobs. On first inspection this is a shocking conclusion, but is it right? A look behind the numbers found that the number of people on welfare included all people who lived in the same house as someone on welfare, whether the other occupants received any support or not. This shows how the words that accompany the diagram matter. Whenever you see a statistic that pushes a particular narrative, remember to ask yourself how they came to that figure. It might well be that the assumptions behind the figures are less reliable and concrete than the initial stat implies.

US Census data on the cost of tuition has regularly been used to create visuals emphasising the rapidly increasing cost of degrees while also showing how graduate earnings have stalled.

While it looks as if the cost of tuition has rendered higher education pointless, these diagrams regularly fail to show what has been happening to the average earnings of those without degrees. The truth sadly is that the cost of not going to university has grown too. This means that while you may pay less in the short term by not going to uni, in the long run, those who do will earn the tuition and more back. According to the US Department of Education, a college grad in 2010 would be expected to earn $1,935,000 over a career, compared to just $1,300,000 who leave education after high school. Even when we take away the average tuition of $95,000, the clear choice based on earnings is clearly to go into higher education.

Another common issue is incomplete data. For instance, any meteorological report from the northern hemisphere in August will have told you that temperatures have increased significantly in the first six months of the year alone. But this is simply because we only have information on half the year, from winter to summer, so of course temperatures are rising!

This last example might appear obvious, but it is a common theme, especially in climate change debates. Deniers have regularly pointed to trends in global temperatures remaining on a constant rather than accelerating path back to the 1950s as proof that global warming is natural rather than man-made. However, with the benefit of more data we can easily find that temperatures have been rising since the Industrial Revolution, and crucially, much faster than at any point in the last 2 millennia. Ensuring you have the full picture before coming to conclusions is key!

Correlation Causing Trouble, or is it?

The difference between correlation and causation is another common pitfall in the use of statistics. Data between 1999 and 2009 found a significant correlation between US spelling bees and the number of people killed by venomous spiders.

Does anyone really think that the number of people killed by venomous spiders has anything to do with the Scripps National Spelling Bee? I doubt it.

And yet the two seem to follow each other remarkably closely. This is just one example of how patterns can appear in all walks of life and as aspiring statisticians (or at least wannabe know-it-alls) we must separate those that just happen to move in similar ways, and those that have a causal relationship. A recent example of this was over the gender pay gap in the aviation industry.

Results from Ryanair in 2018 showed that among their staff there was a 74% gender pay gap. The results for the rest of the Industry was not much better, with nine of the biggest players, including British Airways, above the UK average of 9.7% at the time. If women working for these firms earn less on average than men, does this mean that on average airlines discriminate more on sex than the rest of the economy? The truth is we can't tell from this data, mainly because the stats fail to account for the fact that these men and women are doing different jobs. Most female workers on planes are cabin crew, while only 5.2% were pilots in 2018. This difference in jobs means that average wages are very different, even if male and female cabin crew are paid equally, and male and female pilots are equally paid. This does not mean there is no issue. The fact that fewer women are willing and able to become pilots should be a worry for many, as it suggests they are being deterred from training to become a pilot or are not being chosen to join commercial airline companies. However, it demonstrates how a simple comparison of two sets of information is insufficient to draw a conclusion from. Similarly, if that were so, we could make similar comparisons that cough medicine causes coughs and hand cream causes dryness, as demand for the former and the regularity of the latter often move together!

Look at Sweden!

A more recent classic from the family dinner table, predominantly during the first lockdown, has been the call to 'look at Sweden' as an example of how to deal with the Covid-19 Crisis. As the economic damage wrought by lockdown became more and more apparent, the number of voices questioning whether lockdown was worth it grew, citing Sweden as an example of a country that has done better on health and on wealth.

A good technique for examining someone's evidence without immediately discarding it, is simply to ask more, ask why they believe what they say. In this case, asking how Sweden's deaths and output compared to the UK during the onset of the crisis and lockdown. This can then be followed by questions like, but what about deaths per 100,000 people? Then, what about deaths compared to similar countries to Sweden for a more accurate comparison, like Norway or Finland?

Data from John Hopkins University in early 2021 supplies the answers and reveals how a little investigation of statistics held, uncovers more than what many people's lockdown-weary brains want to see:

Deaths:

United Kingdom: 87,448

Sweden: 10,323

Just looking at deaths, Sweden seems to be the answer, no lockdowns and fewer deaths. But what if we control for the different population sizes?

United Kingdom: 131.52

Sweden: 101.37

The numbers look a little closer now, but still Sweden comes out on top. How about comparing countries closer to Sweden in terms of population density, public service quality and social activity?

United Kingdom: 131.52

Sweden: 101.37

Denmark: 29.69

Norway: 9.73

Finland: 11.20

Suddenly the anti-lockdown stance is looking less successful. When we compare Sweden with its more immediate neighbours, its policy looks far less successful. Some may counter this with the argument that keeping its economy open for longer has meant Sweden has suffered less economically. IMF data from October reveals that again, while Sweden's economic growth forecast for 2020 of -4.7% looks good compared to the UK's -9.8%, Norway is on -2.8%, Denmark is -4.5% and Finland -4%.

Usually, I find by the time we reach the third question, the confidence of the original argument starts to do one of two things. Either the person starts to question whether their argument is right, or they harden and refuse to move their position. Something along the lines of "I don't know, but I read it somewhere and it makes sense". While this might be sufficient in a debate, we must work hard to help improve each other's understanding rather than just silencing people if we are to bridge the gap between opposing sides.

I believe it is this lack of understanding of the figures that leads to the assertion that 'statistics can tell you whatever you like'. For instance, Sweden having a lower death rate than the UK, but a higher rate than Norway does not mean stats are subjective; rather that someone comparing an apple with a pear when there is a fresh bushel of apples nearby is not trying very hard, or keen to sell that apple. We must work harder to understand the evidence before us and make sure we do not abandon evidence at the first sign of complexity. We also cannot underestimate the ability for the crowd to be confused in a way that each individual may not. The argument over debt and deficit is a good example of this.

Slowing Down and Stopping

Since the Coalition government set out to 'balance the books,' the criticism that debt has only increased has been lodged against them. Somehow criticism that the cuts have done permanent damage to social care, communities, policing, etc. has also been lodged. I personally believe that austerity was not the right decision immediately following a crisis (more on this later). However, I find it hard to believe that the cuts could simultaneously not have been effective at balancing the books and reduced the state so considerably, given spending elsewhere. Even when we consider tax cuts, these were too small to compensate the fall in spending elsewhere.

This exposes one of the most resilient confusions over statistics, levels vs. rates. When I apply my car brakes, I do not stop immediately. This is probably a good thing as I do not give myself whiplash when braking on the motorway. Instead

I decelerate first. The same is true for debt, if we are losing money every year, this is known as deficit, a decrease in funds each year. The debt, meanwhile, is the total of all the deficits or surpluses over time. Therefore, when the deficit is being reduced, debt continues increasing. In the same way that while I am applying my brakes the car continues to move forward until I have stopped completely. When examining statistics, we must make sure we are looking at the right ones!

More confusing still is that output (everyone's income in a country toted up) is rising all the time, making the same level of debt smaller relative to output as the days go by. For example, £100 debt may be a lot if you earn £1 a day, but is very small if you earn £1000 a day. As long as output continues to increase, holding the debt constant can be argued to be enough. This is a small comfort given the UK's national debt has grown to over 100% of GDP at the time of writing. However, even that figure can be rationalised. While the government does not own total output in an economy (the state currently stands at about 50%), even if we take an aggressive view, and claim that the government debt is 200% of earnings, this is only as bad as the average UK citizen, earning on average about £30,000 per year and having an average debt of £60,000.

Losing control of a car is dangerous; the same is true for debt. However, if we do not understand the complexities of how to rationalise and manage debt, we are likely to respond with panic-induced instinct rather than thoughtful care. Such actions would be far more damaging for those involved, in the same way that someone who doesn't know how to use the brakes may use an oncoming tree or lamppost to stop a speeding car instead.

Computers to the Rescue?

Some have argued that the rise of big data and machine learning will remove the error and bias in statistics, in the same way that it has improved the efficiency of the stock markets. They assert that this will remove all room for error and opinion, resulting in one version of the truth and no misvalued assets. While more information can be useful and the ability of algorithms to quickly find relationships in data is informing decision-making across the world, one does not need to look far to find cracks in this idea. While computers can analyse more data than ever before, they are still limited by what the writers of algorithms tell them to look for, and what decisions to make once the data is appropriately corralled. A simple example of the former is that a computer accessing mortgage rates for individuals will assign higher rates to non-white applicants given the historically higher chance of default in that demographic. Apart from being morally questionable, this is thankfully becoming more inaccurate over time. Machine learning boils down to giving a computer a million old pictures of a horse and then asking it to find a new picture of a horse among several cows. The problem is that old pictures of a person of colour's creditworthiness are very different from a creditworthiness picture today. As a result, data architects must be very careful that the data they feed into the computer, in order to train it, is accurate and representative of the modern day.

A more tangible example of misuse of big data is the shambolic use of an algorithm to grade UK schoolchildren in the summer of 2020. While the data was accurate, and a perfect representation of exam scores from the year before, the assumptions placed on the data, i.e. the instructions to the computer, were horribly wrong. One example was the higher your class size, the greater your mark would be moderated down. As a result, 40% of students saw their grades downgraded, with those from working-class and disadvantaged backgrounds most badly affected. This shows how big data has not solved the issues with statistics, it has just amplified the success and mistakes we make when producing them.

Technology has meant data is more readily available than ever, but it has also allowed for a quicker spread of incorrect or misleading statistics. One cannot browse social media without seeing a dinner table debate play out across someone's post and in the comments section. I usually find the moments I spend scrolling through social media to be the last times I want to be working the slow part of my brain, and that's fine. Let's just avoid relaying any of these ideas we come across without giving them some more detailed thought. If in doubt, Google is right there for you to quickly search claims others have made. Often, you'll be surprised how easy it is to uncover mistruths.

A report from a national radio commentator in 2020 claimed that those arguing against Trump's attempt to delay the US election due to Coronavirus were hypocrites as the same was being suggested in New Zealand, the leader of which was far more popular amongst those in opposition to Trump. A quick Google, however, found that in fact the opposition parties in New Zealand had asked for the delay, not the incumbent.

Another piece from a national newspaper ran the headline: "Meghan & Harry's Africa trip cost taxpayer £250k" following the couple's departure from the Royal Family. Closer inspection found that the cost of the trip had been authorised by the UK Foreign Office, involved the two attending twenty functions, including participating in charity work, and was part of their royal duties.

Stay aware, the doomsayers and conspiracy theorists of yesterday are in our living rooms today, spouting the same rubbish, but in a way that is much harder to resist. Don't engage with these ideas unless you are ready to scrutinise them, and hopefully the examples above will give you some of the tools you need to pick out the facts, the fiction and the social media rants.

4

I'll Start Dieting Next Week!

Great! I'll never just accept the easy answer or listen to a dubious Facebook post again!

I hope that a few of you have at least considered this in the last few chapters. Some may even have decided that this is a turning point (I can dream anyway!) But how often do we tell ourselves this and never follow it through? How many times have we told ourselves that we'll start dieting next week?

In my family, the main culprit is my mother. Despite being the lightest in the family, just, she exclaims every year that she is going to get fit before the family holiday. This is usually followed by laughter, before one of us points out that she said this last year and the year before. Each time there is a different reason why this year will be different, a new exercise regime perhaps or a new food she won't eat. This is in many ways similar to my attempts to explain why next season will be the one where Manchester United recapture their past form. Both arguments/hopes tend to last about three weeks, before both revert to claiming next year will be different!

Being both overweight and underweight before I was 21 has afforded me some personal experience in this area. As was mentioned in the second chapter, we can see here too, the similarities in being at opposite ends of the scales. Things like the desire to keep my shirt on until the very last minute before getting in the pool, being teased for how I looked, being overlooked for sports teams, because of my size. Whether too big or too small these feelings are often uncomfortably familiar for many of us. Being overweight first, I truly believed that being skinny would stop the abuse and the negative feelings I had about myself. Once I left for university, I told myself, I would stop eating all the 'bad' things that were always available in the sweetie cupboard at home. Whether it was this new conviction, or more likely the lack of spending money I had for takeaways, I did lose weight. Despite my short-term relief at having moved towards, what I thought was the socially acceptable weight, if anything, going the other way, only made the problems worse. I found myself unable to play as much sport as I was used to. I'd feel exhausted before even finishing the warmup. I refused to meet up with friends as regularly and found myself sleeping for more and more of the day. Even my family, who had previously ignored my weight, picked up on how thin I looked, demanding to feed me up whenever I returned home for the holidays.

Strangely, putting weight back on was more challenging than losing it. I felt guilty whenever I ate anything even mildly unhealthy; refusing to have butter or even margarine in my sandwiches and removing cheese from my diet altogether. Eventually I used a mobile application to monitor my calories, to make sure I was eating enough. Even then I would prefer to eat plain foods rather than add any fat to my meals. I regularly ate up to 12 Weetabix in place of a proper meal, water only, no milk obviously, far too unhealthy! Not only were these thoughts wrong but, they stopped me living and enjoying my life. Whenever I did go over the top with food or alcohol, I would be racked with guilt and determined to eat even less the next day.

Fortunately, I am now in a much happier (and I hope healthier) place with food. This is thanks, not only to the support of those around me, but also my increased awareness of the myriad of reasons why so many of us struggle with food. While I experienced a happy ending in this instance, many people across the UK and wider world continue to struggle with food causing all manner of health problems for them in the future. Research has found that 67% of men and 60% of women in the UK are either overweight or obese, etc. Meanwhile 50% of Americans would like to lose weight, and up to 80% have done so but put it back on. But why?

A Map as Long as the Land

Shouldn't the rise of the internet have made it easier than ever to figure out what is good to eat and how to avoid the rubbish?

Classical (textbook talk for old-school) economics would say yes. As long as we are suitably incentivised (and the stat on Americans trying to lose weight above, suggests we are,) then we should simply stop eating what the internet tells us is unhealthy and immediately start shedding the pounds. Many of us, however, have had far too much experience to the contrary to believe this view. A poor joke about the inaccuracy of the predictions of economists goes as follows:

A physicist, a chemist, and an economist who were stranded on a desert island with no implements and a can of food. The physicist and the chemist each devised an ingenious mechanism for getting the can open; the economist merely said, "Assume we have a can opener"!

With regards to achieving a healthier weight, classical economists assume that anyone looking for dieting tips has the time and desire to read all the available information on the internet in order to make a decision on every single food-related dilemma - a longshot indeed. Most of us won't even bother looking at the calorie count on the sandwiches we buy for lunch, let alone produce a long, cost-benefit analysis each time we sit down to eat. Such outdated assumptions about how humans act are often used as a reason to discard economic predictions and modelling, but this is largely because their use is misunderstood.

Maps are useful for telling us about an area we don't know very well. They contain information about major landmarks in an area, as well as roads, buildings and other points of interest. Of course, it omits most of the information that the land actually displays. It cannot for instance, tell us about every house, every tree, every blade of grass. To achieve this, you would need a map as large as the land itself which would, therefore, be pointless to a would-be traveller. An economist's models work the same way. If we were to include every possible variable in our analysis, for example the impact of the weather, or the presence of butterflies on our results, the process would take far too long and be months out of date, thus making it totally useless for informing our conclusions. Also, the point of a model is that it can be replicated for future use. For example, the increase in expected earnings that comes from years of education, where, by considering your child's grades, university choice and subject choice, you can estimate/assess whether your child should go to university. If parents were asked to put in every detail about their child, say, what he had for breakfast this morning, or whether he plays hockey on the weekends, the process would take so long to produce each result (think of the forms to fill out!) that no one would bother.

So, much like a map, economists reduce the detail of the model, in order to remain useful, but make it possible for the target audience to use. So, assuming something implausible about a fundamental part of a model, such as can openers being readily available on a desert island, is not an example of good model building. Assuming there is a rock or stick sharp enough on the island to break into the can is perhaps a better one and would probably be more happily accepted by the chemist and the physicist.

Back to Health

Armed with this new information of realistic assumptions, how do we approach the wealth of information on the internet?

The first, is to accept that some searching is a good idea. Accepting the first pop-up telling you about a new miracle pill for weight loss, is probably not advisable. Equally we know that we will not spend forever on this, we've got avocado to smash!

Like everything, searching has a cost, not necessarily in pounds, but in the time you spend looking through the internet for the right information. Economists call this the opportunity cost; the cost of spending your time doing something instead of the next best available activity. Simply put, while you read this book you could be going to the cinema, or meeting up with friends, or playing sport (unless we are still in lockdown in which case there's no escape!) Choosing not to, costs the benefits you would have gained from doing something else. Another cost is that searching for something without immediate rewards, or when you think you have the answer already, is boring and frustrating. Anyone who has trudged through a shopping centre with their partner, going into every single clothes shop only to return to the first one you entered to buy a pair of jeans you'd swear was no different from the last five they tried, will understand this.

Shops and supermarkets are experts at not only increasing the switching cost as mentioned in the last chapter, but also using search costs to their advantage. Essential items like bread, milk and (for some) alcohol are put towards the back of the shop as the retailers know you will incur this cost for the important items. Meanwhile aisle ends, particularly those by the tills, are full of items you may not have entered the shop to buy but those they hope you will still buy if they lower the search cost for you. More expensive items are put at eye level to save you the cost of lowering your eyes! On the internet, these methods become even more complicated, with firms using past search and purchase history to make suggestions for you, to stop you searching at all. However, search we must.

Being drawn in with impulse purchases and only buying what we have bought before or close to it, are unlikely to result in the lifestyle changes we need to make, if we want to improve our health.

In order to maximise the value in our search we should do simple things like looking for reputable sources of information. Public Health England (if it still exists at time of reading, given the number of recent complaints), provides a good level of information that will work for anyone looking to reach a basic level of health. If you are keen on developing a particular part of your physique for sport or aesthetics, spend a bit more time on that area. Your higher level of interest should be matched by the time you are prepared to look into this. Remember we are looking for a map to fitness, not the whole land, but charging off without any directions at all will equally end in disaster.

Avoiding quick fixes is important, and ties in well with the message of taking time to engage the analytical part of the brain discussed in chapter 2. The borders of websites are full of claims about miracle cures and get-rich schemes. Any product that genuinely helped people lose weight, without having to put in any hard work wouldn't be found in the corner of a page. It would be a household name and manufactured by one of the largest companies in the world, if the current demand for such a product is anything to go by. Ignoring these quick fixes will save you time and mental energy. In the same way, adverts that promote one particular product or supplement should be avoided, as the current nutritional evidence is that a mix is far better than pinning all your hopes on a single miracle food.

Customer reviews are helpful in lowering the cost of search. An advert can make all the grand claims it likes, but if most past customers are claiming it doesn't fulfil those claims, then it probably isn't worth bothering with. Evidence suggests that both customer and editorial reviews lower the search cost to individuals, as they allow us to discard some goods we might otherwise consider. They also promote greater consumer confidence, as reviews help lessen the fear of receiving a final product different from what was advertised.

But what about when sources conflict? 'I heard you can't get enough protein from meat, but others say you can', 'apparently X is good for you, but this says it causes cancer?' 'Should I buy this product?'

I had a similar moment when my faith was shaken, last year. I am a big fan of peanut butter, and have previously claimed it is a healthy option, far superior to other spreads. This belief led me to use peanut butter in everything from porridge to dips. My conviction was rocked while reading an article which extolled the virtues of the Spread when it revealed that it was a potential source of aflatoxins, which are highly carcinogenic. As seems traditional these days, I had just found out that what I thought was healthy, was in fact not so.

Many people use such examples to claim the advice changes too regularly and we shouldn't bother eating 'healthy' foods, as they will be denounced as deadly tomorrow. The truth, however, is more nuanced. If we look at the claims that something is healthy/unhealthy, very rarely do we have about-turns as to whether something is categorically 'good' or 'bad'. Often foods have positives and negatives, peanut butter being a good example. Too much may be harmful, but equally it contains many important nutrients and antioxidants. Therefore, rather than looking for a set of foods that are 100% good for you and never eating anything again, eating a range of foods is a far better way of ensuring you reap the benefits of foods, without overconsumption of their negative traits. Like a well-balanced portfolio, putting your money in a variety of assets means that if one turns out to be a poor investment, you won't lose out completely. Conversely, chucking all your money on one or two goods bears a higher level of risk, if what you thought was a riskless-choice proves to be a dangerous gamble. In an attempt to practice what I preach, I aim to keep my peanut butter consumption to a tablespoon every couple of days. The fact that, previously, I was eating the stuff at least once, if not twice a day, should have been an indication that, whatever the benefits, I was eating too much. Whether I manage this previously insurmountable task of cutting back is another question all together!

Counting Calories

Time for one of the biggest questions out there? Does calorie counting work? At the risk of some angry emails, the short answer is yes, but only if you want to reduce how much you weigh, not necessarily if you want to improve your health.

Our bodies are, at a very basic level, engines. We take in fuel and burn it to move. When we take in high fat foods we take in a higher density of fuel compared to vegetables. If we put more in than we need, the body stores it in the coal cellar, your waist and thighs predominantly. As a result, if you count your calories accurately, and reduce the amount you eat for a sustained period, you will lose weight.

The complexity of the debate online about whether some foods are better for weight loss, whether eating a certain food or drinking alcohol will stop weight loss, regardless of exercise is more to do with the mind than the body. For example, a person taking on 500 calories of broccoli, vs. 500 calories of sweets will gain the same amount of weight. Yes, there might be a minor impact of their genes on how their body breaks down different things, but for people looking to lose weight, I doubt a few grams will make much difference. Similarly, sugar might cause your insulin to spike and convert the energy to fat quicker than broccoli, but if you move the same amount, you will use up the calories of both, in the same amount of time. The reality is, eating the right foods gives you other nutrients you need and, more importantly for weight loss, will probably make it easier to avoid eating again, or as much. Fibre is a good example of such a benefit, where fibrous complex carbs take longer to be broken down and so we 'feel' fuller for longer. This means we are less likely to snack and take on more calories. However, if we grin and bear it and avoid taking in any additional calories, we can lose weight pretty much at the same rate if we just eat sugary foods.

Getting hung up on calorie counting and what foods you are eating is not necessary. If you want to lose weight just remove some of the usual portion from your plate. This has been likened to a self-inflicted period of eating austerity by who else but a couple of economists. The authors present overeating as going into debt, with the results eventually being a default (a serious health problem) or the aforementioned austerity. This presents the simple basis for weight loss, eating less.

If you want to do so in a healthier way, substitute the reduction in your normal intake with healthier alternatives; you may well find your portion sizes increase. For example, a can of baked beans has roughly the same number of calories as 4 squares of chocolate, or over two and a half heads of broccoli. But if we make the simple assumption that losing weight is the goal and that genetics make only marginal impacts for the vast majority, then just sliding a little of your plate into a plastic box for tomorrow, will help you reach your goals.

The internet is full of businesses looking to push their supplements. Yes, if you are already eating the right range of foods and looking to stimulate greater muscle development or struggle to process certain vitamins or nutrients, then a supplement may be the answer. Don't reach for them as a quick solution to becoming healthier though! Often a nutrient deficiency suggests we should eat a greater range of foods, rather than routinely taking the same pill. 25% of UK secondary school children have no breakfast, while two in three 10-16s and 18% of 3-10s regularly consume energy drinks. This suggests that there are plenty of people who need to develop the habit of eating regularly, before simply reaching for a pill (or more worryingly it seems the energy drink) to solve their nutritional needs.

A Burger in the Hand

If our body's mechanics mean that by simply reducing our portion sizes, we will lose weight, why do we struggle to achieve our fitness goals?

As we saw in chapter two, part of the reason is that a burger in the hand is worth more to us at the time, than the future health benefits we gain by reaching for a salad. On top of the issue of discounting the future is something called visceral influences, things such as hunger tiredness and boredom which impact how we value things.

Imagine you are on diet day one. You've had porridge for breakfast, eaten your five-a-day and have rigidly kept to the recommended calorie count for you to safely lose weight. You're on your new daily evening walk and you smell something - It's your favourite takeaway place. Not only does the food smell amazing, but it reminds you of how hungry you are, given you didn't have your usual pudding for lunch. Come to think of it, you probably ate less then you should have anyway, and work today was especially tough, you probably deserve something extra, no harm in looking! You pop in thinking that a small portion of chips is probably okay. But once you start eating you think, I said I wouldn't eat here anymore, I've failed my diet! All your work was for nothing, all that planning. You'll have to start again completely fresh tomorrow and do things properly, but if that's the case, why not have a hot dog as well, since you're here. An ice cream would be great too, especially if you aren't dieting till tomorrow now.

Does this sound familiar?

Here we can see how even the most well-planned change to our lifestyles can be undone by a simple factor like hunger, or boredom, or tiredness from a long day at work.

These feelings make us act against our own self-interest and afterwards make us question why we acted in the way we did. Alcohol and drug abuse is an extreme example of these influences at work. An addict will ignore all other goods he or she would normally value, such as money, a stable job or family that is there to support them, in pursuit of their next high. Even prominent classical economists noted the phenomenon that individuals do not always follow the course of action that would benefit them most, for example:

"At the very time of acting, at the moment in which passion mounts the highest, he hesitates and trembles at the thought of what he is about to do: he is secretly conscious to himself that he is breaking through those measures of conduct which, in all his cool hours, he had resolved never to infringe, which he had never seen infringed by others without the highest disapprobation, and the infringement of which, his own mind forebodes, must soon render him the object of the same disagreeable sentiments."

- Adam Smith, the father of Economics

Or put more concisely:

"Dieting is easy until you get hungry."

- Me

Or even

"We all do dumb **** when we are ****** up"

- Mike Tyson, The Hangover

Padlocking the Cookie Jar

So how do we deal with these sudden and powerful emotions which distort our behaviour?

Sadly, even being aware of these emotions is not sufficient to succeed in overcoming them as individuals routinely underestimate the impact of these feelings on their actions. For example, the ONS found in 2018 that 1 in 3 UK adults underestimate what they eat and across the whole population we underestimate how much we eat daily by almost 60%! Positive and direct action is required to overcome visceral influences. Below I list a few of my favourites.

75

Commitment factors - We can commit to eating less or eating more healthily by effectively burning the bridges to less healthy options. For example, preparing a meal the day before and bringing it in for lunch, rather than buying a takeaway, will not only save you money but remove the option to buckle and go for the less healthy alternative. Leaving cash at home or in your car also limits the chances of you being tempted by extra meals or the nearest vending machine. A shopping list helps keep you from being tempted to buy extras, by committing you to a fixed set of ingredients.

Guilt aversion - This is another emotion which arises when a person believes their action will negatively impact another. This can be directly, such as not wanting to take the last slice of cake when you know your significant other has been looking forward to it all day (however funny their reaction might be!), or indirectly, such as skipping the queue and feeling the hatred of those behind descend upon you, making you feel bad about what you've done. This can work for us, if we tell others our plans for reducing our intake of certain foods. Any true friend will be quick to rip into us, if we fall short of our aims.

Self-imposed taxes:

Governments have tried, with mixed success, to put us off unhealthy eating, by putting taxes on certain products. We can attempt to be more successful by targeting the items to which we are particularly susceptible, for instance by keeping a swear jar for unhealthy eating and inserting a pound for every misstep.

More Influences:

Often the most effective way of battling visceral influences is by putting others to work against it. A hard task is often balanced by the benefits we tell ourselves we will see at the end of it. Whether it's cleaning the house, finishing that essay or sending that honest message to a friend, if we can visualise an immediate benefit, even one as simple as we won't have to worry about it anymore, the inertia of not doing it seems to shrink.

Avoid breaking the seal:

With all these measures or restrictions we put on ourselves to meet our goals, it is important not to let any of these deals we have made slip. If you have promised to avoid chocolate biscuits and then succumb to one, it is hard to argue why you shouldn't have another, they are only small after all? The trouble with this, is that once you have broken the agreement with yourself and not suffered any consequences such as a self-imposed tax or the abuse of those you informed of your plans, then you will be tempted to continue taking small liberties. These accumulate and before you know it you've eaten the entire packet of chocolate chips.

Helpful Nudges:

There are a number of small changes we can make to our diets to nudge ourselves to making healthier choices. Buying smaller packets, bars or cartoons of our less healthy choices reduces the amount we consume of them. Not just because smaller packets mean less food, but that the action of opening another bag sends a conscious reminder to the brain we have continued eating, avoiding our propensity to mindlessly eat our way through an entire family bag in one sitting. Even the colour of what you eat matters! If your unhealthy options are more colourful and diverse, your interest is held for longer and you are likely to eat more. Keeping to a similar set of plain treat foods like plain chocolate will result in you eating less than a selection box.

Gambling Your Life Away

Entering a casino is a unique experience - windowless, bright lights, constant music, rapid food, bars, hotels attached. In short, everything you could need to stay there in perpetuity, provided you have the cash of course. The lengths owners go to maximising the experience for customers is amazing and disturbing. Rarely will you see a clock and often all sight of the outside world is removed, to make sure customers cannot gauge how long they have been gambling. Music is set to the universally pleasing major key to ensure punters are kept happy and spending. A pleasing odour is maintained to relax customers and even stimulate risk-taking hormones. Food and drink are on hand to make sure there is no need to leave before handing over your wallet. If it was not for the damage caused by gambling on the worst affected, the effort that goes into the design would be admirable. With such repetition of a simple message, keep playing, keep playing, it is easy to see why so many people come away with empty pockets.

This level of signal bombardment is also seen in advertising and is another reason why so many struggle with weight. Walking around any town centre reveals the problem if you take a moment to observe. Shop windows, bus stops, billboards, everywhere you look advertising is there, and with food ranking as the third highest spender on marketing by industry (£895 million in 2018, behind Retail and Finance) you can bet many of them will be trying to convince you to eat more. Couple this with a million and one chains nearby ready to serve food immediately and the perfect opportunity to convince people to keep eating is created.

Both industries, food and gambling, make use of these visceral influences, that adverts can stimulate, to increase our consumption of their goods. This is why you see chains so close to each other; they are taking advantage of sudden flashes of hunger or desire for a sugary fix. This, combined with our less than perfect valuation of present and future benefits, makes healthy eating more difficult than it might appear.

This is the trouble when our incentives to push for healthier living, are not aligned with big industries which make more profit from us eating more. The key is to try and align our incentives with industry, or simply to ignore their attempts.

Food adverts are understandably alluring. The information that we receive suggests more eating equals more happiness, often clashes with a medical view of healthy eating. Even supposedly healthy alternatives, like salads, can be laced with fats and oils, making us suspicious of all options. This usually results in us reverting to our preferred and, usually, less healthy option. The number of times I have eyed a tempting chicken salad or wrap and walked away in annoyance to find it is just as calorific as the all-day breakfast alternative next door!

As a result, many have argued that governments must impose restrictions or even outright bans on all adverts of this ilk, but this has proved a complex issue. The reality of banning junk food is much more easily said than done. For starters, what constitutes junk food?

The UK Government has proposed bans on the advertisement of 'junk food', online and pre-watershed on TV, stating that this ban would impact HFSS (high in fat, sugar and salt) foods. However, this definition involves banning advertising on a range of foods we would not normally describe as junk and appears to disproportionately penalise foods often held up as classic British cuisine, which the UK Government has said it wants to promote overseas!

"The government is proposing a total ban on all internet advertising for a huge range of perfectly normal food and drink products. It will cover everything from jam and yoghurt to Cornish pasties and mustard, and will include all forms of online advertising, including paid-for search engine listings, emails and even text messages – at any time day or night.

"No country in the world has attempted anything like this and with good reason. It will permanently exclude businesses large and small from the primary marketing medium of our time. It is an ill-considered policy designed by fanatics who have mis-sold it to politicians as a ban on 'junk food' advertising. It will be hugely damaging to food producers, especially small businesses and start-up companies, and will have no impact on obesity. No one has ever been harmed by an advert for a pork pie."

- *Christopher Snowdon, Institute of Economic Affairs, on the UK government's proposed ban on online advertisement of HFSS foods, 2020*

It seems therefore that junk food is okay if we sell it to foreigners, but not consume it ourselves!

Many people would view a ban as a blunt instrument. Prohibiting any form of advertising would limit the ability of new products and firms to reach their market, restrict competition and the range of choices for consumers. The proposed ban by the UK Government would cost TV companies an estimated £200m a year according to the Institute of the Economic Affairs. Moreover, we can see it is extremely difficult for a government to impose restrictions that fairly and accurately treat the problem they want to solve. The answer is not to destroy the market for such information, but to improve the market for information. Policies such as clearer nutritional information at food outlets together with greater transparency on the impacts of overeating. Equally, a greater focus on the true benefits of healthy eating and how to achieve this would benefit those who struggle with search costs or are vulnerable to the bombardment of adverts. Actions like these do not stop anyone from buying what they want, or firms from marketing and producing what they want. Instead they provide the information that people need to make informed decisions on how and what they eat. As with statistics, we must not simply turn our back on advertising, or on becoming healthier. Instead, we must find ways to improve the current system, keeping the benefits, while minimising the negatives.

The Bottom Line:

Sticking to a healthy diet is undoubtedly a challenge, just ask my parents. As I write this, my partner and I are currently visiting. On my right my father holds a plate stacked with three different tubs of ice-cream. On my left, my partner repeatedly nudges me to pass her one. This is unsurprising, however, given the medley of confusing and contradictory health messages we receive from the internet and the adverts that repeatedly pop up on our TV screen (although I'm not sure ice cream has ever been held up as top of the nutritional value table). Even more understandable is our regular overconsumption as a result of our disregard for future costs. We are assailed by various emotional influences that alter our decision-making, be it a tear-jerker convincing us we need a pick-me-up, or a bore fest that sends us to the kitchen for some relief.

The same tactics are regularly used in the political environment. We are bombarded with simple messages and soundbites. We find it so much easier to back the side that offers the short-term benefits, that appeals to our emotional responses, like tax cuts over future investment, new schemes over improving existing infrastructure.

Using tools like commitment factors and self-imposed taxes will help limit the impact of visceral influences. Looking for credible sources and nuanced analysis over quick fixes will also improve our abilities to search for the right answers, whether they be nutritional or political. Have your head free of emotional influences and you will be better placed to make decisions on your next meal and your next opinion. If we all discarded outside influences, we might well find that our arguments become less divisive and more likely to reach an informed compromise. We might well find that such a change is easier than losing that stubborn belly fat!

5
Freeriding on the Planet

My university first year accommodation saw its fair share of scandal. I came very close to falling out with several members of my living quarters and once we had the option of moving out of our shared accommodation, we all went our separate ways. Strangely this didn't involve any late-night parties or alcohol. In fact, the subject that caused my hall of residence to split, was the cooking.

It all started so well, the group was divided between those with some cooking experience and those without. The fact that I needed a recipe for cheese on toast tells you which group I was in! We agreed to help each other out with the cooking and cleaning the kitchen, which included taking out the bins - my specialty. After a few weeks of peace, unwashed dishes started to sneak into the corners of the kitchen and bin bags to pile up. Speaking to members of the flat it became apparent that someone, no names of course, had begun to leave their jobs undone, preferring instead to let everyone else keep the social space clean instead.

Aside from being very annoying, this freeriding from my flatmates is a good parallel with the environmental problem we face today. While many of us agree that something must be done to reduce the build-up of greenhouse gases, climate change and extreme weather, we are yet to halt the build-up of CO_2 in our atmosphere. As a result, rare weather conditions are becoming more dangerous and far more common. Someone must still be asking for help with the cooking, but not doing the washing up!

As was the case in the previous chapter, we have an issue with a long-term benefit being deemed less immediately important than the short-term costs. Today there are a lot of people whose jobs rely on our current energy sources, not just the CEOs, but their workers and the businesses that serve them. It is easier for these people to let everyone else slowly push for renewable energy, while trying to avoid any direct costs to their own business. For example, reducing operations, sacking staff or explaining to shareholders why profits are down. The same is true for politicians who have a million and one policy options they would like to enact and only a limited amount of time and money in which to do them. They also know that people are far more likely to support a project that will save them money now, rather than possibly saving other people's lives long into the future. Even more problematic is that the people who will benefit from green policies in fifty years' time are not likely to be able to vote for politicians now, making them far less valuable than those currently walking into voting booths. As a result, all manner of excuses will come forth to delay hard decision making. Everything from denying the existence of global warming, to arguing renewables cannot replace fossil fuels, to claiming we could survive the effects, even as forest fires and hurricanes reeked destruction across the US in Summer, 2020. But surely, these climate delayers (if not outright deniers) are in the minority now and we can move on regardless? Recent occupants of The White House provide good evidence that this might not yet be the case.

Let Sleeping Cards Lie

My first introduction to game theory (one of the more immediately interesting disciplines in economics) was a game of cards. Each member of the class was given two cards, one black, one red (suits didn't matter). We then had the option of handing in the red or the black, face down. Keeping the red would give the individual more points at the end of the game, giving up the red would give the whole group more points. In order to win three quarters of cards handed in had to be red. If not, all players would lose, regardless of the points they had amassed individually. In the first round most of us dutifully handed in our red card and easily won the round as a team. Once our teacher pointed out that several of the group had gained more points by keeping the red and letting everyone else sacrifice themselves, the team fell apart immediately; everyone kept their reds and we promptly started losing games.

This is why neither side can ignore the other and continue to push their own agendas, without understanding the other. If parts of the economy start to incur costs from going green while others free ride from the effort, the green firms will feel disadvantaged and likely reduce the scale of their ambitions. If we cannot convince everyone to work in the same direction, the efficiency gains of all moving as a unit will be lost, and the size of change achieved will be too small.

As soon as one person leaves out the bins, who is going to bother doing the dishes?

Sadly, the situation in my dorm room did not improve. People moved their crockery into their rooms, the cleaner complained about us, and the main offenders' dishes cultivated mould, some poetic justice at least! A possible tactic to avoid this would have been to charge people for leaving the bins out, or not doing their dishes. Once people received a small fine for missing duties, they'd surely stop the free riding, or, in the case of my more affluent flatmates, start paying for the clutter they were leaving behind them. Sadly, such a suggestion received the reaction you might expect in a student flat; no one was interested in risking fines. They simply didn't like the idea of an individual interrupting their lives. It would have taken a higher authority, like the university, to impose such a system. Even then, parents and students would probably have seen this as an unnecessary impingement of student rights.

I hope to prove in this chapter, that a bridge can be built between both sides on the green issue, and maybe grease the wheels of environmental conservation. I'm sure, however, that solving university hall arguments is beyond the reach of this book and most others. I will start with some evidence on climate change and its effects on people today, not just decades into the future.

Proving the Point for the Hundredth Time

Whether we agree/disagree on the extent to which climate change is human related or part of the world's course, we can still improve our situation by not increasing the speed of change. Evidence provided by ice cores (long cylinders of ice drilled from glaciers), show that carbon dioxide and other greenhouse gases correlate strongly with air temperature, and that current levels of the former, is unprecedented for over 420,000 years.

Some will argue that these levels are not out of place in the wider context of Earth's history. While this might be accurate, the speed at which change is occurring is far from being in line with normal global climate movements. Moreover, just because Earth has been in a similar state of CO_2 and temperature before, does not mean we want to return to that era. That period of history (the Pliocene) was inhabited by 50-foot sharks, 4 tonne sloths and most pertinently, not humans. While this comparison is borderline flippant, it is important to point out there is value in avoiding speeding up a natural process.

Another issue with this debate, and mankind more generally, is our temptation to regard our species as immortal given our current dominance. We talk about destroying the planet and forget that we will destroy ourselves much more quickly. A brilliant quote from the always philosophical Ian Malcolm, in one of my favourite books (and films) of all time, goes as follows:

"Let's be clear. The planet is not in jeopardy. We are in jeopardy. We haven't got the power to destroy the planet—or to save it. But we might have the power to save ourselves."

-     *Ian Malcolm*

And for those arguing that humans are not so brittle, remember again that the aim should not be to make our time on this planet any more difficult than it already is for so many.

Evidence from 355 studies between 2011 and 2019 which looked at extreme weather around the world found that 69% of extreme weather events were made more severe or more likely by human-initiated climate change. 9% were fortunately made less severe/likely by human impacts. This means that at least 78% are affected by humans and the vast majority are either worse or more regular because of us. Among these events, extreme heat events were made more likely or severe by humans 93% of the time. For flooding, this was 54% and droughts, 61%.

And what does this mean for the people on the ground?

During the 2003 heatwave, temperatures were at their highest since 1540. An estimated 506 of the 735 fatalities in Paris that summer were due to climate change being made more intense than would otherwise have been the case. Since then, Europe has had its 5 hottest summers in 500 years in the last 15. Each time, more avoidable casualties are recorded. In 2018, Scandinavia recorded 950 deaths due to record-breaking heat levels. This in a country that had not required air conditioning until this century!

Thinking back to the stats chapter, we know that one event having a particular outcome does not tell us much about the causes of that outcome. In other words, correlation does not necessarily imply causation. Fortunately, the sample size and repetition of this investigation across many weather events means we can be sure of human impact on extreme weather, which in turn makes our lives more difficult.

A good, if Americanised analogy, is supplied by the American Meteorological Society, of a baseball player who starts taking steroids. If the player begins hitting 20% more home runs than before, it would not be possible to say for sure whether a particular home run is because of the steroids, or the player's ability. However, it is possible to say how the steroids have altered the likelihood that the player hits a home run, by comparing their current and historical performances. As the report put it:

"Given that steroids have resulted in a 20% increased chance that any particular swing of the player's bat results in a home run, you would be able to make an attribution statement that, all other things being equal, steroid use had increased the probability of that particular occurrence by 20%."

So, while these studies do not claim to prove an event was caused completely by climate change, the repetition of results does prove that the severity and likelihood of such events have increased due to changes in our environment brought about by increased emissions.

This evidence has led to a greater understanding of the scale and complexity of the challenge. It should also start to establish the basic premise that the problem exists and bring people from across political divides together. It should also prevent one side simply declaring global warming a myth, or that every time a flood occurs, it's due to idiots building on floodplains, rather than a wider global problem. Our ability to put a human cost on our actions will also help us move from philanthropic arguments to quantitative discussions on how we solve these issues.

"A few years ago, after [hurricanes] Irma, Maria and Harvey, the cleanup was $265 billion. Wouldn't it have been smarter, folks, to have reduced odds that you're going to have that kind of storm? And the costs of treating kids for environmentally induced asthma, largely from coal plant emissions: We spend $55 billion a year to hospitalize and care for those kids."

John Kerry, US Special Presidential Envoy for Climate

But while the arguments over whether we contribute to climate change are largely over, the arguments on how we deal with the issue are still largely open to debate.

It Takes Two to Tango, and to Save the Planet

"Capitalism tends to destroy its two sources of wealth: nature and human beings"

– Karl Marx

On October 31st, 2018, Extinction Rebellion was formally announced as a global environmental movement outside the Houses of Parliament. Since then it has inspired thousands to engage in peaceful protest, and enjoys support from 47% of 18-24-year-olds, as well as public displays of support from celebrities from Emma Thompson to Radiohead.

However, the Rebellion has also cost the taxpayer millions in police arrests and the overseeing of protests. It has also defended members accused of all manner of criminal damage, including on one occasion, floating a house down the Thames, because they claim such actions are necessary to stop climate change.

Most divisive of all has been its take on the current capitalist system. Many of its critics claim that the group wants to destroy capitalism and usher in an era of de-growth and permanent recession. While officially Extinction Rebellion claims to be beyond politics and not a socialist movement, the mixed messages from its leadership, including claims that "capitalism must die" has done little to dissuade its opponents from seeing it as a threat to our dominant economic system.

This link between environmentalism and anarchic economic policy is one particularly pushed by the extremes on both sides. However, as we saw in Chapter 1, supporters and detractors of movements or political parties are often far less zealous than the leaders of groups like Extinction Rebellion. Many people who marched through London to oppose climate change did not want to bring down our current economic system. Equally, many who have denounced their actions as unhelpful, damaging or even actions akin to terrorists, do not believe that nothing more needs to be done to preserve the environment. Therefore, we must look beyond the angry headlines and realise that neither maintaining the status-quo, nor political anarchy, will garner the support or the effective action required to solve this problem.

There are many inherent issues in our current economic system, some explored in later chapters, but they are not necessarily here because capitalism is fatally flawed. Rather, the current incarnation of a system that has pulled billions out of poverty and destitution has strayed from its founding ideas. This has happened for a mix of reasons, from established interests to our fundamental flaws as humans.

For instance, the simple concept of supply and demand is based on the idea that we understand all the costs and benefits of a purchase involved, and that we only impact ourselves, when completing the purchase. The reality, however, as was discussed in the previous chapter, is far from this.

For example, when I buy a chocolate bar for my breakfast rather than preparing a proper meal, I understand the cost of the bar and the benefit of how it makes me feel. I may not notice until much later, however, that this less than optimal habit may be impacting my health. How do I value the impact of each individual chocolate bar on my waistline? What's more, if I really let it go and end up in hospital for weight-related issues, I will not have factored in the chance that such questionable food choices will eventually cost the taxpayer.

Capitalism and classical economics usefully provide the cash incentive for business owners to produce different breakfast options. These concepts also explain my own internal cost-benefit analysis that ultimately results in my misguided meal decision, as it is driven by my sugar-focused self-interest. However, their assumption that we have perfect foresight and understanding of all the benefits and costs is limiting. The reality is that we do not and so the issue is not with the system but with ourselves.

Sadly, this means we cannot rely on altruism alone to solve our problems with the environment. While many may care enough about the planet to lower their consumption and push the companies that supply their demands to do the same, we will still find it next to impossible to correctly gauge the future costs of our consumption, especially when the fast parts of our brain are allowed to take over!

Altruism at the government level can also be misguided:

Imagine first a city that is not within the jurisdiction of a local government. When extreme weather events occur in a specific district, such as flooding on an area built alongside a river. In such a city without the jurisdiction of a local government, capitalist economies will send price signals to the housing market to reflect the hazardous nature of living in this section of the city. For example, the cost of home insurance in such an area will likely rise if the flooding becomes a regular occurrence. This will discourage people from living in this area and so the impacts of extreme weather events are mitigated by the private sector. Meanwhile, if the same city is supported by a local government, outcomes might be very different. If the government steps in to protect and repair damaged property, people will be encouraged (or at least discouraged less) from settling in this area, and the costs to the taxpaying population of protection from flood risk will rise.

While some blame undeniably lies at our feet, another problem is the push from businesses for us to consume more than we need. Advertisements plastered across our towns and cities are testament to the efforts, by firms, to make us consume more than we need. Think bargain-bucket prices on food, multi-packs in supermarkets, frequent flier miles. This overconsumption means we are working through our natural resources far quicker than necessary, as well as fuelling a debt mountain, as we spend more each month than we currently earn.

The challenge for leaders across the world is therefore how best to deal with the imperfections both of large companies and ourselves, within the current capitalist model. An example of a failure here is the attempt by Australia, at a carbon tax, which cost companies millions, increased energy prices by up to 6%, and decreased emissions by less than 2%. This proves that governments struggle effectively to internalise future costs into today's world too. However, this does not mean we should allow our current form of capitalism to forget about all the costs and benefits of their actions. Capitalism at its core, spurs economic growth through competition, and understandably, reducing costs is part of this competition. Simply imposing artificial costs will not necessarily alter behaviour. As in Australia, if not properly considered, policies can simply result in the consumer paying higher prices without any change in emissions. That said, making sure we include all present and future costs of production is not moving away from traditional capitalism, but rather creating a more accurate version of it.

If we make sure the environment is just another area of competition for companies, we will have maintained our current economic system which has achieved so much good. At the same time we will avoid waking up in 20 years' time a lot heavier and a lot hotter, which is the future we face if we don't include all the costs of our actions, whether its buying chocolate or forgetting about emissions.

Readers probably know a friend or relative (if not themselves!) who laments 'the good old days' as my father would say, 'before health and safety went mad!' They argue that government and regulators have no place in the economy, whether it's on the environment or any other type of interference in the market. They maintain that the 'people who have actually worked for a living,' will always be more effective without government officials, 'who haven't spent a day of their lives in the real world!'

"The nine most terrifying words in the English language are: I'm from the government, and I'm here to help."

Ronald Reagan

Government slip-ups and projects accused of being white elephants like HS2 (which will remain a debate for now) and the O2 (which isn't) add credibility to these views but are not the end of the story.

While government involvement in all parts of the economy is not desirable, neither is leaving our economies open completely to the market, and both sides must accept that we will never be arguing for one of the two extremes. A crucial example of this comes from the supposed hey-day of free markets in the UK, the Industrial Revolution. The birthplace of modern economic growth was a time of low regulation, and as I have argued before, it was the greater freedoms of the middle and upper classes that drove this growth in Britain first. But would we still want the low level of government interference that was prevalent back then? There are very few I imagine, who would argue for the repeal of the laws banning children from as young as four, becoming chimney sweeps, as was permitted in Victorian England. Even workhouses, horrible places where debtors and orphans alike worked to earn their generally appalling housing, were still a form of government 'support'.

On the environment the same was true, even in an era of factories and satanic mills. As early as the 1870s, slaughterhouse owners were regulated to limit the emissions of the stench of their work to within their buildings, rather than allowing it to waft through the streets. The Public Health Act (1866), while lacking legal teeth, instructed corporations to minimise and eventually remove the causes of smog across the country.

So before we discuss, to what extent the government should be involved in making for a greener economy, we must accept that some level of regulation will be required and that across all areas of the economy, we have never lived in a purely free market economy. One does not need to look far to see how over-government involvement will damage an economy (the next chapter is a good start). We must attempt a more nuanced discussion than just saying we must ignore the private sector when designing our future economy. Equally, we should recognise government will also have a role too. The extent of each is still up for grabs but must be decided now!

What Will it Take to Make People Pick up Dog Mess?

Lockdown has resulted in the majority of household outings of the last year, being long walks up and down the promenade of my seaside hometown. This increase in more active trips than say, to the cinema, or to restaurants has resulted in far more fresh air, sunlight in our lives, not to mention the extra activity – a definite plus. However, with so many people doing the same, many of them dog owners, we have not returned every time, particularly in the early morning and late evenings when visibility is low, without an unwanted addition to the bottom of our shoes. This issue of having to spend walks around local parks and green spaces, eyes peeled for mess, has been a bone of contention with my father in particular, for years. He has deemed the issuing of fines as insufficient, even at the current £1000 level of my local area. He points to our recent missteps as evidence it is not enough to deter selfish dog-owners. He has even suggested a policy of installing snipers on the top of various hotels and flats along popular thoroughfares, to search for any dog owners not keeping to the rules on mess. The punishment of instant death for the dog, or its owner (he's still working through the details) would surely be enough to ensure no mess is left in public places.

Sadly, for him and thankfully for dog-owners, this is not seen as a credible option. The fact remains, however, that dog mess continues to be an issue.

So why don't fines work?

A study in Israel, which looked at the impact of fines in the day-care industry, has some interesting answers to this question:

"Specifically, we studied the effect of fines on the frequency with which parents arrive late to collect their child from day-care centers. Our data include observations of 10 day-care centers over a period of 20 weeks. In the first 4 weeks we simply observed the number of parents who arrived late. At the beginning of the fifth week we introduced a fine in six of the 10 day-care centers. The fine was imposed on parents who arrived more than 10 minutes late. No fine was introduced in the four other day-care centers, which served as a control group. After the introduction of the fine we observed a steady increase in the number of parents coming late. At the end of an adjustment period that lasted 2–3 weeks, the number of late-coming parents remained stable, at a rate higher than in the no-fine period."

These results surprised the researchers and I suspect us readers too. Why would a fine increase the regularity of lateness?

This work uncovers not only the difficulty of setting effective fines, but also introduces us to how contracts work between parties, and how conflicting interests can result in poor outcomes for both sides, if the contract is not well developed, (Contract Theory for the boffs).

When we agree contracts, it is often the process of agreeing a good or service in return for a price. When you walk into a coffee shop and order a latte and a muffin to go, you have entered into a contract with the firm when you hand over the money. You have not sat down and signed a contract to say you will give this money, and in two minutes you will receive the goods you paid for, but that is the bargain you have implicitly agreed. Obviously forcing everyone to write wavers for every transaction would be a huge drain on time and so, many contracts are implicit or simply ignored by customers (when was the last time you read the terms and conditions?) However, this leaves grey areas in many aspects of our lives. What if I don't get a coffee for ten minutes, or an hour, or five days? Rarely does the process of ordering a coffee involve agreeing the exact time of delivery, as a more traditional contract might. Instead, firms employ common standards across their branches, such as refunds for late or missed orders, so that customers can be sure they will receive a good service. If they cannot enforce these standards, people's faith in the firm will fall, and eventually, customers will stop coming. This reliance on implicit sections of contracts means changing the rules with fines and other measures can result in adverse results, if we attempt to fill in these grey areas.

In the day-care example, the explicit part of the contract was that the firm would look after the child for a set number of hours, and the customer would pay them for that time. The implicit section was that parents should not be late picking up their children and if they are, there should be a good reason. Equally the firm should not dump their child outside, the second the agreed time of the service expires. When a fine is imposed on late comers that grey area disappears. Parents view being late, not as failing the implicit standards (in this case we might call such an amorphous thing a social norm), but as an acceptable part of the arrangement, if they pay the fine. As a result, latecomers will increase provided the fine is sufficiently small that parents would rather pay the fine, than be kept to a firm deadline.

The same is true for dog mess. Imposing a fine disrupts the social norm that we expect people to clear up after their pets.

Instead of feeling guilt for not picking up the mess, owners may see it as their right to do so and that if caught, they will just pay the fine. Unlike the day-care example where the fines were small, fines for leaving dog mess can be large. However, unlike the day-care example, the chance of being caught is far less certain. As a result, the expected cost (the fine multiplied by the % chance of being fined) of allowing dogs to go wherever they like is much smaller than the fine itself. As a result, fines may not deter certain actions, if they are not stronger than the social norms they replace.

If we are to use fines or taxes to change people's behaviour with regards to the environment, we must make sure that the expected cost of the fine/tax is large enough to have a more powerful impact on behaviour than the social norms we currently have in place. We must also make sure therefore, that the likelihood of being caught is large enough that would-be wrongdoers regard it as a credible threat. In the latter two examples, we can see that fines will need to increase for day-care, if we want the desired reduction in lateness. Alternatively, the firm could simply revert to relying on social norms and accepting some lateness. For dog mess, we need to improve the likelihood that someone will be caught to improve adherence. Novel methods such as DNA tracking are already being tested, or, as some would suggest, there's always the sniper option.

Smoking, Driving and Plastic Bags

Climate change is often described as The Long Emergency. Humanity is excellent at dealing with immediate dangers, whether it be natural disasters or going to hospital for a broken limb. It is less effective with long emergencies, such as global warming or yearly check-ups. For example, 1 million people miss GP appointments every year. Data on people not turning up at A&E when they suffer from a broken limb is harder to find, but I imagine the number is rather smaller.

It is understandable, therefore, that we are slow to address the environmental challenges we face. In chapter five we covered the ways in which we can make future costs be felt in the present and so make us more likely to deal with them. In the case of global warming, at the national level an individual's actions make little difference. Government must be the force that brings the future costs into the present. Libertarians will argue that, gradually, costs will grow to the point that private industry will adapt to meet these challenges without government help. Further, the free market will solve these problems individually. Environmentalists will point to the logic of the card game outlined above, and the problem of free-riders like my old flatmates, as an example of why people won't be more responsible. We can get caught in a feedback loop where bad behaviour elicits more of the same, rather than incentivising better behaviour. They argue government should take control, nationalise power generation, ban emissions beyond a certain level and use other blunt instruments that may prove effective. Conversely, the other side will argue this causes many unnecessary stresses on the market. For example, carbon limits might be okay for some industries but not others, and even if we make the jump to electric, where does electricity come from? While we still need fossil fuels for power, the idea of moving to all electric is merely delaying the inevitable.

What both sides have, so far, failed to realise is that there is a way they can both be right. Government can intervene in the market, but not to limit its influence, but rather facilitate its extension into the environment.

Smoking is a typical example of government extending markets rather than meddling in them. Without taxes on cigarettes a smoker pays for the good and consumes them. But he does not pay for the external costs of those around him, who must suffer the cost of the smoke produced by the activity, or the smell that is left behind. Equally, simply paying for the cost of the cigarettes alone, will not cover his or her increased chances of needing public health assistance to deal with the many implications linked to smoking. A tax on goods that cause negative externalities on those around us, either now or in the future, actually assigns the costs of consuming a good to the consumer, rather than allowing them to free ride on the health and taxes of those around them. The way cigarettes are sold also makes it easy to enforce this tax, meaning that adherence is maintained. Whether the tax is sufficient to change behaviour is questionable given the addictive nature of cigarettes. It is argued that those worst affected will not give up and are simply being hit with a double whammy of tax and health effects. The evidence for this has credibility but, in this example, we can see that even if behaviour is not changed, the proceeds of the tax help mitigate the impacts of the behaviour, as long as the proceeds are put into the public services that deal with the impacts of smoking (namely health).

An action that has attracted praise from both sides of the aisle is the plastic bag tax, and even more incredibly, from both my mother and father. Before these bags were priced, a whole market was not being utilised, people used far more than they needed, supermarkets lost revenue, and our oceans continued to fill with plastic. By pricing the bags, and appealing to everyone's aversion to paying for an unnecessary good (I remember one skit of a customer avoiding paying 5p for a bag by stuffing his shopping in ever more unnatural parts of his clothing to avoid the minimal cost of the bag). Again, we see here how government is actually opening up areas that the market has failed to price. If a greener alternative to the taxed good can also be supplied (in this case the revelation of a reusable bag) then the effects of even a small tax can be huge. In 2014, the year before the tax was introduced, consumers used more than 7.6 billion bags, equalling 61,000 tonnes of plastic. Fast forward to 2020 and sales of single-use plastic bags are down by 95% in England's main supermarkets.

Capitalism to the Rescue?

Can this methodology be extended further to help reduce our consumption of fossil fuels?

One way to answer the question is to look at the sector which is most responsible for our current level of pollution, transport. Our dependence on cars, planes and trains for getting around has meant that they are the largest source of emissions in the UK and much of the West. Also, its progress towards cutting these figures has been comparatively slow, with most sectors cutting emissions by over two-thirds in the last 30 years, while transport pollution has fallen by just 2%.

Whenever we set out in our car, we know that driving will cost us in petrol, but sadly we often also pay the cost in lost time by sitting in traffic. Like the card game, we face the dilemma - if everyone else avoids driving and takes public transport to miss out on the cost of the traffic jam, we can gain from being the only car on the road. Everyone thinks this way and so everyone ends up in a traffic jam. Even attempts to increase capacity often result in encouraging more traffic and so more congestion.

There are no winners here, everyone is paying a cost, and no one is benefitting, especially not the planet, (most of those engines are still belching fumes while sat in the queue). Road pricing, the process of charging each car for using a certain road electronically, rather than with a toll, but with the same effect, changes the cost from one of time, to a monetary cost. Everyone using the popular road pays for it, and this cost can include the long-term cost to the planet of driving. Meanwhile, the increased cost will push some people to avoid driving where possible, or into using less direct routes, spreading out drivers. the traffic jams will disappear and those prepared to pay for their direct and external costs, enjoy a jam free drive. Proceeds from the taxes can also be used to mitigate the impacts of the pollution, for example by subsidising renewable energy development or similar R&D. Moreover, evidence from the plastic bag tax suggests that small costs are equally effective at both ends of the income distribution. It turns out we can all be stingy, regardless of how much we have in the bank! This provides optimistic evidence against the criticism of such schemes that they are regressive and will result in only the wealthy using the most popular roads.

Once again, the government has brought the costs of the future into the present to reduce the chance of disaster later. More importantly (if those pushing for environmental conservation are to succeed), they will do so by facilitating the market, rather than restricting it. There is no silver bullet for convincing others, nor is reducing traffic jams the solution to global warming, but it is a start and a method we can apply to other areas. Reducing consumption gives us more time to develop cheaper renewable energy as well as storing power. Once the cost of green dips below fossil fuels, the market will take the momentum and there will be more of a push to leave oil and gas behind, as has already been the case with coal. Until then, government must continue to create new markets to ensure the polluter pays for their consumption and emissions in a way that appeals to those who disagree with government intervention. This is because I believe the debate has moved from whether climate change exists, to the manner in which we solve the issue. While an outright ban on emissions would be more immediately effective, I believe the creation of new markets has a better chance of political success.

When Government Should Lead, Car Engines, Wind Turbines and Plastic Bags

Governments have the power to impose change whether companies like it or not. The UK government, for example, passed the world's first legally binding national commitment to cutting greenhouse gas emissions, committing to cut emissions by 80% by 2050. This has since been increased to 100%. This includes five carbon budgets between 2008 and 2032 which allow the Committee on Climate Change to monitor the UK's performance. These simple blunt deadlines provide a clear target, rather than the uncertainty of aspirational policies to reduce certain types of pollution, without a clear goal set. Other instruments, such as taxes to increase the cost of producing emissions, allow governments to make sure the additional costs of emissions are felt by the polluters. In the same way that we might stay in to binge-watch series if the price of cinemas goes up, the expectation is that businesses will adjust their spending towards production that doesn't pollute in order to avoid the additional taxation.

Another example, courtesy of the European Union, is the introduction of an emission trading scheme for certain industries. This allows trading of permits to emit a certain amount of CO_2 and other greenhouse gases. The number of permits is set, so regardless of what happens to the prices of these permits and how much of the cost is put onto consumers, this allows governments to limit total pollution across these industries indefinitely.

The UK government has not shied away from implementing blunt instrument policies on other industries either, such as banning new petrol and diesel car production by 2030.

So, regulation is one method, but it's not all bad news for business. The UK government has become a leader in wind energy production. Famous for complaining about the weather, and for politicians that produce plenty of it, the UK has increased its offshore capacity 20-fold in the past ten years, far ahead of other countries with green ambitions such as Germany, Denmark and Japan. Part of this has been the award of subsidised contracts which have won the country massive investment in subsequent years from the likes of Siemens and Orsted.

Not limited to wind, the UK invested £42.1bn in low carbon electricity generation, much of this going towards contracts with private companies to improve our renewable production.

Finally, the average citizen. Government has pushed schemes on the UK people, some welcome, some less so. Policies range from recycling (which had a very mixed response in my household), to the aforementioned plastic bag tax. The latter was received with gusto by people like me who would rather look an idiot carrying everything haphazardly down the street and dropping half of it, than paying 5p.

So, the government has the tools to impose change on a population that even today's industry juggernauts would not be able to manage. For those who doubt the limits of industry power, just look at what happened when producers tried changing the size and shape of a famously triangular chocolate bar and were met with unbridled fury from consumers, before quickly reverting to their original method!

Over the past decade, as a result of these measures, UK CO_2 emissions have fallen by 29%, fossil fuels collectively account for a record-low of 43% in 2020 and 54% of electricity generation is now from low-carbon sources.

When Business Should Lead, Poaching and Plaice

The unique power governments hold, does not mean that business should be removed from the equation altogether. One particularly memorable example comes from a question I encountered when applying for the UK Government's Economic Service went as follows:

Question 4. Give economic reasons why banning the sale of ivory might endanger elephants as a species.

By making it, in effect, illegal to rear elephants as a 'cash crop' this decreases the incentive to breed and protect elephants as an asset. It may also decrease the return to protecting elephants from poachers.

[50%]

Banning sales will reduce ivory supply and could drive-up its price. Hence increasing the incentive to poach elephants.

[25%]

The banning of ivory sales may reduce its demand by increasing awareness of ethical considerations. But this may not result in more elephants; there would certainly be less, not more cows, if the sale of dairy and beef products were banned!

[25%]

Some might argue that ethical reasons should be sufficient for maintaining a good population of elephants. It is difficult to argue with the point that our demand for milk and beef, not our ethics, is the reason cows are not facing extinction too though!

Another example concerns the rights to a finite resource. If a lake of fish is open to all fishermen, then each individual has no interest in fishing sustainably, because he knows the next person may not be so noble. Handing the land over to a private company might well have a more desirable result. Where fishermen are charged for the fish they catch, allowing a sustainable population to be maintained. In this way, assigning property rights to the private sector can lead to more responsible actions, by making people's self-interest work with, rather than against, the environment.

The ability of the government to encompass all the costs and benefits of people's actions can be limited too, due to the true nature of production in the modern world. We might want to tax carbon emitted in the production of goods, but what about those that come from other countries? Do we place tariffs on all these goods to reflect the pollution involved in their production? If so, how are going to measure these foreign production methods?

A single government acting alone may find it difficult assigning property rights too. As was all too obvious during the Brexit negotiations, rights over fishing are difficult to regulate, given that fish do not adhere to national boundaries.

A solution, not necessarily precluded by Brexit, is to work across borders. Common sets of standards can be agreed, to encourage companies to produce responsibly, no matter where they are based.

A mix between government regulation and free market policies is required. This allows the market to produce goods effectively, while also internalising all the costs of production, not just to the consumer, but to the planet in general. Government must act like a referee in sport, providing and enforcing the rules which allow the players to perform at their best, rather than allowing the game to degrade into a lawless brawl, with the ultimate winner being all us spectators.

Coal, a Case Study:

In 2019 the UK burned just 8 million tonnes of coal in its factories and power stations. While this still sounded like a lot to me, it was the first time the UK's dependence on the black stuff had been this low, since the creation of James Watt's steam engine in the second half of the eighteenth century. A hallmark of the Industrial Revolution was that as much as 200 million tonnes was being used by the mid-20th century. Such was coal's importance in driving the first industrialised society, powering its cities as well as shrouding them in smog, that is seeped into the lives and lungs of the population for generations to come.

"Civilisation … is founded on coal. The machines that keep us alive, and the machines that make machines, are all directly or indirectly dependent upon coal."
-       Down the Mine, George Orwell

In 1971, 88% of electricity supplied to the UK market was still powered by coal. By 2018 the size of the industry had shrunk to 5%, largely replaced by renewables and gas turbines. This change has greatly improved the green credentials of the UK and massively improved the air quality in our towns and cities, providing an example to the rest of Europe and the World.

"The British experience shows that any country can actually do it [end coal power], it's a question of putting the policies in place to do it,"

"Had Germany decided to tackle coal first rather than nuclear [which it has committed to phasing out by 2022], I think Germany could be in a similar position to the UK."

-   Richard Black, director of the Energy & Climate Intelligence Unit

So how did a country, whose history has been tightly entwined with one of the most polluting fossil fuels, largely wean itself off the stuff after centuries of dependence?

Josh Burke, policy fellow at the Grantham Research Institute on Climate Change and the Environment, claimed in an interview with the Financial Times in 2020 that a "confluence of market drivers and regulatory interventions" worked together, particularly since the start of the 21st century, to all but end our use of coal.

Regulations forcing new coal plants to be constructed with expensive carbon capture technology and the carbon tax imposed in 2013 helped bring the external costs of coal back to the producers, making its use far less competitive compared to cleaner fuels. The rise in the carbon price coincided perfectly with the fall in the use of coal, tipping the balance in favour of natural gas and renewables.

Government has played a huge role in the reduction of the country's use of coal for decades. Since the Clean Air Act of 1956 coal consumption in the UK has been falling as the government encourages people to use fewer polluting alternatives in an attempt to reduce smog. This century billions in public money has been spent growing the Nation's wind farms, resulting in 37% of our electricity coming from renewable energy. Arguably the final nail in the coffin for coal, came from the government, with the 2015 announcement that it would cease to be used by 2025.

Not to be outdone, the incentive-lead and profit seeking private sector also had a key role in upscaling the alternatives to coal. In the 1960s, diesel and electric trains started to replace those run on steam. Far more efficient, they quickly replaced all mainline passenger trains by 1968. In the 1990s the UK electricity industry was privatised. Regulations on the use of natural gas in power generation were relaxed, leading to a private sector-led surge in North Sea gas usage, rising from 5 to 30% of the UK's electricity capacity. Renewable energy has lower running costs than coal, meaning that once their construction was complete, they were prioritised over coal when supply from a single source was sufficient to meet demand (for example over the summer months when fewer of us have the heating on). New advances in battery storage technology have also meant that while wind and solar remain less reliable than fossil fuels (The UK's weather is anything but consistent) the National Grid have stated that any volatility can easily be smoothed out by stored power.

Sadly, there are still losers from these progressive steps. Steelmakers, who must have access to coal in the production process for specialist products in the aerospace and automotive industries, have argued an outright ban will result in this production moving overseas with the jobs and the money they produce going too.

This example sets out the positive and negative actions governments can take in the area of conservation. A mix of internalising the external costs of dirty energy creation and investing in clean renewables can make positive change, by working with industry. Blunt instruments and outright bans, rather than providing the opportunity for firms to negate the external costs of their output, such as carbon sequestration technology, result in adverse effects such as profitable companies closing down or moving overseas unnecessarily.

As we must come together to understand and work towards solving the problem of climate change, so government and industry must become more closely aligned to avoid freeriding. Otherwise we will have more to deal with in the future, than a few angry flatmates and overflowing bins!

6

Economics Cliché No.1 – A Chapter on China

Fans of a particular office-based series will remember a particular episode, where the generally clueless manager, Michael reads a report on China's growing economy and population at the dentist, largely due to the lack of comics available. The discussion, as is often depicted in comedies featuring American foreign policy, devolves into a debate on where to bomb China first. While we are far from having a Michael in the White House (depending on when you read this of course!) this sensationalist attitude to the second largest economy in the world, is widespread across the US, for both obvious reasons, and some more subtle ones.

As of Spring 2021, China appears to be beating this book to the punch by uniting both left and right, by attracting criticism from both sides. Concern, from Australia to the UK, that the use of Huawei technology could be used by state-sponsored hackers as backdoors to strategically vital networks, such as sovereign countries' power stations, has led to the Chinese company being blacklisted across the globe. This traditionally right-wing priority of national security and defence spending is supplemented by the left's criticism of human rights abuses conducted by China. The reports that China has detained over a million Uighurs, in the years leading up to 2020, in 're-education camps' has led to widespread criticism. Further accusations of forced sterilisation of Uighurs drove the UK Foreign Secretary at the time, Dominic Raab, to denounce China's actions as "gross and egregious" human rights abuses.

I risk uniting both sides further (in opposition to this book, an odd strategy I concede) by claiming that the second largest economy in the world is not to be feared. Not because it hasn't committed industrial espionage or human rights offences, but because its economic power, the strength of the Communist Party and its geopolitical influences have been overplayed in recent years.

First however, a short history, and the understandable list of arguments why China could be seen as a dangerous adversary.

The Dragon Rises

The Chinese Communist Revolution, led by Mao Zedong, began in 1946, spurred by an invasion by the Japanese and a resulting wave of nationalism, in the largely rural and incredibly unequal society (10% of the population had as much wealth as the bottom two-thirds). It ended with the creation of the People's Republic of China, which was led by the Communist Party of China under Mao for the rest of his life. He quickly embarked on a plan which aimed to improve the productivity of Chinese agriculture and massively increase the size of the industrial sector. The ultimate aim was to copy the move Britain and the US had made in becoming modern economic nations. This plan, known as The Great Leap Forward, was a failure, on a scale, that dwarfs many of the odd policy decisions we see across the world today. On the industrial side, farm workers were instructed to construct furnaces and retrain as steel workers overnight. Such an order makes the poorly timed advert about those employed in the arts retraining in cyber, wrongly attributed to the UK's Culture Department in 2020 amidst the Coronavirus Crisis, seem reasonable.

These untrained workers were given quotas for steel production, which could not be filled with the amount of raw materials they had available at the time. This resulted in bizarre reports that ex-farmers were melting down tools and cutlery to produce enough goods for the quotas, including more of the same cutlery; using forks to make knives!

Meanwhile new agriculture policies included planting more crops in the same number of acres, leading to crowded fields and lower yields. Arguably this didn't matter given there were now far fewer farmers, meaning not all crops could be picked. While this appears comical, it sadly led to the death of between 10-60 million people from the resulting famine.

In 1978 Deng Xiaoping took over control of the Communist party and the country. He inherited a nation that was starving, but the success of his reforms meant that when he left office in 1989, it was with the title "Architect of Modern China".

Agriculture productivity shot up under Deng, leading to the excess supply of workers required to build the industrial power Mao had hoped for. Despite the attempts of the previous regime during the Agricultural Revolution, in 1978, 80% of the Chinese population were still working in the fields. By 1994, only 50% were. Deng's open-door policy to foreign investment meant that the level of investment from overseas, which had been negligible before 1978, rose to nearly US$100bn in 1994, up from 1% of fixed investment to 18%.

Deng's focus on economic success over ideology meant that between 1978 and 2017, GDP grew nearly 24 times.

"It doesn't matter if this cat is black or white, so long as it catches mice"

- *Deng Xiaoping*

Crouching Tiger, Hidden Dragon

This success has earnt China many plaudits, and sceptics, since the turn of the century. The recent issues, whether unsubstantiated conspiracy theories on Coronavirus or more reasonable criticisms on human rights, have ignited a long running feeling of unease in the West about China. Be it currency manipulation, or attempts to absorb more of the surrounding lands into the country, like Tibet and Hong Kong, fear of China seems only to have risen with its economic might, but are we already too late to act?

In May 2020, the World Bank reported that, for the first time, China's total real (inflation-adjusted) income was slightly larger than that of the US. And it's not just dismal scientists predicting a changing of the guard. Elon Musk predicted in February 2020 that China would eventually become two to three times larger than the US, noting that given the population difference between the two (330million vs. 1.3bn), that a GDP per capita of only 50% of the US, would make China twice the size in economic terms.

These observations, particularly over population difference, and the country's ever more active role in geopolitics, are usually at the heart of why so many people fear the rising power of China. Additionally, there are a number of long-standing grievances that countries have with the People's republic. Some claim that several unfair practices are a route cause of China's rapid growth story. Overproduction of materials like steel to export and flood foreign markets in order to weaken or remove existing producers, is one example. This 'dumping' of products can be likened to a chain store that lowers its prices to put local shops out of business, before jacking up the prices once it is the only show in town. China has also been guilty of buying and selling reserves of foreign currency in order to influence their exchange rate. Interestingly, this practice halted before Donald Trump's 2016 election success, making the period during which he'd labelled China, a currency manipulator, one of the few recent times when they hadn't been. This can also give Chinese exporters an unfair advantage over domestic producers in other countries, as the Yuan has historically been kept artificially low. This makes goods from China cheaper than they would otherwise be, even if the government was not effectively subsiding its products.

China has also regularly invested in developing countries to gain soft influence beyond its borders. I vividly remember hospitals and other infrastructure being constructed by China, during my brief time living in St Lucia, in the Caribbean. Sure enough, a steady stream of island nations have aligned with China's political views, from denouncing the existence of Taiwan as a standalone state, to more recently, 15 nations siding with China in opposing the US-led efforts to recognise opposition leader Juan Guaido as Venezuela's interim president. This catalogue of less than spotless foreign policy decisions explain why many believe China should be viewed with more suspicion than ever before. Many others have gone so far as to say that Donald Trump's rhetoric on China and the proceeding trade war was not just warranted but greatly overdue.

Missing Scales

A reading of history like this would make anyone question the US's position as the economic Hegemon of the future. However, a closer look exposes several weaknesses in the Eastern powerhouse.

Let's start with trade:

Most people my age grew up in a world 'made in China'. Everything from my train set to my Walkman was made in China. Probably the only thing I knew about the country as a child was that it produced a lot of stuff. This still holds true today, with 28% of the world's manufacturing taking place in China, compared to just 17% in the US and 7% in Japan.

This rapid growth in exports didn't occur overnight, but by international standards it was growth at lightning speed. In the 1990s the surplus of goods and services exported over imports was just 1.6% of GDP.

Exports spiked following China's admission to the World Trade Organisation in 2001 and by 2007 exports accounted for 36% of its GDP. The mix of a cheap labour force (the minimum wage in January 2020 was below $3 or £2.20 per hour), less stringent laws on pay and labour rights, and a well-established network of suppliers and distributors has facilitated this dominance in manufacturing. This much is common knowledge, due to the made in China badges we remember seeing everywhere. What might be more of a surprise is that by 2011 China's surplus was back to just 1.8% of GDP. Since then it has remained largely stable and in fact shrunk further by 2020, ignoring Coronavirus for a moment (if you can!).

If we stick to the prevailing view of the Trump administration, this is a story of sneaky Chinese producers taking advantage of open American markets and flooding the World with cheap products in order to put hard working Americans out of work, before being beaten back by good old fashioned US hard work, with the help of a few tariffs too of course. What this argument misses, is the simple fact that this falling surplus was well established as early as 2011.

The truth is, that as mentioned in the earlier chapter on how countries first industrialised, the idea that trade is a game only one side can win, and that we should limit imports while maximising exports is misguided, in the same way that refusing to buy milk for your coffee business is misguided. Wealth does not come from simply holding on to money, but by putting it to use in the most effective way. My first economics teacher taught this lesson in a vivid manner by burning a £10 note in front of every new class, emphasising the point that economics is not about cash, but how we can best use the resources we have available to get maximum output. If a country holds on to its earnings from exports and does not spend them on goods and services, the living standards of its inhabitants will not increase; the equivalent of obtaining a promotion, but not putting any of the money into more comfortable living arrangements, better education for your children, and so on.

Therefore, it makes sense that such an imbalance was always likely to even out as Chinese incomes grew, and with them demands for greater living standards. The surplus itself was created by weak labour laws, and a huge supply of cheap labour which kept wages low meaning little consumption of imports occurred. Another contributing factor was the lack of public support for Chinese citizens, which led to the need for higher savings for retirement. Imagine how much more you would be saving if you didn't have a pension to fall back on. Rather worryingly this is the situation for many already and will be explored, you guessed it, later!

However, greater state support, wages, and openness, in the last decade has evened this out. As any German car maker, or French jeweller will tell you, the Chinese are definitely spending on foreign goods now!

Add to this the huge amount of Chinese tourism, either in the traditional sense, or for education, and you can see why the surplus has drifted away. This is good for China and the world. Chinese students spending money on university means income for the UK and the US, which in turn means we can pay higher wages for lecturers, finance better research and of course, send it straight back to China for more of their goods and services. This will only continue as China's population ages. Spurred on by the one-child policy, the average age is set to increase massively in the coming years, resulting in a shift from savings to spending, as workers retire.

Even more pertinent to the arguments over trade, is that the average value of goods produced in the western world is much higher than in China. This is because while China has been catching up with the developed world since the 1980s, there is still a big gap in the level of design and research conducted between the countries. For example, while China excels in assembly, testing and packaging, this only accounts for a small percentage of the value of the final product. In the production of, for example, semiconductors, a big feature of China's exports, only 10% of the value of an average product is derived from China's contribution. This means that for every iPhone 7 exported by China, valued at $225, only $5 of that value was added in China, the rest was supplied by the raw inputs from other Asian countries, and from the original design by Apple. This also exposes the issue of how imports are measured. All $225 are registered to China. Whereas, in fact, most come from other countries. This is why trying to reduce a trade deficit with one country is fairly pointless. As the US has found out, rarely is that country solely responsible for the deficit, and any barriers to trade with that country will likely see the deficit shift across to others.

The US deficit with China in May 2020 was already down 18% from its 2018 high, when President Trump began taking aim at it. However, the US trade deficit in manufactured goods with all countries, was largely unchanged over the same period, as importers in the US simply moved their business from China to other countries. As a result, the trade deficit with the EU hit a record $177.9 billion in 2019. This meant the overall deficit remained 22% higher than in 2016, the last year of President Barak Obama's administration. Commentators in the US have also suggested that a number of these imports from other countries, remain ultimately Chinese imports and that they have simply been passed through third-party nations to avoid tariffs.

These actions also miss the wider point that trade is not as simple as swapping goods between two countries. The US may have a deficit with Asian countries, but a surplus with European countries. The Europeans may have a deficit with the US but a surplus with China.

This reveals the true value of trade. It is the ability of countries to import (or offshore) parts of the production process that they are less good at, and thereby focus on the things they do best. Due to their head start, the developed countries have the lion's share of added value.

So the first question we must ask ourselves when reassessing our feelings about China in the light of their more malignant moves on the world stage is, are we actually hurting ourselves by reducing our use of China as a warehouse for the less profitable and less popular parts of our production process?

Currency Controversy

"Of course, they fiddle with their currency!" Another common quote that is regularly used across dinner tables and in political debates. Many argue that China is a currency manipulator, but what does this actually mean?

Many countries have the power to change the value of their currency and regularly exercise this. Whenever the federal reserve, the Bank of England or the European Central Bank change interest rates, their currencies move too. This makes sense, as just as when we make decisions over which bank to put our savings in, if international investors see the rate of interest on investments in a country go up, as the central bank interest rate goes up, they will be tempted to move their money to that country. Putting your money in a British bank requires its conversion to pounds, which creates additional demand for pounds which (like with any good) leads to a rise in its price, which for money, is the exchange rate. So, in fact all countries manipulate their currencies.

What China is accused of, is going further by buying foreign reserves of cash such as dollars. In this way they are able to keep demand for other currencies up and therefore China's Yuan by comparison, is kept at a low price. The reality however is, as is maddeningly often the case in the worlds of economics and politics, more complicated. Moreover, the fears about China's actions over its currency are not just overblown, but historically have been seen as a sign of weakness, rather than of game playing.

The Holy Trinity of Eating

On the cusp of leaving for university, I suddenly became aware of the need to learn to feed myself, having previously taken no interest in where my meals came from and having no catered accommodations to choose from at Warwick. Such was my ability at this point that my mother packed me off with instructions on everything from beef chilli to the cooking time for a baked potato (I'm not joking).

Despite my initial limitations I quickly took to cooking. Whether it was the lack of ready meal options on campus, (even I became bored with microwaved burgers and frozen pizza), or more likely the fact that I would rather spend my limited income in the bar after matches rather than on expensive meals out and Deliveroo, I started making all sorts from scratch, even baking my own bread in second year.

Once I had mastered the basics, I realised that home cooking was the only way to achieve the three main components of an enjoyable, but sustainable meal plan, that is tasty, healthy and cheap. While eating out may give you the first two and eating nothing but rice and peas (my brother's tactic upon starting university) might give you the second and third, cooking from scratch was the only way to reach the trinity.

Sadly, in economics, especially in the world of central banks and exchange rates there is no such answer. Governments across the world have struggled with a similar problem of maintaining control of three things, exchange rates, interest rates and free capital movement. While not as immediately important as what's for dinner, this has proved a real challenge for policy makers more times than I've had Sunday roasts. International agreements on how to keep exchange rate fluctuations under control have been repeatedly attempted since the Gold Standard and they have ranged from the Bretton Woods system to, more recently, the Exchange rate mechanism, the precursor to the euro. The problem with all these systems is that countries have attempted to use them to keep all three plates spinning and under their direct control, with dire consequences.

The most well-known examples of these failures have been in South and Central America, where governments have routinely fallen due to spiralling debt, as their currency plummets. This has been caused by their attempts to keep their exchange rate fixed, and interest rates low. Much like someone trying to eat tasty and healthy food without cooking, the result is a huge outlay of cash. While for us this is because we are eating out all the time, for those falling foul in South America, it was the constant spending of foreign currency reserves, to keep their exchange rates steady. Without new money coming in from overseas (the artificially low interest rates haven't appealed to those looking to invest their savings somewhere), eventually they face letting their currency devalue to the level dictated by their interest rate, or run out of foreign currency, where they are forced to devalue anyway.

Whether it be the British pound in 1992, the Mexican Peso in 1994 or the Thai Baht in 1997, governments have blamed speculators betting against their innocent currencies as the reason for their foreign reserves running dry, and an enforced depreciation. The reality, however, is that speculators rarely manage to create an irrational panic on a currency, instead they simply point out the implications of the unsustainable policies highlighted above.

As a result, economists have been reasonably firm (for once!) that economies cannot keep all three of these plates spinning at once, two must be chosen and one let to fall, lest one inevitably comes crashing down anyway.

China's recent past is cluttered with failed attempts to keep all three plates spinning. The country's hoarding of foreign-exchange reserves (artificially keeping its currency low) was once a symbol of its economic might. In June 2014 the reserves peaked at $4 trillion. Looking back in hindsight, it is possible that this unsustainable purchasing of dollars encouraged the high levels of foreign investment at the time. Investors predicted the Yuan eventually appreciating, leading to demand on the Yuan increasing, resulting in pressure on the value to rise, leading to the Country's central bank buying more dollars. This spiral came to an abrupt halt in 2015 when China's economy began to slow. Fearing the Yuan would lose value, people began moving their money out of the country. This created downward pressure on the Yuan and the foreign reserves started falling. The threat of a run on the currency forced China's central bank to reduce the currency's value by 2%, the largest change in 20 years. This depreciation did not stop people pulling their money from China, leading to the Country restricting capital movements to other countries. This has limited its ambitions of challenging the dollar as the world's reserve currency, as trust that people could always access their cash in Chinese accounts evaporated. Despite China's greater leniency on its currency, in 2018, President Donald Trump began a trade war, claiming that the country remained, a currency manipulator. This restarted the flight of capital from China, resulting in its central bank lowering the value of the currency again. During the Coronavirus pandemic, China has outperformed much of the developed world, restoring faith in the Country and so facilitated the rise of foreign reserves again. However, the past 10 years have shown that large reserves are no guarantee of safety if the fundamentals of the trilemma are not followed. If the speed of recovery slows and confidence is shaken, investors will pull their money, which could cause a run on the Yuan. Equally, if China's central bank were to attempt to sell off these reserves, the Yuan would appreciate, leading to its exports becoming less competitive and slowing growth. In short, China's history is one of attempting and failing to game the system. It must now decide whether it will continue attempting to control its exchange rate regime and risk having to adjust its interest rates to maintain this, with the resultant risk of slowing growth, or allow its exchange rates to move more in line with the market and risk its dominance in exports. The latter may well be an unavoidable destiny for China. As it continues to reach for developed economy status it may find itself falling into the consumer-driven, low-growth future the West has already reached.

This demonstrates the very real limits of China's influence against the dollar. While the greenback has weakened in recent months, the US's monopoly of gold reserves, a steadfast guardian of value, even during times of currency turmoil, remains dominant. As of September 2020, the US is still the largest hoarder of the metal, with 26% of the world's reserves. China, meanwhile, sits at only 6%.

It also exposes the limitations of even the most authoritarian economies. Much like trying to control the tides, China is limited by the economic fundamentals of the Trilemma.

The State is the Bank

Another challenge for the world's number two is its debt mountain, which is largely hidden by its banks. In most political systems in the West, bank bailouts are public knowledge as are debt mountains. In China this is not so well understood.

China's debt has been on the rise for over a decade, reaching $27 trillion in 2015, 249% of their GDP. This is roughly in line with total debt in the UK and US. These are simple statistics, but deserve pondering over given the amount of time we spend worrying about our debt levels, the amount of US debt China holds, and the investment by China in the UK.

So how is this possible?

Firstly, most Chinese firms are not in debt. It is only a minority who are piling it on to such an extent that they increase the average, partly because these are disproportionately the largest firms in China. They are also disproportionately state-owned. Following the crash in 2008, 41,200 Chinese state-owned enterprises were loss-making. By 2018 this number had risen to 76,100. These perpetually struggling companies are often dubbed 'zombie firms', companies with low or no profits, only supported by lines of credit, which in China largely comes from the state. As their number has risen since the Financial Crisis, these companies have sucked more debt financing from the state. Other more profitable companies have not been able to obtain the loans they need. As a result, the effectiveness of credit allocation has dropped, with $0.48 required to generate $1 of output, vs. $0.14 in 2008.

So, with all this inefficient credit, how are Chinese companies and individuals able to invest so much in other countries?

Some development is in developing countries in return for soft power, as mentioned earlier with hospitals in St Lucia. The vast majority in developed countries, however, is from rich individuals and entities trying to find a more secure place for their funds than their home country. One only has to look at Jack Ma's Ant Group's treatment by the Chinese government to understand why firms and rich people do not feel comfortable keeping their money in China. In November 2020 the Chinese government rejected plans for a record-breaking £26bn stock market Initial Public Offering (when a company floats on a stock exchange for the first time) from Ma's finance company, Ant Group, just two days before the proposed float. Ma was also pulled from reality TV shows in the Country and only resurfaced after almost a 3-month disappearance. All of this was sparked when he gave a speech criticising the country's financial watchdogs, saying that "China's financial sector basically doesn't have a system". Within days Ma was summoned by regulators for questioning. He joins the list of people, from property managers to actors, who have had their business and private lives drastically changed, after questioning the state.

This capital flight has been a boon for the UK and one reason why it has been able to sustain a consistent trade imbalance. For every pound we send overseas to pay for goods, the same is coming back in foreign direct investment. The UK's long-standing, independent and transparent institutions provide security for people's money. As a result, the UK received more FDI projects than any other state in Europe from 1997 to 2019. In the coming years, the Chinese government may clamp down on these transfers (although they have already been trying for some time). Conversely, they may continue to open up further to the World and give their privately owned companies the freedom from intervention they need. Until then, however, a trade deficit is not necessarily something to be feared, if we can maintain the superiority our western institutions enjoy, that makes us a safer option. Brexit, and the current lack of faith in democracy in general in the US, could potentially threaten this however.

By peeling back the curtain we see that investment in China is largely led by the 'Crazy Rich Asians', and by the subsidising of public industry, from not so private banks. The country's high inflation levels have also been mitigated by its unprecedented growth levels. As explained in Chapter 4, debt levels and inflation become less significant over time if your income rises. However, if China's growth rate continues to slow, the impacts of inflation and debt will have more bite on future generations. Economic growth is crucial to the happiness of the population and so the electorate's acceptance of the one-party regime and vast inequality levels. It may well be the case that as growth slows the Communist Party will be forced to cut loose some of its zombie firms that rack up this debt, allowing greater private enterprise. This will move the country ever closer to the market economies of the West. Otherwise, growing unrest, for which Hong Kong has already been a testbed, may spread across the Country, ultimately resulting in China either becoming a more open economy or a far less dynamic one.

Where's the Spark?

The trade, debt and exchange rate issues reveal that China suffers from similar issues to the developed world, with one crucial difference. China is still to reach the point where the productivity of its people and so the average wage meets the wages of the US and Europe. The reason that this has not been the case is down to the same lack of entrepreneurial spark that limited the USSR in the 20th century.

My introduction to Communist doctrine was during history A-level. My teacher, who looking back, was obviously keen on stamping out any form of socialist uprising in the classroom, set in place a special way of grading the class, in the term before we started on Russia in the 20th century. Instead of the usual means of grading each person on their work in isolation, he collected each grade and took an average across the class, before handing this score to every member. This obviously had mixed reactions. Had this been French, or Spanish, I would have been a firm supporter of the policy; my foreign language skills being among the greatest shortcomings in my knowledge at the time. Sadly, it was one of my preferred subjects on which this policy fell. More interestingly, however, was how this policy led to the average grade in the class falling steadily throughout the year. Even though my teacher took a clear average of our work and made no changes to the policy, including keeping the difficulty of the tests and coursework the same, grades fell. What became obvious was that those at the bottom of the class realised that they were getting higher grades than their work merited and saw no reason to increase their efforts. Meanwhile, the top of the class slowly became unhappy revising and preparing for lessons, when it only helped out the rest of the class, and their extra work was not properly merited. Accordingly, the top marks dwindled, and the average gradually fell.

This is a common criticism of a state-run company or country; without proper incentives, the whole system will slowly diminish.

China has included a greater blend of private enterprise and less equality of outcome (more meritocracy) allowing it to surpass the heights reached by the former Soviet Union. It remains, however, a country that stifles free-thinking - just look at its treatment of Hong Kong. As a result, it will only ever emulate the present and never create the future. Like a student who copies the work of others, China has been able to catch up quickly in terms of output, supported by its abundance of land and labour. It has good institutions for doing so, including strong government support for businesses that have amassed scale due to protectionism, and can now compete overseas. Also a comparatively weak rule of law, for example on patent protection, which allows intellectual property theft. I remember a famous British television car show, which compared Chinese car designs with others. There was a remarkable likeness between existing European cars and new Chinese ones. It was remarked that when the Europeans asked Chinese regulators to investigate the similarities, the response was simply that the cars looked nothing alike.

While China's aggregate output is impressive, the average citizen remains far less effective at doing their jobs than workers in other countries. Having only copied the work of others, and with any attempts to create new ideas crushed or taken over by the state, the worker is similar to those at the bottom of my History class. The strong state influence and lack of protection for private enterprise means that the incentive for innovation is weak across the country, as is the relative performance of its tertiary education and research.

The US faces a similar challenge with its tech monopolies purchasing any would-be threats. If the US continues on its divisive route towards refusing the ideas and views of many amongst its population, it may well be surpassed by China as the World's economic leader.

In the USSR, workers were disincentivised to keep working at their maximum as they saw no reward for their work. In China, while profits and high wages are possible, they are only permitted alongside intense scrutiny by the state. Communist party members occupy boards and committees everywhere from top companies to universities. Without the freedom to innovate, the value of the country's output will be limited, exacerbating the slowing productivity it will face as its population begins to age. Developed countries have struggled to find the productivity required to support its ageing population, and so too will China, to an even greater extent perhaps if nothing is done to overcome their stifling levels of state intervention.

The developed world suffers from a productivity problem because it too, has allowed the strength of its markets and institutions, to be restrained. Between 1980 and 1999 US economy-wide concentration (meaning the amount of market share that the small number of biggest firms enjoy) fell. By 2017, however, The Economist reported that of 893 US industries analysed, 2 in 3 had grown more concentrated since 2007. On the ground this meant that the top four firms in any given industry, on average, saw their share of total market revenue rise from 26% to 32% between 1997 and 2012.University College London found in a separate study that profits for publicly traded firms rose from 18% in 1980 to 67% in 2014. While companies have become less competitive, social mobility has also been falling in the US since the 1970s. In the UK the Social Mobility Commission (I assume they know about this stuff!) accused the government of delivering on only 23% of its proposals since 2013. Meanwhile child poverty in the UK has grown between 2012 and 2020, with only 24.7% of disadvantaged students obtaining a good pass in English and Maths GCSE compared with 49.9% of all other pupils. An economy where those with the greatest ability are kept from rising to the top will always fail to progress as quickly as those that advance people on merit rather than birth.

"We all know, in our hearts, that as long as there is deep poverty living systematically side by side with great riches, we all remain the poorer for it."

-       *David Cameron*

It is for those who believe in their system, be they 'gammon' libertarians, or 'leftie' democrats, to stand up for democracy and the way it promotes openness, competition and success. This does not mean declaring wars on China (in trade, tech or worse), nor does it mean surrendering our economies to a more aggressive form of state-control. Competitive markets, supported by the state may be a complex mix and hard to get right, but it is ultimately the success story of our current system. Bringing out the best of both the private and public sector is the West's best chance of out-competing and possibly converting China into a democratic and open ally, rather than demonising it into a dangerous adversary.

7

You Can do Whatever You Like, as Long as its Maths

"Of course, maths and science are what matters."

"Unless you want to be able to speak to people!"

This was a typical exchange growing up in my household. While my father eventually relented and agreed that my performance in English, at least until GCSE, was important, my maths and science grades were by far the most scrutinised marks in my end of term report. No amount of As in art, drama and geography (I rarely got high marks in these anyway!) could make up for a botched chemistry mark.

This led to an understandably brutal view of other subjects by the time I reached A-level, with only history managing to sneak in from the humanities, and not an art in sight. It was not only my father pushing this narrative. By this time I had spent a number of weeks work experience in local banks (mainly because I had heard they made a lot of money) and most of the managers I met there had suggested maths as the primary choice, with economics coming a close second. I remember regular arguments with my housemaster at the time, me asking for his opinion repeatedly on what the most useful set of A-levels were and him, gradually in a louder voice, responding that "it was up to me!" "What did I enjoy?" As every know-it-all student, I promptly did the complete opposite and started studying economics, with maths and physics joining history to complete my choices.

Fortunately for me, not only did I take to the new subject, but continued studying it through university, all the time declaring geography to be 'just colouring-in' and drama as 'a good way of making yourself unemployable'. This short-sighted view of subjects is becoming less accurate all the time. I hope the following chapter may absolve me of some of my previous big-headedness. Moreover, little did I know that the problem was not just about which subject I had picked, but with the wider UK education system that fails to prepare young people to join the workforce and saddles them, and eventually government, with rapidly growing debt.

The End of Humanities

Having both a brother who studied English and close friends with masters' degrees in history, geography and theatre studies, I am no stranger to making jokes about the humanities. However, the seemingly harmless comments about job prospects (or supposed lack of) hide a worrying trend and a classic case of false conventional wisdom.

Many traditional degree courses are in retreat, largely due to the rising number of alternatives offered by universities such as computing and data science. However, since the 2008 financial crisis, humanity subjects, ranging from modern foreign languages, to history and archaeology, have been left most firmly, um, in the dirt.

In the US in 2019, history majors were down 45% from their 2007 peak. This is partly explained by the fact that overall university enrolment dropped following 07/08, however, even accounting for this, humanities are falling behind. According to the American Historical Association, the most popular four humanities, philosophy, history, languages and English are all at risk of dropping to below 100,000 degrees for the first time in 20 years.

Research by The American Council on Science and Health (probably jumping at the chance to show off to those Humanity grads) uncovered that, as far back as the turn of the century, some humanities and arts had been falling in popularity in the US. This has only increased following The Great Recession which began in late 2007.

Many-a-smug Mathematician or Physicist, (and me until recently!) would say this is because the recession has made the job market more competitive and now only 'proper subjects,' will earn you a living.

However, another look at the evidence immediately preceding the crash revealed to me my own naivety and vanity, perhaps exposing one of the reasons why employers do sometimes prefer humanities to the sciences!

Data from the Institute for Fiscal Studies shows that there is a gap between sciences and humanities in earnings 5 years after graduation. From 2017, medicine and dentistry have been at the top, with an average of £46,700 and creative arts at the bottom, with £20,100. However, this gap has been consistent since before 2007 and has even narrowed in recent years. Therefore, the increased speed of students abandoning the humanities and arts cannot be explained by the wage gap between subjects. If this were so, this reduction would have occurred long before 2007.

Studies from New York University demonstrate that in fact it is not just the arts and humanities that are under threat. The traditional subjects are too, as the more applied topics, such as engineering and computer science continue to take up a greater proportion of applicants.

What's more, the gap in employment levels are also small, tiny in fact. For people aged 25-34 in the US, the unemployment rate for those with a humanities degree is 4%, but for engineering or business degrees it is still 3%. This means a difference of just one person in every 100!

"It's technology married with liberal arts, married with the humanities, that yields us the result that makes our heart sing."

- *Steve Jobs*

So why aren't we seeing more English and History students enrolling at universities?

As I think back to the various jokes I made at my brother's expense during his years studying English, I begin to worry that it is this flawed view, held by so many, that may be contributing to people not applying for the subjects they excel at.

Is the dropping enrolment caused, not by a fall in expected earnings, but merely the perception of such?

One way to test such an idea would be to take a group of students who didn't need to worry about employment after graduation, or paying for tuition. This is a common tool for isolating a certain factor's impact on something, in the same way a scientist may use a control group in an experiment.

Fortunately, one such group exists, students with military bursaries.

West Point, a US military academy, offers full bursaries to students who have agreed to join the military after graduation. This supplies a unique set of students who are not impacted by the effect (or perceived effect) of their degree on their future earnings. Another report by New York University in 2018, highlighted that the proportion of students taking humanities was treble the national average at West Point and has remained almost unchanged since 2007.

This trend is seen not only in military academies, but also in other places of higher education that offer guaranteed jobs for graduates; another common example being US culinary schools. This suggests that one reason for the fall of the humanities is our negative perception. It's had a more damaging effect on enrolment in the last 10 years than the median earnings gap has had in 50. While this may not be the only reason, it is certainly one we could easily avoid with less propagation of false truths.

Arguably the biggest offenders in this regard are economics students, for in lecture halls across the country, (although mine could have passed for a small basement), lecturers teach that (at least in theory) the subject we study at university doesn't matter!

It is a Tale, Told by an Idiot, Full of Sound and Fury, Signifying Nothing

When a person goes to university, they invest time and money in the hope of signalling to an employer, that they will be a better employee.

A similar situation arises with warranties. When a firm which produces high-quality cars offers a warranty, it signals its quality. This is because if the car breaks down the firm will lose money, therefore it is worth offering the warranty if most cars don't break down. If a lower quality firm were to offer the same warranty however, they would lose more from offering a warranty, as more cars would fail prematurely. As a result, you are less likely to see lower quality goods with warranties. The assumption that people and cars are the same is perhaps why this theory does not hold so strongly for some degree-holders.

Moving back to universities. Obtaining a degree will only be worth the three additional years of education, if the individual is sufficiently determined to achieve a good grade. Therefore, someone obtaining a first in English has demonstrated a higher work ethic and interest in the subject than someone with a third in chemistry. As a result, the type of degree shouldn't matter, compared to the relative quality of the institution and level of work required to gain it.

This will be less of a surprise to those who consider how often we actually use our knowledge from university. Many people complain about never using algebra after school, my university colleagues complained about classics students landing investment banking jobs at Goldman Sachs and writing this book is the first time I have needed to look back at my Topics in Economic Theory notes. Employers care about quality, not the course.

For those less sure of this, particularly those in jobs that do use what they learned at university (looking at you medics), I accept that some jobs require specific higher education. For the majority of job applications, however, a candidate with any degree subject is sufficient, with many employers arguing that the key to success is simply that the candidate demonstrates (or signals) the propensity to learn.

So next time I am tempted to joke about English to my brother, or a parent considers discouraging their child from taking History of Art, remember that their passion for a subject may well be more likely to land them a job than the degree course typically seen as more employment-worthy.

Degree Inflation

If the degree doesn't matter, just the skill and determination of the individual, why do we study for so long? For some subjects like medicine, it is obvious. I would feel safer knowing someone operating on me has had 6 years of study and practice in hospital over none. Equally while 6 years work experience might be better, what about the unlucky people who are operated on during the intern's first day?

For the majority, however, the skills we need are learnt on the job. Rarely do we need to remember the relevant chapter of Adam Smith's, The Wealth of Nations or Plato's The Republic, to do a good job.

I believe this is part of the reason why wages for STEM graduates are higher. It is not because they are inherently more complex subjects, but that the years spent studying them are more closely aligned to their final job than other subjects. They also have the added benefit (as do you all) that I cannot simply decide to be a doctor tomorrow, while I have been able to do this with writing! Required qualifications, which create barriers to entering these professions, and the closer link to the final job may explain the higher entry-level wages, but does this mean the rest of us should be signing up for university when we could start working earlier, and avoid the graduate tax that is a student loan?

This idea of not studying for so long, or even going straight to work (imagine!) has not been a popular one to date. Going to University has been linked with social mobility, greater equality as well as higher incomes for years.

Student numbers almost doubled between 1992 and 2016, spurred on by both sides of the political spectrum. Tony Blair's aim to have 50% of young adults in higher education was met in 2019 making 5 years in which the proportion of the population attending university rose.

Even while introducing higher tuition fees, David Cameron spoke of increasing the representation of those least able to pay for higher education, as part of his '2020 agenda for BME communities'.

The success (in take-up at least) of student loans provides further evidence of this narrative that university is always the answer and a good way for disadvantaged people to pull themselves up. Any arguments that rising debt is an issue have been swept aside by the argument that the loans are guaranteed by government and will have a limited impact on their income in the future, unless a certain level of wages is reached. While this argument is correct, the fact is the loan acts more like a tax on graduates, and anyone who has passed through university will know that the costs do not stop at the lectures and seminars.

One of the many things I owe my parents, (especially considering I have rewarded them with a book that paints them as constantly arguing extremists) was them paying for my food, drink and accommodation while studying. I met many students who were working while studying to feed themselves. They had already taken out any additional loans available to cover accommodation and textbooks (Economics tomes are as expensive as they are dry). This meant that while we were able to study the same subject, when it came to applying for internships, going to networking events, and crucially, having time to relax and recover from studying, I remained in a privileged position.

This can be seen in wider society too. While 59.1% of black young people now attend higher education, due to the drive by successive governments to improve equality in this area, there is still a 20% Attainment gap between white and black students. This shows how significant barriers to success still exist when disadvantaged groups enter university.

As a result, student loans are simultaneously not helping aid social mobility as well as we thought, and certainly contributing to degree inflation.

If I offered to pay for your coffee, unless you'd just won the lottery, you'd probably start drinking more (I certainly would, I never buy scratch cards, too much student debt!) And while subsidising the first coffee may give you a much-needed pick-up in the morning, over-consumption of free coffee would likely result in a lot of unnecessary shaking around the office. To many students, the idea of earning enough to be able to pay off their loans must feel like a lottery chance. As a result, student loans, like any promise to subsidise something, has led to overconsumption, as people spend more time in higher education than they would otherwise have, further contributing to the national debt. While the importance of our debt mountain will be explored later in Chapter 12, we can be sure that it will remain controversial. We will always need to allocate our spending carefully, and so should not be wasting our limited fiscal firepower on pushing degree inflation further.

The signalling effect is also in play here and highlighted by Cambridge economist Ha-Joon Chang as early as 2010. Many argue that the massive improvement in the economic situation of many Asian countries is linked to their improvement in educational attainment. However, there is precious little evidence of this. The argument seems simple - a more educated person will be more productive and so this should work on a national scale. If we look closer at the miracle Asian economies, in 1960 Taiwan had a literacy rate of just 54%, while the Philippines was at 72%. Despite this, Taiwan has managed one of the highest economic growth rates in human history while the Philippines has not. In 1960, the Philippines had almost double the per capita income, while in 2010, Taiwan had 10 times the per capita income. Meanwhile, South Korea had a 71% literacy rate in the 60s, compared to 91% in Argentina. Korea has since grown much faster, from an economy one fifth of Argentina's in 1960, to being over three times larger today.

Investing more in education is no guarantee of producing more output either. Between 1980 and 2004 sub-Saharan Africa literacy rose from 40 to 61%, despite its per capita output falling by 0.3% per year during the same period. So, if education is so important why do we not see it in the figures?

Firstly, many subjects do little to improve productivity, for example, history, literature and music. This does not mean that we should abandon them; they benefit our wider social development, but sadly not our economic development. Furthermore, even the STEM subjects do not necessarily improve productivity. Investment bankers after all, rarely use their biology knowledge in their day-to-day work. On-the-job training is widespread as even the job-orientated parts of education are insufficient to make a worker effective in their chosen employment.

Technology has further limited the importance of education in making us productive workers. Cash registers mean that workers in shops do not even need to be able to add up, a skill their predecessors definitely required. Anyone who has received incorrect change when buying an item from one of those rare shops without a till will know! This is true even in the more technical jobs. Anyone who has seen a certain car show special will have seen mechanics across the world with greater ability in repairing vehicles, (even the ones trashed by the show's team), and almost certainly at a fraction of the price that we pay in the developed world.

The signalling effect is instead, the reason for the unhealthy zero-sum game of young people being pushed to apply for university to secure a decent job. As more people go to university, those who haven't look worse in applications, so more go, so those who remain look even worse and the circle continues. Even when you do graduate, the pressure is now on to obtain a masters, then a doctorate and so on. Everyone spends more time before starting work, and yet no one comes out with a better job than they would have done before everyone started going to university. This can be seen in the job market, where roles that are currently done by people without a degree require new entrants to have one.

Therefore, the trouble for governments is, how we value a university degree, or a year of education, or one seminar?

Work by the IFS on the impact different degrees have on expected wages, present a start on this. It estimates that over the course of a lifetime, women can expect to earn about £250,000 more if they have a degree, and men £170,000. But this is just the start, as university is about much more than the graduate's wage.

The career-driven culture at Warwick, coupled with free time over Christmas and Summer meant I attended two insight experiences with banks, as well as an internship for what became my first employer. If I had started working immediately, I would not have been able to apply for these experiences, decide that investment banking was not for me and have a graduate scheme lined up before leaving Warwick. As well as this I learnt to cook and how to become involved in teams and groups, without the help of the school or my parents forcing me into social situations. I met people from different backgrounds and with different ideas, which have since moulded many of the views I have developed and expressed in these pages, particularly on inequality and race. These benefits, both professional and social, were key to my development. Crucially it also helped me find my place in society through helping me find a job I enjoy and the hobbies and friends that have stuck with me since then.

These benefits of university suggest that time spent there is not wasted, but do we need to be spending so much time and money there?

Capping the cost of tuition (most of the time!) appears to be making university more accessible to all, given the explosion in the number of students enrolling over the past two decades. However, as explained earlier, the additional costs that come with university such as accommodation mean social mobility is not guaranteed. The real impact of capping tuition is that universities can only improve profits by expanding the number of students they admit. This has resulted in numbers being preferred over the quality of teaching and outcomes for the students. If signalling did not exist and the push to go to university was solely on the value a university added to your ability to work and progress your life, then this would result in fewer people going. However, the continued push for degrees means that even as the standard of education has dropped, demand has risen. More flexible pricing and various periods of study would allow universities to differentiate by price. This would make the options more obvious as well as separating out the professional and life experience degrees.

If we expose the limitations of universities and some degrees, we will encourage more people to enter the workforce early, learn more relevant skills and reduce debt. This will prevent universities putting up their prices without the quality teaching to back it up, as students will be more informed on what prices make a course worthwhile and will feel they have an acceptable alternative to simply paying up. The IFS have taken a good first step in this direction, by exposing universities that offer courses which result in expected earnings five years after graduation, up to 66% lower than the average course.

Some have gone so far as to argue that tuition fees should also be restricted for underperforming universities, whose students fail to find a job post-graduation, who regularly dropout. This would incentivise better education standards and open the door to a greater range of degree term options, such as only one or two-year courses for non-professional degrees where the focus would be on putting graduates into jobs rather than keeping them in education for as long as possible. This greater level of competition would prevent escalating prices, without the need for caps, and reduce degree inflation, as it would be easier for employers to choose between applicants with different degrees.

Just a Stepping Stone

I vividly remember while practising for my university interviews, asking my teacher, who was espousing the benefits of the 'institution' I had applied for, whether in fact university was simply a stepping stone to a job. While the many life experiences I enjoyed at university suggest otherwise, I believe we have become infatuated with university.

Afterall, how well do universities fulfil even their primary role, preparing students for their futures outside education? In May 2017 an all-party parliamentary group for education found 44% of students due to complete university in 2014 had no idea what they wanted to do after graduation. On the supply side, under 30% of firms believe employees have the required digital skills, with this problem only magnifying in the future. According to the World Economic Forum, 65% of children entering primary school in 2017, will have jobs that do not yet exist, and for which their education will not have prepared them. ONS data from 2018 shows that there is a large disparity between the dreams of 16 to 21-year olds and the realities of 22-29s today:

"While the variety of available jobs has grown with the advent of digital technology, it seems the jobs that young people aspire to has not changed. In 2015 to 2016 the top five jobs that 16-21-year-olds wanted to do when they were older was unchanged from the top five jobs being sought by the same age group in 2010 to 2011."

- *Office for National Statistics*

Many of the most popular jobs that 16-21s aspire to are traditional (e.g. in literacy and media, teaching and health), but the reality of today's job market is very different. Teaching is the only occupation, among the top five, that young people actually find themselves in, by the time they are 22-29. Instead, jobs such as sales assistants, carers and in marketing are among the most likely jobs for people in secondary education. The fastest growing industries for employment since 2011 have been in IT & telecoms, and Business, finance and related jobs.

These statistics show our education system is out of date. From as early as secondary school, young people are developing incorrect impressions of the job market from their educational experience.

If you had ICT classes like mine, you will understand this. The subject that teaches the necessary skills, not only for the fastest growing job market for young people, but also the skills used in many other jobs across the country, was restricted to once per week. This largely covered how to make a simple chart in Excel, with nothing at all on data analytics or coding. With no regular practice sessions, I barely understood my inbox by the time I left school. This disconnect and lack of focus from educational institutions is less than ideal, but entirely understandable, as the incentives for schools and pupils are misaligned. Does my school benefit from me getting a job after leaving? Not really.

Does my university gain more from me finding a good job, or staying on for another year while I make up my mind into which industry I should go?

The fact that most educational institutions list how many of their students are in jobs or (more pertinently) in further education after graduation should tell you the answer. The percentage of students with a certain set of grades is what matters in schools. Therefore, the incentive is to perfect how to pass exams, rather than prepare us for future work, or even for future learning. Incentives for schools can be so warped that modernising teaching methods can feel counterproductive, as many teachers have learnt a specific syllabus and changing would likely lead to lower grades in the short term as they learn the new methods. This is far from the teacher's fault. They have been boxed into a set curriculum, rather than having greater autonomy over what they teach. If less emphasis was put on exams and getting into a top university, teachers would be able to focus on teaching students how to enjoy learning, and help them work out what skills they have and where they might enjoy working for the rest of their lives.

We have the issue of degree inflation, the fact that people spend too long at university, becoming saddled with debt, and that many still don't know what they want to do when they leave!

Overall Grade: Must do Better!

Universities and schools need to change, to align their aims with the students they should be serving. Rather than deriving their earnings from selling years of education, universities should be incentivised to ensure that students know where they want to start their careers before graduating, and have the skills to succeed once they do.

When developing a new education system, as with deciding on our own development, the key is to start with the desired outcome. People should train to do the job they want, or at least, for their chosen industry, and work backwards. Universities that are incentivised to qualify students for these arenas will be crucial. So too will schools that guide students to the right universities. Governments and parents that understand the value of all subjects and career paths, as well as funding them appropriately, complete the chain. Supporting kids to do what they need to get the right job for them, not just pass exams will be key.

How can we be sure of the right strategy? We need only look at the countries that often produce the best outcomes for their students, principally in Scandinavia.

Finland, 10-time best schooling country, only has one standardised test for students across their entire school career, the results of which are not publicly published. Children do not start full time education until they are 7 and are not separated into sets based on past performance. This encourages learning, over pressurising kids with tests. Despite Finnish classes being relatively large, and teachers being paid moderate salaries compared with other OECD nations, Finland has impressive PISA scores. This has resulted in Finland, and similar countries, Norway and Denmark, having the best value-for-money education systems in the world. Coincidently the brightest student of my university cohort (and a key reason for my final year results) also came from Finland.

The UK is a world leader in passing exams, but if a teacher gives his students the answers to every test, whilst they may look good on paper, they might not necessarily be any good in their future jobs. Government and education watchdogs should focus not on individual grades, but on how many students are able to find a job after graduation. They should also exclude those who have simply stumped up more cash for the privilege of avoiding the labour market for another year. The push for exam success also results in some schools employing dubious methods, such as removing failing students from cohorts. Better incentives, greater transparency at the university level on the value of a degree, and more informed views on the value of vocational subjects need to be enforced. Competition is not, in isolation, a bad thing and can drive new ideas in education, and across industries. However, misdirecting the incentives that drive competition will result in hitting a very different, and often ill-desired target.

In the UK, the intense level of competition and high student numbers hide the reality that we are training students to pass tests, not to excel in life. The number of diplomas has increased by 400% since 1990, and those leaving with first-class honours is up from 7% in 1997 to 30% in 2019. This massive increase in human capital that political parties like to fantasize about, has done little, however, to drive economic growth, productivity or wellbeing because of the confusion between academic skill and the ability to pass a test.

The strict curriculum has made it easier for tests to be passed but has led to higher stress levels for students, and poor motivation among teachers. This has resulted in more teachers leaving the profession, with 50% leaving within the first 5 years. The average age of teachers in the UK is 5 years below the OECD average and only 18% remain in the profession after 50, this compares to 34% elsewhere, meaning a less experienced workforce available to teach our children.

In Finland and other leading countries, the curriculum is flexible, teachers have greater autonomy, pupils spend less time doing tests and more time learning soft or vocational skills. The constant focus on marks in the UK reduces teachers' role to one end-of-year exam a year, greatly reducing feelings of self-worth. Countries where the profession has more respect achieve higher levels of job satisfaction and so quality of teaching. In China and South Korea this is achieved through authoritarianism, in the Nordics by ensuring teachers are highly trained and obtain qualifications on a par with doctors.

Teachers in the UK and US have, on average, longer hours than the majority, and far more than in Scandinavia, however, they bizarrely spend less time teaching. Teachers in the UK work on average 46 hours a week, but only 20 in the classroom. This is because of the focus on testing results in teachers spending more time per week marking and lesson planning than actually teaching their students!

A lower focus on competition results in greater social mobility, lower degree inflation and less pressure on the government to chuck increasingly massive sums of money at education. Greater supply and respect for vocational learning (utilised by 40% of students in Finland) would provide the practical skills needed to facilitate everything from finding a decent plumber to running megaprojects like HS2 on time and on budget. Sadly, instead of championing this alternative to university, funding for UK schemes has fallen by 16% since 2011 and is 25% below funding for the university route. The snobbish UK view that university is the only path for young people to achieve success is a self-fulfilling prophecy, where those who don't go, are overlooked for jobs, are less able to support their families, and so their children are less able to attend in the future. Work placements, both before and during university should be made more mainstream. Less than half of UK students in the 16/17 cohort completed a work placement during university, compared to 87% in France.

Turning something the size of the UK further education industry around quickly will not be easy. We can start by offering more honest information on how useful university is and removing caps on tuition to allow prices to reflect this. I believe greater scepticism of these companies that claim to be the answer to social mobility while providing little evidence of such is a good thing. In the same way that we should not force our children to do a subject just because it is perceived as superior, we should not force them to attend university because of the perception that by not doing so, they face a career death sentence. This will halt the oversupply of places, reduce the debt burden to government, and increase output, as the number of people attending university falls. While learning to a higher level will always be useful, many in-work qualifications exist that, once achieved, supplant university degrees.

I believe that in the majority of cases, further education does not give us the intellectual tools to work, but instead is merely a stepping stone to our careers, when there are many other options available. We simply have to sweep aside the imperfect information and dangerous narratives around the further education industry. We will then see more clearly what is required for our future development, and what is superfluous, hopefully during the last years of secondary school, not after completing our doctorates!

8

Rise of the Machines

The Terminator was the first 18-rated film I ever watched, much to the dismay of my mother, as I was under 12 at the time.

It quickly became a favourite along with other fiction blockbusters such as Lord of the Rings and Jurassic Park. These films share a similar problem in that recent attempts to rejuvenate them have been hit and miss at best. One only needs to look at the online reviews for Jurassic Park 3, to find out what an attempt to flog the same narrative with uninspired additions can do. Understandably, it is difficult to balance sticking to the winning formula of the originals, without becoming predictable. Here, the Terminator series has had arguably most trouble. In each film, another machine is sent from the future to bring about the end of humanity, making each story and its conclusion predictable. At the same time any possibility of future attempts being different decreases. With every new Terminator appearing in the present, the chance that the future can really be changed, and Armageddon averted, becomes less and less likely. The rise of the machines seems all but inevitable within the series. If you look through the technology sections of newspapers today, you could make a similar argument for the real world.

While few are arguing that the development of Artificial Intelligence will result in immediate nuclear war, there are plenty of warnings abound about the damage ever more powerful computers could wreak, from meddling in elections to putting us all out of work.

The threat to jobs has been particularly in focus in recent years. The ONS estimated in 2018, that 1.5 million jobs (7.4% of the labour force) in England were at high risk of, at least some of their duties being automated in the future. Women, young people and part-time workers were those found most likely to work in roles that were at high risk of automation.

A study by economists Frey and Osborne found that 47% of US jobs were at risk of automation. A later survey by the OECD produced a significantly lower figure, estimating just 9% of workers were at risk. However, this still translates to roughly 13 million jobs across the US. Furthermore, job losses are unlikely to be evenly distributed across countries, meaning the impact at the regional or local level could be several times the disruption at the national level. One example is the massive job losses in the Detroit car industry, caused by increased automation since the turn of the century.

The uncertainty caused by the Coronavirus Pandemic left many people unsure whether to return to their workplace. Predictably there were, and still are, news sources that are determined to make up their mind for them, with titles akin to, "back to work or lose your job" or "[Downing Street] urged to beef up its 'back to work' message." The temptation many of us can fall into, especially for those who have been working throughout lockdown, is to read these headlines and imagine a world in which everyone is skiving off work and attempting to use every opportunity to avoid being pushed back to earning their living.

This explains why, sitting in a coffee shop at weekends writing this book, I have overheard several people suggest that these workers should be replaced with robots to 'teach them a lesson'. While I did not hear any clear arguments to support this assertion (people are obviously too polite, or aware of the nosy so-and-so in the corner to engage in such a thing) I did hear the opposing argument, that the Government should be doing more to support these people, to stop firms taking the opportunity to weaken worker rights and use Covid as an excuse to replace them with machines. In both cases, while the sentiment and solutions were different, the result was considered inevitable, that eventually technology would lead to mass unemployment, whether this was something to fear or cheer.

This narrative paints a similar picture to the Terminator series; a feeling of inevitability, many disagree on whether the outcomes will benefit or cost the economy,

but the future seems written and cannot be changed. Are they right?

Just a Hologram

If we are generous, we can assume that the writers of these 'back to work' headlines, repeated in coffee shops across the country, have forgotten that many people are already back to work, and that not being in the office does not equal not working. UK HMRC data shows that the number of people supported through the JRS (furlough scheme) had dropped from 8.9 million to just 4.8 million by the end of July 2020 and that by late August it was 3 million. This did rise to 4 million following the start of further lockdowns over the winter but still only accounted for 12% of the UK labour force pre-crisis. If furloughed workers from the food, accommodation and retail industries (many of which only closed due to government instruction) are removed, only 1 in 15 workers were on furlough by the end of 2020.

Looking at those working from home, figures from the Resolution Foundation, August 2020, showed that in fact, many of the poorest and highly unionised areas of society were largely back in the workplace, while professionals and IT workers were resolutely avoiding returning to the office. Despite the figures above proving that the vast majority of the labour force have continued working during lockdown, many people have allowed themselves to believe that there are vast numbers of layabouts refusing to go back, rather than accepting the less appealing truth that, in fact, returning to the office is not as easy as some have claimed. For example, social distancing makes it impossible for 1000s of employees to go back to the office if only 1 person can use the lift in a 20-storey building. It also makes it difficult for such densely populated office blocks to be at full capacity when only two people can use the toilets at a time.

So, most people don't deserve to be replaced by machines for 'shirking the workplace', but will they be put out of work regardless?

It may be tempting to fear lockdown as the catalyst for more white-collar workers working from home and robotics replacing blue-collar workers, thereby creating a new level of inequality. However, this forgets a fundamental premise in economics, that even the biggest sceptics like to quote, the law of supply and demand.

Like so many people during the first lockdown, I found the empty weekends and lack of commute gave me more time for hobbies, for me this was baking - not very original I know! To begin with, this was more challenging than I would have predicted. With so many deciding to do the same, I found there was little flour available. What was left, I found to be organic flour produced by the ancient family miller of somebody, from the untouched fields of such and such, and thus cost triple the usual flour.

As restrictions were lifted, and as with so many hobbies, people quickly became bored and gave up, I found the availability, and so the price of flour became far more favourable. This led to a glut in my breadmaking, to the appreciation of my flatmates and family.

And it wasn't just flour. In the first month of Coronavirus-induced lockdown, sales of supermarket essentials rose by 8%. With people having more time on their hands, the prices of cooking ingredients such as rice and vegetables saw big increases, while quicker meal ingredients, such as sauces, saw their prices fall. This, coupled with UK households making 80 million panic-induced, extra trips for groceries in March compared to the same month in 2019, meant that in total they spent almost £2bn more than the year before!

Even more worrying are recent reports that three of the biggest UK supermarkets are considering trials of electronic labelling on products. This would allow suppliers to change prices in seconds, to respond to changes in demand, for example, ice cream during a heatwave.

So the old adage of supply and demand still has some clout then.

The same is true for workers. The worrying numbers in receipt of job seeker's allowance, and unemployment rising each month during the Pandemic ``suggested that workers were more plentiful than ever. News outlets and unions repeatedly claimed that some owners were taking advantage of the situation to depress wages. If this was the case, why would any employer invest in expensive machinery, when workers were so cheap? In fact, the truth about machines, throughout our history, is that they do not always replace lower paid workers and spare the highly paid, but often increase the productivity of workers and replace the expensive, inefficient ones. Therefore, whatever might be said around the coffee or dinner table, the rise of the machine is far more nuanced than The Terminator would have you believe.

Returning to the Past to Save the Future

Automation has been threatening livelihoods for far longer than the first Terminator film. As early as the Victorian era, we find reports on the number of employed shoe binders dropping by 90% in England, due to mechanisation. In this case sparked by the introduction of the US Singer sewing machine.

Fast-forward 20 years and telephone operator was one of the most popular jobs for young women in the labour market in the 1920s. By 1940, most phone networks used mechanical switching, resulting in 50-80% permanent job cuts over the period. The same level of cuts is estimated for cashiers and customer service workers by then end of the 1940s, due to similar mechanisation in retail, according to the Bureau of Labour Market Statistics.

Did this early 20th Century automation result in a huge wave of unemployment for this demographic? The answer for new cohorts of young women was a resounding no, as the group simply moved to fast growing and similarly paid roles like typists and secretaries. The story was less positive for incumbent workers, who were significantly less likely to be employed a decade after the automation of their roles. Even here machines were not the sole cause of this loss of jobs. The high turnover rate in these roles (up to 40% a year) before mechanical switching was introduced, and views on women's roles in the family unit at the time are far more likely suspects for the high levels of unemployment for incumbent telephone operators than automation.

Some may applaud this limited level of job destruction; surely unproductive workers deserve to be unemployed? Sounds harsh, but also sounds like your average tabloid headline, or even me, circa 5 years ago!

The truth is that mechanisation doesn't even achieve this level of disruption with surety. In the (not too) distant past of the 1970s, books were already being written about rising unemployment in the US caused by tech-led productivity gains. However, a more entertaining, and easier to follow story on this, comes from the 2005 film adaptation of Charlie and the Chocolate Factory.

In the film, Charlie's father loses his job at a toothpaste factory, when a machine which is able to work at a much faster rate, is introduced. This has immediate, devastating effects on the family, whose income drops to nothing. By the end of the film however, his father secures a new job, maintaining the machine that replaced him at the factory, with a much higher wage to go with it.

The first part of the story is what was predicted, by many writers in the 70s, on productivity in some industries in the US, and now by mechanisation doomsayers today. What is forgotten, is that for every lost job in one industry, whether due to robots or some other kind of increase in productivity, there are often new workers and jobs becoming available within the economy. When we take a step back from the headlines on steel or automobile jobs, we see that, on aggregate, overall jobs in the UK and the US (2020 excluded) have consistently grown for over a decade, and much longer when we exclude temporary spikes in unemployment, which were far from machine-driven. For example, I don't remember many sparing the bankers in 2008, to blame machines for the Credit Crunch.

Come with Me if you Want a Coffee

While Arnold Schwarzenegger proved himself adept at blowing up police cars and machines alike, never once did we see him make coffee, or give someone a haircut.

While the threat of robots replacing us all has been around for decades, little progress has been made, particularly in sectors such as hospitality. Human beings appreciate interaction with others, and do not adhere to set patterns; you should see the number of changes my family make to a Full English Breakfast order! The result, while routine jobs have seen their hours eaten up by machines, personal and health services have seen the proportion of UK worker hours in these fields increase, since 1993.

Tech has been, comparatively, far more successful in running the fancy modelling and equations, that we used to pay people to solve. Risk analysis and insurance are now largely a case of running an algorithm, rather than doing any complex equations ourselves. As a result, we are starting to see the rise of industries like FinTech (financial technology), taking over the roles of traditional jobs, like actuaries and bankers.

The diversity of the workforce in developed countries is also a bulwark against mass unemployment, with education the biggest employer in the UK by sector, and yet only 11% of the total. This is followed by manufacturing at 10% and retail at just 9%. While some of these are at risk, it is hard to imagine teachers, carers, etc being replaced so easily by machines.

There are plenty of people who would, can and are arguing that the pace of technological change and the sheer power of machine learning will mean this time will be different. They predict a tsunami of job losses and economic destruction, rather than a ripple. However, we humans appear, at times, programmed to expect new things to be bigger and better than anything that has come before, overegging everything from the newest smartphone to the latest signing to our football team.

Take for example, the creation of the telegraph in the 19th century. Before this invention, it took three weeks to take a message across the Atlantic by sail ship. With the telegraph this time, for messages under 300 words (so plenty for social media people), was reduced to under 10 minutes. This was an increase of over 2500 times the original speed of sending a message by ship. In comparison, the internet increased, the then fastest method of sending messages, the fax machine, from ten seconds to 2 seconds. This is an increase in speed of just 5 times!

Even when we focus on longer documents, which would have taken the telegram longer of course, we find the internet is still over a factor of twenty-five out from meeting the speed increase set by previous technologies.

There is more to the internet than speed, but it still displays the temptation for humans to overhype the 'latest thing'. Moreover, the IT 'revolution' has not led to the wider benefits to society, that people who care about more than the speed their status updates go online, have been arguing.

As early as 1987, Robert Solow, Nobel economist, was questioning the value of the computer to national productivity:

"You can see the computer age everywhere but in the productivity statistics."

While much has changed since then, the jury remains out on whether the latest technology adds real value to our lives. It is easy to question the effectiveness of social media on our productivity. Many would even argue the opposite has occurred. Deeper than this, technological advancement since the 80s, has remained resolutely obscure as to its improvements to society, whereas green energy, medicine and other technologies are much more transparent.

Productivity fell sharply during the 2008 crisis, particularly in Britain, where it remained below its pre-crisis trend levels as late as 2018. This 'productivity puzzle' has remained even as the immediate effects of the crisis have faded. In fact, productivity in the UK was falling before 2008, causing many people to suggest that recent advances have not been as successful in improving our productivity, and so our lives, as previously. Unlike GDP, which is often difficult to connect to ordinary people's living standards, productivity presents a far clearer benefit to people's lives. After all, the faster we can finish our weekend chores, the quicker we can get on with the important stuff, like taking a well-earned break!

Solow himself later reflected that judging the impact of the internet and its associated technologies like AI, against older inventions which have had longer to have impact, is unfair, given that new technologies take time to move from the laboratory to the factory floor. Despite this important qualification, I think the current rate of impact that computers, the internet, and now, robotics and AI is having on the world's economies is perhaps not as impressive as we might first assume. Even if we allow for some more time for their full potential to become evident, the above suggests these inventions are in line with what has come before, and not some next level threat, to jobs and livelihoods.

And how good are these robots anyway?

As alluded to before, often it is the expensive, inefficient jobs that are replaced by machines. This suggests that algorithms will be replacing bankers, not barristers. Some may argue this is a good thing, remembering the wild assumptions and calculations of fixed income associates at banks, in the lead up to the Great Recession in 2008. However, more recent disasters, such as the UK government's attempt to grade students by algorithm, show that we are far from perfect, when designing machines to do our work for us.

The supposed super-advanced algorithm made as obviously questionable decisions as downgrading a class's grades based on the number of pupils in the class, or the ability of the students the year before. This adds to the earlier warning about how using yesterday's data can bring yesterday's prejudices into today's decision-making, such as basing a loan decision on the applicant's race.

This exposes a weakness in yesterday's bankers' risk assessment and today's algorithms. They are only as effective as the assumptions and considerations that those who set up the models make. Without people in the loop, who understand the consequences of one assumption over another and who have the power to stop the wrong decisions being inputted into the model, we are destined to bring about our own doomsday through incorrect decision making.

Crawling but Still a Threat

At this point, the unstoppable terminator is starting to look a bit haggard, perhaps, as in the first film, it has lost both of its legs. Despite this weakened state, however, it proved a sizeable threat to the protagonists. In our world too, just because fewer workers will be displaced than the headlines would have you believe, this doesn't mean there will be no technological driven job displacement, nor that automation won't have economy-altering effects.

Where jobs have been lost to mechanisation, there has been a disproportionate loss of routine, middle-income jobs in developed countries in particular. This has resulted in a fall in employment in what was, traditionally, the centre of the pay distribution. Despite this, average wages have not fluctuated accordingly. Over the last 20 years, while traditionally low and high paid jobs have filled the gap in falling employment from the middle, the rising living wage has kept the number of people in what were, historically, seen as low, middle and high pay jobs, largely the same.

New jobs have also helped fill the gap in the traditional middle. For example, administrative roles declined by 2% overall between 1993 and 2015, but new roles emerged in science, IT and health that have contributed to filling this gap. Jobs in education, the police and the armed forces have also occupied this void, but it is worth noting that these incomes have dropped from the higher level to fill the middle, rather than appearing from nowhere as totally new jobs. There has also been a rise in business and media roles in the middle of the pay distribution. This is possibly because secretarial roles now classed as professional business roles, as more graduates take on these positions. The overall story of pay changing little, even as job types move around, shows the limited impact of technology. It also links well with the previous chapter on education, particularly on degree inflation. We can now see, in the labour market, graduates doing the same roles that non-graduates did before, resulting in a hollowing out of the middle-skill occupations, as even those on middle incomes remain in what are officially classed, lower-skilled jobs.

'Finally, the fact that caring has emerged as the growth occupation replacing the majority of the hours lost in the bottom half of the pay distribution should also urge us to view automation more cautiously in our accounts of occupational change. In this example at least, changes in demand due to demographic change, as well as changes in supply due to the rise in female employment and availability of migrant labour over this period, have had impacts that are more significant than technological change.'

– Resolution Foundation, 2020

This paragraph sets out nicely how many jobs are not lost in a sudden wave of mechanisation, but instead are slowly retired, as the workers themselves in these occupations leave the workforce.

A slow disease can be just as crippling as a fast one however, and research from Massachusetts Institute of Technology shows that while the average wage has not changed much in recent decades, the total wages paid out to the working population have grown noticeably slower since the 1980s, than in the 40 years before. This is because the % of income from the production of goods and services that has been paid to labour as opposed to capital has fallen. As a result, a worker producing a widget is taking home, less of the final price paid for the widget, than they were in the 80s. More is going to the machines' owner, and to other aids utilised by the worker to produce the widget. As mentioned in earlier chapters, the pay split has also become more unequal, with more educated employees taking home a higher % of income than those with a lower level of education.

This is due to a shift in the balance between the rate of job creation and destruction caused by technological change since the 80s. Prior to the 80s, the two rates matched, as noted in the movement of call operators to secretarial and other roles. Now, however, the gap between job creation and job destruction has widened significantly, resulting in greater levels of unemployment caused by automation.

The Marxists reading this book will claim this is proof that capitalists are reducing worker influence, so that they can be marginalised, and paid ever lower sums for their labour. As we saw with my bread making however, supply and demand deems that, in fact, the decision over whether to utilise labour or capital in the production process is much more about the relative prices of the two than some master plan.

Since the 80s the relative cost of capital has fallen significantly compared to labour, and so it appears tax policy is far closer to causing employment Armageddon than machines.

"Employers often ask whether a machine or a person is better suited to do a job, based on factors such as speed, precision, and what's technically possible. But one of machines' biggest advantages over a worker may be how they are taxed."

- *Daron Acemoglu et al., MIT*

There's Always Something to Worry About!

My partner is a persistent worrier. Whether it's a mysterious noise coming from the car no one else can hear that heralds an imminent break-down, or whether she has bought the right amount of presents for her friends for Christmas, there is always something keeping her on edge. It has become customary, therefore, for the rest of the family to claim that she isn't happy unless there is something to worry about. She will be reading this now and having been severely upset that it appears that automation is not an immediate worry, she will have been relieved to hear that there are still challenges to the current economic system that threaten workers across the globe. There is an uncanny resemblance here with the warnings in the media over the dangers of automation. Both seem happier to find a malevolent and unstoppable force to explain their problems, than the more mundane explanation. With the world press this makes sense, as an unforeseeable adversary is far more interesting to write and read about, than misguided tax policy. What reason my partner has for constant worry, I fear I will never know. Indeed, it will not take her long to realise that another thing we have not addressed so far, is how to deal with the movement of workers from an outdated job to a new one. Just because a worker is made unemployed on one day and will find a new career on another, does not make the morning after redundancy any less painful, even in a tight labour market where there are not many other unemployed people to compete with. For example, a ballerina one day cannot simply start a job in cyber the next.

Automatic stabilisers, such as unemployment benefit, are already in place and offer a softer landing for those made redundant at any time, regardless of the cause. These have limited impact however, particularly as unemployment benefit in the UK is below the National Living Wage. Even so, the emergency $600 per week extra unemployment benefit in the US, following shutdowns caused by Coronavirus, was criticised by some commentators, most prominently Republican senators and President Trump's aides. They argued that paying people not to work, would result in people not feeling the need to look for a job. Incredibly, these same commentators can be relied upon to demand subsidy support for jobs at risk due to automation or foreign competition, such as in American steel and agriculture. This odd dichotomy of not wanting to support those out of work, but protect those who are yet to be made unemployed is not a uniquely American problem, nor is it based on strong evidence.

Recent studies of the Universal Credit benefit have found that the scheme did not disincentivise work. In fact, those who benefitted most from the scheme were just as quick, on average, to return to work, as those who benefitted least. This fits in with the simple theory, which is that a temporary benefit helps people find jobs, as it gives them support and therefore time to research new job opportunities, and if time-limited, will still incentivise job search.

While arguments that unemployment benefits damage the labour market don't hold much sway in the UK, it is still the case that even the highest earners (and therefore greatest tax contributors) only receive a level of benefit below the minimum wage, if made redundant. This means any impact of automation is likely to be felt strongly, whether you are rich or poor. The German system by contrast, employs something far closer to the current furlough system for the first year of unemployment. Those made redundant receive a percentage of their earnings rather than a flat amount. This has three major positive impacts for the labour market.

Firstly, those made redundant or who become unemployed have a greater level of support, regardless of their incomes, as even those at the bottom receive more than their UK equivalents. This is a temporary position and so maintains the incentive to look for a new job. Rather than spending time in any job that will take them, and moving their family to a bedsit with all the time-draining implications these bring, they can actively look for a job better suited to their talent, rather than one that simply pays the bills.

Secondly, this system receives more backing from the middle and higher-income brackets of the German labour market, as those who pay more tax, have greater support in their time of need. Not only does this mean the system is better supported and therefore funded than in the UK, it also allows for a certain amount of subsidisation of lower incomes. For example, higher tax receipts allow for a higher percentage of earnings being paid to those at the bottom of the pay distribution, meaning those already close to the poverty do not drop below it, as was the case in the early days of Universal Credit.

Finally, greater protection for the unemployed is a more efficient method of adapting to the changing demand for certain jobs than subsidising industries that are either old fashioned or uncompetitive.

No industry has perhaps garnered more attention for the size of its subsidies than agriculture. In the EU, wheat subsidies in 2005 averaged at 20.4% of the total price, on dairy it was 13.7%. In 2010 the EU spent 57 billion euros on agriculture, 39 billion of which went on direct subsidies. In 2020, the EU budget was 168 billion euros, 35% of this being spent on agriculture and fisheries.

But beyond agriculture, the UK also spent £10.5bn in support of fossil fuels in 2019, the highest in the EU. An often-touted opportunity of Brexit is that the UK can pull itself away from such levels of support. Doing so would force outdated industries to modernise more quickly.

"A temporary increase in borrowing is a price worth paying to save lives and protect businesses and jobs from a one-off shock like coronavirus. But the government needs to wean the UK off this extraordinary level of state subsidy as soon as possible."

"This huge amount of intervention will distort the economy, undermine market incentives, and ultimately hold back the recovery."

> -   Julian Jessop, Institute of Economic Affairs, May 2020

Subsidies, to their credit, have proven an effective tool for countries looking to grow new industries without foreign companies using their incumbent power and size to throttle such growth. Much of the success of Asian countries has been built on government support for industries that have since become world leaders in arenas such as steel, ship building and many others.

However, as we saw in chapter 7 on China, subsidies on established, unprofitable and indebted companies, often termed 'Zombie companies' have proven ineffective in helping companies return to profitability. Instead they cement their place as inefficient firms, unable to sustain themselves without continued support.

Rather than keeping zombie industries, government should support the retraining of workers to enable a quick transition into new roles, when necessary. Buy-in from workers and the private sector will also be crucial. A report by McKinsey in 2018, found that 62% of US executives surveyed, believe they will need to retrain or replace their workforce between 2018 and 2023 due to automation. 82% see retraining and re-skilling as at least half the answer to this need to retrain, with 94% of European executives believing the same.

Reminding a Fisherman Where he Left his Rod.

It is a common argument from big business, that government should keep its nose out of their companies, and limit regulation and intervention in markets, unless of course, it's to bail them out. One example is the intervention by famously anti-big government President George W. Bush, who authorised $700 billion in spending to stabilise banks during the 2008 financial crisis. In 2020 firms accused governments of imposing draconian rules on them in response to the Coronavirus crisis, while also accepting £66bn in grants and loans, and a further £73bn to support their workers through the furlough scheme. Historically, the great power of capitalism is that it utilises competition to drive growth. Companies that ask for subsidies to protect their industry are looking to slow competition, to make their time of it easier, much like the proverbial fisherman, who having been taught to fish, asks that the government sends him fish, to keep him in the job.

By reducing handouts for these fishermen, but funding schemes that will teach them new skills, we can keep the competitive edge classical capitalism provides, while also enabling quick transitions, as our economy continues to modernise. This will prevent deskilling of our workforce, by limiting the time spent unemployed, as well as upskilling workers. As we saw in the education chapter, skills are what makes workers valuable rather than the specific topics they have studied. For example, an applicant's skills of communication and leadership are likely far more useful in leading a new team than their knowledge of degree-level mathematics. Recent studies have found that previous experience in a job is a poor indicator of the long-term success of an individual in a similar role, despite this being a regular metric for recruiters in assessing the suitability of an applicant. With more support for the unemployed in terms of reskilling and job search, we will keep our labour market dynamic and save much more money than keeping out of date industries on life support.

The historic role government has had in driving the development of new technology, should give policy makers confidence to support job-creating advances. Since the Second World War, government investment has been the driving force for invention. The first computers and antibiotics, the internet, and companies like Apple and Google have all benefited from government support early in their development.

Advancements in technology also provide the greatest spillovers to other companies, where the techniques or products produced to answer one problem, can be used to solve many others. These positive externalities stretch from the useful, such as memory foam and freeze-dried food from the government-sponsored NASA missions (turns out the non-stick pans claim is a myth!), to the critical, such as the development of microchips which now power everything from jets and satellites, to cars and fridges .

Much like the wider benefits achieved by green energy, government should champion job-creating technology that benefits the wider population. Leaving this to the private sector would lead to underinvestment as private companies do not value spillovers as highly. As has been the case with the environmental problem, governments and voters should work to encourage a social awakening to the idea that technology is something that has good and bad elements and that, we all have a role in promoting the positives over the negatives. The success of populists claiming to defend manufacturing heartlands from automation and globalisation, shows that there is an awareness of the problems in labour markets, and people are being left behind. However, the true danger, poor policy subsidising capital while over-taxing labour, is still to be fully understood. Information therefore is power.

Once there is a greater acceptance that some technologies are more beneficial to wider society than others, governments should move to invest in technology that augments and improves labour, rather than replaces it. As with emissions, measuring this will be a challenge. Something akin to measuring the % of labour in the added value of the new technology's product, would be a start. This may sound like government unfairly intervening in the market and yes, it is a form of intervention. However, it is no more intrusive, and is far better targeted than the UK's plans to 'level up' left behind manufacturing regions. If we do not invest in job creation technology, it will not matter where the government invests.

Spending money on robots in Leeds or Chicago is no more use to the people in those areas than human jobs in already established employment centres such as London or New York.

Fear of the power of governments was turbo charged during the Covid-19 Pandemic, as people questioned who should have the ultimate say on a person's actions, the state or the individual? Playing these two off against each other is a useful argument for libertarians, although drawing the line as to who receives which freedom is difficult. Who should have the greater freedom, the individual to visit a shop, or the owner to only admit people wearing masks or with a 'Vaccine Passport'?

More research from MIT finds that the power of the state can bolster the power of the individual. For example, laws and policing which uphold our rights to property, and protect us from those who would do us harm. If power was left solely to individuals, those with the most money and power would dictate what is right and wrong. This was the case during feudalism, and remains the case in some extreme regimes today, where the political and judicial rights of individuals (particularly of those on the margins of society, such as ethnic or religious minorities) quickly suffer as a result.

The Storming of Capitol Hill and the rise of authoritarianism in China show how delicate these institutions which support individual freedoms can be. However, if countries work to preserve them and spread their influence to areas such as big tech, we can secure the rights of individuals on everything from fair pay to data protection. Such protection is not possible without the independent scrutiny of the state and its independent bodies.

A more effective tax system which does not allow for multinational companies to avoid tax by basing operations overseas, must also be implemented. This will be, by far, the most difficult policy for sovereign nations to enact, as it requires cooperation with other countries. Having left the European Union, the UK finds itself at a particularly clear set of crossroads in this regard. If future governments want to maintain a level of tax income from tech companies, they will have to find a way of working with foreign nations, to strengthen the mechanisms which prevent these companies from avoiding tax. As well as maintaining their ability to spend on public goods such as schools, hospitals and prisons, such an effort will enable policy makers to rebalance the relative costs of labour and capital. This, in turn, will halt the recent march of a more destructive type of technological progress, which is, in part to blame for the rising inequality, currently plaguing western societies.

These commitments combined with a stronger, but also more targeted welfare system will enable people to better adapt to technological change. Just as industry helped fill the gap in employment left by the agriculture productivity boom during the Industrial Revolution, greater provision of public support and training programmes should help workers displaced by automation find new roles.

We can see now that firms make decisions between machine and man in a calculating, cost-focussed way rather than some grand capitalist plan. Also, those arguing for 'pro-business' support in response to unemployment are closer to pushing for communist China-style subsidisation of uncompetitive industries. This knowledge should mean we are less afraid of automation, while harbouring a newfound respect for the impact technological change can have. This, combined with the right policy decisions can keep our economies dynamic and productive, rather than slipping back into the rent-seeking, subsidy-ridden economies that existed before the evolution of capitalism.

9

Whites, Women and Wokeness

Many of us have that family member who makes comments at the table that make us wince. The talk of life being better in 'the good old days' quickly turns to complaints about immigration and the country being too full. Any news of a crime or violence committed by a non-white person is quickly highlighted as a sign of British values being eroded, regardless of how long the person has resided in the country. Even as I wrote this chapter for the first time, back in mid-2020, I could imagine these misconceptions being reinforced by people focussing on the colour of the perpetrator of the horrific September stabbings in Birmingham, even as the killing of a 15-year-old in London was also being reported on at the same time, the killer this time being white.

The evidence for this discrimination expands beyond one or two personal examples. A study in 2019, found that 71% of people from ethnic minorities reported having faced racial discrimination, compared with 'just' 58% in January 2016 before the EU referendum vote. Hate crimes have increased year on year since 2013, doubling to 71,251 incidents in

England and Wales in 2018, according to UK Home Office data.

Less overt discrimination remains an issue for many protected groups. The gender pay gap (the difference between average hourly earnings) in the UK in April 2020, was on average 15.5%, with 90% of women still working for companies that pay them less than male colleagues. For ethnic minorities, while the pay gap in 2020 was at its smallest since 2012, at just over 2%, double-digit pay gaps remained for 4 of the major ethnic minority groups.

Disparities on everything from loan applications, to the likelihood of conviction for the same crime, continue to exist across the globe.

A recent study published by Oxford University found that even small acts of kindness do not go unaffected by race. The social experiment involved people of different ethnicities being given a travel card with zero balance. They were asked to use a bus without paying, by asking the bus driver whether they could have a free ride. While the good news (unless you own a bus company) was that two thirds of drivers offered free rides, they were twice as likely to give white test subjects a free ride, as non-whites. This suggests that inherent discrimination is just as evident in informal situations as formal ones, and while this can be harder to track, it is also far more difficult to extinguish. It also receives far less attention in both the media, and academic research.

What many don't realise is that immigration and a multicoloured society have been with us much longer, than those who pine for 'simpler times' believe.

British History, in Black and White

Black men and women have been living in the UK from as early as the 12th century, but it was colonialization and the slave trade in the 17th and 18th century which led to a significant increase in their numbers. By the time of the Industrial Revolution, people of colour were not an uncommon site in the UK, particularly in slave-trading hubs such as

Liverpool and Manchester. By the second half of the 18th century, there were reportedly 15,000 black people in England alone, 0.25% of the population, or 1 in 400.

It is worth noting at this point that in the 270 years since then, the black population in England had grown to just 3.3% at the 2011 census, and 3.6% according to experimental data from the ONS in 2017. I can confidently guess that this number is smaller than most of you would have imagined. It also suggests our understanding of the current racial complexion of the UK is almost as bad as past ones.

Unsurprisingly perhaps, two of the few dates we Brits can remember on race are, 1807- the abolition of the Slave Trade, and 1833, when slavery across the British Empire was banned. Both these British-led moments can be held up as pivotal and positive action in the history of racism. What may be less well known, as it is rather less impressive, is that the British government paid £20 million, worth around £17 billion today, to compensate slave owners for freeing their slaves, the debt from which was only paid off in full, in 2015. Moreover, while these acts may look like Britain leading the way in ending the movement of black people from Africa to the Americas, this was less a matter of leading and more of being one of the few countries engaged in the slave trade in any meaningful way. Britain and Portugal alone contributed 70% of all Africans transported to the Americas.

Greater awareness of black history in the UK only begins post-World War Two. Soldiers from the Caribbean settled in the UK (including the now infamous 492 arrivals on the SS Windrush). Despite fighting for the freedom of the country, they became the targets of race riots immediately after their arrival. There is an interesting parallel here with the popular British trope that France has never quite recovered from the apparent embarrassment of needing to be liberated by the UK and US, while under Nazi-occupation. In the same way we accuse the French of sabre-rattling to make up for their historic failings, we are still to fully deal with our own historic failings, of the very people who helped us overcome fascism and racism on the continent. This is worth remembering, especially the next time you hear people claim that racism in the UK is a past evil. You may feel compelled to ask these people, whether or not war embarrassment explains the French's political motivations for their grand standing and hard stance during the 2020 Brexit negotiations. History matters, and we must continue to talk about it.

Despite the continued hostile environment for people of colour in the UK, many names have broken into our recent history and made serious contributions on this subject, and to our lives today. Take Dr Harold Moody, an energetic campaigner for black rights and founder of the League of Coloured People in 1931. The LCP fought racial discrimination in the NHS. It is hard to believe given the current diversity in the service, but Moody was unable to find a job in medicine in the early 20th century, despite acquiring a medical degree from King's College London. The protection of mixed-race children orphaned by the World Wars, was also a hallmark of Moody's work. His name sits alongside others who dared challenge the status-quo of the 20th century. These include Walter Tull, the first professional black outfield footballer, and later military officer in Britain, Evelyn Dove, the first black singer on BBC radio, Margaret Busby, the first British black female publisher and Diane Abbot, Britain's first black female MP.

Key legislative changes came in the 1960s, starting adversely with the 1962 Immigration Act which actually restricted immigration from the Commonwealth. However, in 1965, just weeks before Martin Luther King's famous 'I have a dream' speech, the organisers of The Birmingham Bus Boycott, triumphed in overturning the bus company's decision to discriminate in interview based on colour, despite support for the firm from local all-white unions. Partly spurred on by these actions, the UK Parliament finally passed the Race Relations Act in 1965, after the bill had been put to Parliament for an eighth successive time. This outlawed discrimination on the "grounds of colour, race, or ethnic or national origins" in public places in Great Britain.

Despite the success of these movements, the higher propensity of people of colour to be made unemployed during the 80s recession, coupled with the 1984 'Stop and Search' policy, which disproportionately targeted black people, maintained the perception that people of colour were lazy and prone to criminality. A study this century by the Journal of Mass Communication and Journalism found that in one US state, black males were connected to the crime story 70% of the time, despite only making up 31% of arrests.

Holes in History

Knowledge of this recent history is crucial, as the majority of the population, particularly those in higher management in business and politics, were alive during this time. While I believe few in the UK go to work with overtly racist feelings, the lazy and criminal perception has driven an unintentional feeling about certain groups within society, known as unconscious bias. Unconscious is the operative word here, as with only 11% of GCSE students in 2020 studying modules that reference black people's contribution to British life, we are far more likely to hear and so believe the stereotype of the lazy or criminal minority, than we are to hear about the work of Dr Moody or Ms Dove.

What was so surprising to me when reading about these people and events, is that despite studying history all the way through to A-level, I had not studied this section of history, nor had I heard of many of these people or organisations. In fairness to my school, I did study the American Civil Rights movement in my final year, but nothing in recent UK history. If we want our schools to be teaching UK colonial history and black history, this needs to start long before A-level, otherwise only small groups of history nerds like me will be learning about these events.

"The US struggle against racism is globalised into the story of the struggle against racism that we should look to for inspiration – eclipsing the black British story so much that we convince ourselves that Britain has never had a problem with race.

We need to stop lying to ourselves, and we need to stop lying to each other."

-    *Reni Eddo-Lodge*

This lack of knowledge of our own history explains, not only the rose-tinted view of Britain's past, and fear of immigration, but also why we have been so poor to-date with reconciling our colonial past with our more tolerant present.

Greater representation of the history of ethnic minorities in the UK, as well as our history as a colonial power would do much to help us understand the issues that still exist today. Fortunately, there is a great opportunity for change here, given the support for more focus on Britain's colonial past. Both those who wish to expose the atrocities of the British empire and those who wish to reminisce of when Britain 'ruled the waves', want to have this portion of history explored. While both sides will argue for very different focuses on this teaching, a balanced view would surely appease both groups (or at least not be totally unpalatable to them), as well as providing much needed context for the situation in which we currently find ourselves.

The growth of the Black Lives Matter movement, much like the MeToo movement of 2017, has given rise to another split in opinion, with the middle seemingly impossible to hold without receiving abuse from both sides. You must either support the idea that the treatment of ethnic groups across the UK and US has remained structurally racist, and so find yourself labelled on the left of the political horseshoe, or that racism is a topic for the history books and find yourself on the right. As mentioned in the early chapters of this book, this polarisation of opinion has become a regular feature of the western world in the last decade, as culture and identity have overtaken economics to become the heart of what defines our political image. This, however, is an over-simplistic view of how someone forms their opinions. With regard to race, the idea that racism does not exist, is as irrational as the argument that the UK has remained as structurally racist as it was 100 years ago.

Many opponents of these waves of sentiment for greater de facto equality in our societies argue that campaigns for minorities to be heard have morphed into campaigns for the 'silent majority' to be quiet. Whether it's through 'wokism,' 'cancel-culture' or 'a denial of freedom of speech', they argue this is an attempt to police people's thoughts and opinions to the point where our entire economic system devolves into some 1984-style dystopia.

Look into this in more detail, however, and we find little evidence of a thought police influencing our lives.

Recent interviews with prominent opponents of 'the wokies' have exposed, with the exception of the transgender debate, that the only examples of genuine impacts of this campaign against freedom of speech have been trivial if not comical. These include such 'outrageous scandals' as, the suggestion of a female Doctor Who or James Bond, the arrival of a vegan sausage roll while the original still remains available, and complaints that statues outside parliament were boarded up during the BLM protests, when in fact this occurs during any major demonstration, including the pro-Brexit marches and anti-Iraq war campaigns.

Once you strip away the conspiracy theories and the genuinely difficult debate on transgender rights, one can quickly see these complaints add little and can provide cover for less palatable views. This is most obviously exposed when we consider the irony of national newspaper columnists complaining that they do not have a platform to put forward their views and are being 'cancelled' whenever their more extreme views are challenged.

If we are to grasp the real issues in our society, we must push aside pointless arguments and prevent such strawmen being the reason we don't find practical answers to the problem of race in society.

In the words of former-professional footballer Slaven Bilic when asked to comment on something he didn't think was the crux of the issue:

"You're sounding very neutral there Slaven?"

"To be fair I don't care... you are getting angry, I don't know why, I'd rather talk about Courtinho's goal!"

- It's worth a watch, even Roy Keane cracks a smile!

As was touched on in the introduction, a lot of this polarisation comes from the inequality in our society. Lip-service has been paid to helping support ethnic minorities, while in reality the richest, and therefore whitest, have seen their incomes grow fastest. As a result, those at the lower end of the pay scale and in the traditional working class feel under attack from both sides. They see those above them growing their wealth, while all the new opportunities seem to be going to other under-privileged groups. This frustration drives a lot of today's discontentment. It also opens the door for the minority of genuine racists in our country to push an incorrect narrative, namely that foreigners, and by dint, anyone who looks different to the majority, are the reason for today's problems.

The latter half of my second year of university was a frustrating time as I attempted to secure an internship for the summer. My university was dogmatic in its approach to students securing jobs after graduation. The golden ticket to this was experience in the industry of your choice, before completing your course. Dutifully, I applied to 20 different firms in economic and finance-related industries. Rejections came thick and fast, some within minutes of applying. As I became more desperate, I started looking at a wider range of opportunities with these firms, outside the standard graduate schemes, only to find that many of the remaining opportunities were limited to those from disadvantaged groups. It was at this point, I felt that very real frustration of feeling left behind, as my opportunities appeared to be fading away before my eyes. This view was misguided, as the vast majority of people who are offered such roles, come from privileged and white backgrounds with 70% of employers in 2019 identifying increasing diversity and social mobility as a key priority for these schemes. This is before you even consider the disproportionate number of privileged individuals who enrol in Russell Group universities in the first place. Despite these very real facts, having been pushed to achieve or bust, and seeing headlines on tokenism mixed with what looks like discrimination against whites, it is hard to escape the frustration which has driven much of the polarisation, in the western world, for the past decade.

The question we must deal with, therefore, is how we push for greater equality in our societies, without further alienating the crucial sections of the electorate that feel left behind?

Colour-blind to the World

Evidence that in the right conditions, ethnicity doesn't matter (typified by the election of Barack Obama in 2008) leads to the rise of the argument for colour-blindness, the idea that if we ignore colour, prejudice will disappear.

This idea is appealing as it appears meritocratic. If we can remove colour from the equation, we will promote, based on ability and convict, based on evidence. The issue of social mobility in general, it is argued, could be solved in this way, by achieving equality of opportunity. We can see easily, in the case of segregation in education, that it is not only morally wrong, but also inefficient, to have the worst candidates going to universities, simply because of their colour. Those today who campaign against quotas use the same argument, as this may lead to the best candidates being turned down. Also, equal opportunity should not be taken for granted, given how little of human history we have enjoyed it. From Confucianism through Georgian Britain to Apartheid South Africa, someone's birth has been a major factor in their future opportunities.

"No one who buys bread knows whether the wheat from which it was made was grown by a Communist or a Republican, a negro or a white."

– Milton Friedman

The hope for the colour-blind group has therefore been that the market will drive out racism, as firms who pick based on such base and inaccurate feelings as white supremacy et al, will quickly go out of business, driven out by more open minded and therefore successful firms. HA-Joon Chang's '23 Things They Don't Tell You About Capitalism' uses the example of Japanese car makers in South Africa during apartheid to explain this point. The Japanese were given honorary white citizenship and not subjected to segregation. This was done to entice them to stay and continue building good cars for the white supremacists to drive. Surely such power to overcome such established views should be enough to defeat discrimination?

While this is a compelling argument, many prominent sociologists in the UK and the US are extremely critical of colour-blindness. They argue that an attempt to ignore race, in fact allows the more covert forms of racism to remain in common discourse today. By claiming to 'not see colour', even if we do so with good intentions, in fact we are also averting our attention from the less obvious, but still damaging forms of racism.

This is exemplified by the pushback against the expression 'white privilege'. Many people believe that they have worked hard for their position in life and the idea that it was somehow a fluke, or worse, a conscious use of racism, is painful. This definition of white privilege is wrong, however. It is not an innate advantage whites have over others; it is simply the absence of the disadvantage experienced by non-whites. This is a crucial distinction, as it both accepts that being white does not mean life is easy, but also acknowledges that whites have fewer hurdles to jump to finish the same race. The same is true for other disadvantaged groups, whether women, LGBT, or those from a poorer socio-economic background. It is crucial therefore, we recognise the additional barriers, as simply ignoring problems, are unlikely to see them disappear.

It appears that equal opportunity is not always easy to tie down. As we saw in Chapter 4, if we do not control for all possible impacts on a result, we cannot be sure we have come to the right conclusion. For example, if a child does not perform well at school because he has not been fed properly throughout the year, (this is particularly pertinent, given Marcus Rashford's heroics, regarding the provision of free school meals during the school holidays), and as a result does not achieve the same grades as others in his class, this does not mean he is less able. Many economists have argued this means a degree of equality of outcome is required, where every household must be given enough to provide the basic level of support for their children, thereby allowing them to take full advantage of equal opportunity. I would argue this is simply an extension of equality of opportunity rather than a move to equality of outcome. Regardless, if more work akin to the Manchester United striker's can be done to ensure support for those without equal opportunity, the better and fairer outcomes for all.

A common saying in South Africa is that despite the end of Apartheid, discrimination remains in what is known as, the Cappuccino Society. Much like the coffee, the colour of those on the bottom of the pay distribution are predominantly black, with white froth on the top and a sprinkling of black (cocoa powder) above that. While equal opportunity to go to the best schools now exists for blacks, the schools in their local areas, the employment rates for their parents, and often the lack of food and time to be productive at school, means that the chances of a black child attending a top university and securing a good job as a result, is still far from even with their white counterparts. Sadly, in the UK this is also the case, as we learnt from the statistics at the beginning of the chapter.

Despite the remaining challenges for ethnic minorities, some will argue that if the state focuses on supporting the economy, by reducing taxes and backing job creators, an improvement in living standards for all, will be far more effective at lifting lower earners out of poverty, than attempting to pull those at the top down and into line with those at the bottom. This is the approach taken by proponents of 'All Lives Matter', or in a wider economic sense, Trickledown Economics.

The theory of trickledown economics can be imagined much like a tower of glasses erected in a pyramid, often seen at fancy dinners. If we allow enough champagne to pour into the top glass, it will eventually overflow and 'trickle down' into the glasses beneath it, until all are full. The trouble with this analysis can be seen before we even leave the analogy! Not only will attempting to fill the glasses below, by overfilling the top one, result in a fair amount of waste, but also relies on there being enough champagne to fill the top glasses, long before the bottom sees a single drop. I would cautiously suggest therefore, that such a move, which usually takes the form of tax cuts in the real world, would in fact be an incredibly inefficient way of helping the lower earners and unemployed, regardless of their colour. A better analogy would be the idea that a rising tide lifts all boats. Here, instead of the biggest boats rising first, it would be the smallest that would float first. In the same way, support should be targeted at the bottom of the pay distribution, if we want to maximise its effects.

To be clear, I am not suggesting an all-out war on the rich in society, merely that if we are going to use the limited public funds available, it should probably work from the bottom-up rather than top-down. Also, that this is not a call for greater income support for one minority group alone, but to all those lower down the wealth distribution. In the same way that historic grievances and unconscious bias disproportionately affect women and ethnic minorities, so too would such progressive support. For example, greater spending in underperforming schools, or greater education for businesses on the negative impacts of unconscious bias, would impact lower paid minorities most, and any others unlucky enough to find themselves struggling to pay the bills.

Life is not Two-tone

This push for equality, not just for historically disadvantaged groups, but for anyone who finds themselves in financial difficulty, will prevent us supporting those who aren't in need but are in the target demographic (an inefficient policy if ever I saw one!) Also, it will receive greater buy-in from the population who have shown in recent elections and referendums that they feel unsupported by governments, which they believe are only catering to the 'fashionable' disadvantaged groups. While the statistics suggest otherwise, this attitude that our institutions now disproportionately favour minority groups exists, and we must face it if we are to overcome the issues in politics today.

Some may argue that non-whites are always the ones to suffer from maltreatment, but unconscious bias proves we all have this capacity for prejudice. Evidence from the National Basketball Association shows that unconscious bias, the propensity for us all to allow our preconceptions on people and things to unfairly influence our decision-making, is measurably present in everyday life, regardless of the race of the individual.

"Players earn up to 4% fewer fouls or score up to 2.5% more points when they are the recipients of a positive own-race bias. We find similar results when aggregating to the team level, with the racial composition of the refereeing crew having an appreciable effect on the probability of a team winning. In an average game, one team plays around 15% fewer minutes with black players than their opponents. For this team, the chance of victory under an all-black referring crew versus an all-white crew differs by about three percentage points.

The bias in foul-calling is large enough so that the probability of a team winning is noticeably affected by the racial composition of the referring crew assigned to the game."

This tells us two things:

The first is that own-race bias is not just for white people. This tallies with my own limited experience of spending some of my education in the Caribbean. In school, I was the ethnic minority, and I was subject to stereotypes and occasional maltreatment. One only had to leave the local school and head to the beach to see the qualifying point to this evidence. A long row of hotels populated the area's most popular beach and while people of colour would often be asked at the entrance what business they had there, as a white family, the explanation that we had come for lunch or for a day by the sea was sufficient for us to be allowed to spend an afternoon on a private section of beach, or in one of the hotel's pools and restaurants. This shows, as does the NBA example, that whoever holds authority or power in a situation is the one whose unconscious bias matters. Thus, in the western world, where the majority of business and political leaders are white males, it is their unconscious bias which impacts the majority. It may only have been as small an infringement as mocking my foreign expressions, or teachers not believing me over a black student, even with no evidence in their favour, but my Caribbean experiences have only made me more determined to work for true equality of opportunity and to remove unconscious bias. I believe that this can be achieved, not by focusing on a particular group or race, but by concentrating on improving the position of all lower earners. This would naturally, disproportionately, target ethnic minorities, who due to past failings and overt racism have found themselves clustered at the bottom.

The second point is that, far as humanity has come on racism, we appear predisposed to some level of positive bias towards people who look and act as we do. Much like in chapter 5 on eating healthily, the quick-thinking part of our brain is programmed to help our decision making by making generalisations. These are still useful in some cases today (remember my pre-determined preference for certain ice-creams and how this speeds up the queue), but we must internalise these feelings on more complex decisions and utilise the slow moving part of our brain to combat unconscious bias.

For example, hearing a foreign sounding name may conjure up automatic feelings of unfamiliarity or distrust, even in formal situations such as at an interview. It is crucial therefore, that we do not ignore these feelings, as like it or not they will impact our decision-making. Instead, we should focus on them and develop ways of negating them, by considering what preconceptions we have of a particular name and taking a conscious step to allow greater leeway if the applicant appears to fit our perceived caricature. Alternatively, in the case of the sifting process, simply not read the name and ethnicity during the process, to halt bias from the start.

So unconscious bias training for all, right?

No, according to UK policy makers. Training for English civil servants was scrapped, after a report from the Government Equalities Office stated there was no evidence that the training had improved workplace equality.

So how do we ensure greater social mobility and equality for ethnic minorities?

In keeping with the arguments above, an approach that benefits the equality of opportunity for those who need it most will benefit all. This will also disproportionately benefit ethnic minorities, while being unlikely to foster the same level of denouncement as blunt instruments like quotas.

Fortunately, a report by the OECD in 2010, not only has a comfortingly similar subtitle (Intergenerational social mobility reflects equality of opportunities), but also highlights the countries with the greatest track record in these areas, namely Australia, Canada and the Nordic countries. As proof, the report shows how, in the UK, at least 50% of the economic advantage that high-earnings fathers have over low-earning fathers is passed on to their sons. By contrast in Australia, Canada and the Nordics, this figure is just 20%.

As was suggested in Chapter 8 on education, the sheer amount of schooling, and inputs, (such as a reduction in class size) is found to be only weakly associated with student performance. Teacher quality, achieved through higher levels of teacher training and pay in the successful countries, has a much bigger impact on both student performance and future equality of opportunity in secondary and tertiary education. As a result, countries with the biggest disparity in funding between their private and public education sectors also see lower levels of social mobility.

Early childhood care and education is also important for the development of cognitive skills in later life. Hence, compulsory enrolment in quality early education is another reason for the greater level of social mobility in the successful countries. Correspondingly, evidence across OECD countries shows that grouping students by ability at a later age further enhances social mobility. For example, moving the practice of streaming from 10 to 16, is estimated to reduce the influence of the school's socio-economic environment on students, by two thirds.

These are just the beginning of a long list of policies to improve our meritocracies. Other, similar moves for later in life, including employment and welfare support would further improve social mobility and so equality of opportunity for all disadvantaged groups.

It is only by removing many of the disadvantages in today's society that reinforce historic stereotypes, that we will make people more aware of the fact that our unconscious bias drives us, not reality. If we see that given the same opportunities black kids do just as well as white, we will have no excuse to prefer one over the other. If we maintain differences in opportunity, either by maintaining the status quo, or by going too far on equality of outcome, we will never kill off the feelings of unfairness, accusations of tokenism, and general scepticism over the treatment of different races.

Role Models and Role Firefighters

Here are the top 10 childhood dream jobs for American men and women from a survey of over 2,000:

TOP 10 CHILDHOOD DREAM JOBS FOR AMERICAN MEN

1. Professional athlete
2. Doctor/Nurse
3. Musician
4. Police officer
5. Business owner
6. Superhero
7. Teacher
8. Movie star
9. Architect
10. Firefighter

TOP 10 CHILDHOOD DREAM JOBS FOR AMERICAN WOMEN

1. Teacher
2. Doctor/Nurse
3. Veterinarian
4. Movie star
5. Writer
6. Artist
7. Fashion designer
8. Musician
9. Business owner
10. Chef

One can see instantly a few differences between the groups. While some job aspirations are shared, others stand out on one list but not the other.

For men these are:

Professional athlete

Police Officer

Superhero

Architect

Firefighter

For women:

Veterinarian

Writer

Artist

Fashion designer

Chef

We can see instantly that these roles fit into common preconceptions on what boys and girls like, macho, physical jobs, vs. fashion designer and chef.

We can also see that traditionally female jobs rank higher for girls like teacher and doctor/nurse, while business owner ranks higher for men.

Some might argue that this is proof of different biological preferences for jobs, given that even at an early age, boys and girls have separated themselves into traditional gender roles. A more worrying suggestion would be that they have already had these gender roles unconsciously imprinted on their minds, so that by an early age, boys already see their role as more physical, while women see themselves as more caring or creative.

Sadly a six-year study by Johns Hopkins University, looking at data from 10-14-year-olds across 15 different countries, found that even in children at an early age, the views that "girls are vulnerable and boys are strong and independent," were already deeply rooted.

Further research in 2019 found that 45% of people experienced gender stereotyping. Of these, 51% felt it had constrained their career choices, while 44% said it harmed their personal relationships. The result, just 8% of STEM apprentices are women.

There is some evidence that great gender equality leads to greater differences in what the sexes value when surveyed. However, even if the average woman wants something different to the average man does not mean we should force these desires on the whole gender. It is also important to note that just because values differ, does not mean people want to be treated differently. Just because the average Brit likes to go to Spain for their holidays and have chicken tikka masala on the weekends, I don't think we should all be encouraged to do the same, let alone have our other options restricted in the way the opportunities for women in certain industries are.

It is important therefore, that in both education and in work, we provide a balanced view of the opportunities for men and women, people of colour and white. If girls see only nurses and teachers portrayed as common female jobs, that will influence their decisions later. If black boys see only white business leaders and politicians whilst growing up, they will not perceive those careers as for them. It is the responsibility of all of us to point out positive role models for children. This should be consolidated in our jobs and workplaces, starting with the basics like learning to pronounce each other's names correctly.

While any 10-year old can string off the names of his (or her!) favourite football team's players, without stumbling over the pronunciation of names like Didier Drogba or Adama Traore, then why do we struggle with names or similar ethnic origins in the workplace?

This proves that it is not some impossible feat to adapt to greater diversity in the workplace, or to present this reality of the world to our children, rather a lack of commitment and interest on our part. Hopefully we can overcome this unconscious bias by providing the right institutional framework to make sure there are greater opportunities for more Didier Drogba's to make it to the top of their prospective fields, as well as Janet Yellen's and others, in order to provide the diverse world that the next generation desperately needs to see to further push progress in this area.

Crosses and Noughts

The novel Noughts and Crosses is set in an alternative universe where dark skinned people (Crosses) are the ruling class and pale skinned people 'noughts' are an underclass, previously enslaved to the Crosses.

One does not need to go far to find those in the media and across the dining room table claiming to be afraid that at the current rate of progress people of colour will be in control of traditionally white societies. Aside from being wildly inaccurate (as we saw from the % of the UK's black population for one) it is also paradoxical. If as many on this side of the argument espouse that the UK is no longer a racist country, then why would it matter who leads it? Only by accepting that there remains a benefit to being white in our society does it make sense to fear a loss of control.

As discussed in chapter 7 on China, rather than closing ourselves to other ways of thinking, we must be confident in our liberal views, and our state-supported market economies are the best way to maximise welfare for our inhabitants. Anyone who believes that British, or at least Western institutions and laws, are preferable to less free and equal parts of the World, should feel confident that people who come to this country of any colour or creed, will integrate happily.

Equally we should be confident that people who refuse to accept our rule of law will be punished. My hope is that a more open and confident society, which sticks to its principles, will not only reduce radicalisation, and improve social cohesion but also improve the attitudes and actions of all its people.

This is evident in one of the most acute cases of social decohesion – extremist terrorism. The London Bridge attack in November 2019, threw into sharp relief the failure of the current UK deradicalization strategy. Usman Khan killed two people near the London landmark, despite completing two deradicalization programmes during eight years in prison, before the attack. The focus since then has been on extending jail sentences for terror sympathisers. Arthur Snell, former head of the UK government's anti-extremist Prevent program, has argued this won't solve the problem however:

"If you're not rehabilitating prisoners, whether you let them out in two or four years isn't very important."

"Much like the war on drugs in the US, simply further ostracizing groups of society leads to a greater feeling of 'us and them'. This in turn inevitably results in greater decohesion and extremism, as more of the minority population feel under attack. Given the rise in hate crime in the UK since 2016, who can blame them."

Other countries, meanwhile, which boast far lower rates of re-offending than the UK and US, offer a very different life to terror suspects and perpetrators. One 'centre' has a swimming pool, art therapy classes, and offers housing and other support on release. The reader no doubt is imagining a nice Scandinavian style prison. Others might say this type of incarceration would 'certainly never work here', but they would be mistaken. In fact, this is the description of a rehabilitation centre for jihadists in Saudi Arabia, which claims to have an 80% success rate. Whatever you think of the Country and the numbers it claims, the fact that we are not only behind other OECD countries, but also countries we often accuse of having poor standards on human rights, in supporting rehabilitation in our prisons, should be a worrying sign.

"They almost universally were young men without much sense of direction or status, and by joining the insurgency in Iraq, they felt for the first time in their lives that they mattered, that they were doing something important, almost heroic," he said. "So basically, it's a mental health issue."

- *Arthur Snell*

The 'freedom of speech' argument reflects the fear that by being overly accepting of other views, traditional ones are being silenced. People who face criticism for what they say and write will argue this impinges on their freedom of speech. However, what we are really seeing, on Social Media and the news alike, is more freedom of speech. as a wider portion of society enters these arenas and feels free to judge others' views rather than stay quiet, and allow an echo chamber for views to persist.

Once incitement to violence is removed from public discourse, all views should be allowed and challenged. Those who argue this might lead to a dominance of the majority, must first explain to 48% of the UK why it has left the EU. Afterall, the current footballification of public discourse in the UK means supposed 'champions of free speech' are often to be found on the same 'team' as those who voted to leave the EU.

Summing up, all these challenges to race and other forms of discrimination, whether it be historical disadvantages, current unconscious bias or the naysayers and fearmongers of tomorrow, equality of opportunity, through improvements in education, employment and our attitudes to each other in everyday life hold the key. Simply declaring an end to discrimination helps neither the oppressed, nor those either wilfully or subconsciously oppressing. True equality will prove to us all, finally, and undisputedly, the strength and intellectual ability of all groups in society, a fact obscured by centuries of division and lies from those seeing opportunity in other's pain.

"No one is born hating another person because of the colour of his skin, or his background, or his religion. People must learn to hate, and if they can learn to hate, they can be taught to love, for love comes more naturally to the human heart than its opposite."

-       *Nelson Mandela*

10
Financial Fair Play – What do Football Clubs and Investment Clubs Have in Common?

Sticking true to form, my family has settled on each member of the group supporting a different football club, rather than insisting that the younger members follow the same team as their elders, thereby stimulating competition. Free marketeers to the end! As a result, my mother, the least keen of the bunch, usually finds her team changing on a yearly, if not monthly basis, to make sure we maintain top four representation. She had moved from Manchester City, to Leicester, to Spurs, not to mention brief stints with Wolves in the last few seasons.

This leads to plenty of discussion on the prices and wages of footballers in our prospective teams. My father, for instance, still maintains that my team's new attacking midfielder is not worth his wages and that 'anyone can score a penalty'. As a long-time Manchester United supporter, probably sparked by the fact he supports Liverpool, I remain hopeful that the player continues to perform. While it appears hard to mount a convincing defence of the wages paid to footballers, the theory is relatively simple. Fans at the ground, and watching on television, stimulate a huge demand for the rights to advertise products during the game. This in turn leads to a huge clamour from broadcasters to televise the games. As a result, clubs that can attract the most eyeballs, or have the best talent, are paid exceedingly large amounts for the privilege. In order to secure the top talent, clubs are prepared and able to offer huge wages. This simple chain of demand, from the punter on the street, to the club wanting to secure the next top striker's services, explains why the best players are paid so much. But why does all the money end up with a bunch of (in fairness, very talented) 20-somethings, while fans pay hundreds for season tickets?

Pokémon and Gladiators

Many crazes make their way across the school playground, ranging from pogs, to conkers to Tamagotchi. One popular phase at my school was a particular set of trading cards, but in reality, all of these crazes work for this example. So feel free to substitute your own! It all started when someone brought them into school and the popular strapline 'gotta catch them all', did the rest. Suddenly everyone was after them, particularly the most famous characters, and predictably, the rarest ones. I remember it being a regular sight to see someone giving up stacks of cards for either a rare one or a famous name. Scarcity combined with perceived value drives high prices. The combination is important as everyone values water but will not pay a fraction of the price of a diamond for it, until there is a drought. In the same way, top quality footballers are scarce, and unlike school crazes, good football has been of huge value to people across the world, for generations. As a result, it is not a surprise that those at the top of the sport, particularly those with discernible value, highest goal scorers, assisters, clean sheet-earners, etc, are offered so much money.

This is the nice, clean side of markets, where value and scarcity are rewarded with a high price. Sadly, however, this is not the end of the story when it comes to the market for footballer' wages.

Most professional sports can claim the stakes are high today, but none can surely compare to the gladiatorial games of ancient Rome? Small margins, and often a fair amount of luck, could mean the difference between life and death. In that world, the rewards for success were large, but there was certainly rarely room for second place. As a result, any would-be gladiator would be truly incentivised to try his absolute best, far more than his meagre wage at the start of his career would normally stimulate. This was not only because to bunk off training might well result in death, but also because the potential increase in prestige and earnings were massive. The same, to a lesser extent, is true in football. Every Saturday and Sunday, thousands of young players go out to play or train, often paying for the privilege rather than being paid the millions the professionals receive, hopefully because they enjoy it. The reality for many, however, is that in the back of their minds there will surely be the hope of winning the lottery, that being paid the wages of a top player is like. As a result, the high wages of the top players are not only down to their brilliance and scarcity, but also because they provide a goal that makes every young player give up their time and effort for nothing. This provides clubs with a constant stream of new talent, happy to take anything offered, for the chance at the big time.

This tournament model of competition, where those at the bottom are incentivised to work hard for the chance of earning the big bucks, presents a problem for top clubs and companies; What is the incentive for those already at the top? Whether it is a football player or a CEO, once they have started earning the money, why should they try anymore?

Some would argue that players that play badly or CEOs that do not perform will be sacked, but sadly, it is not that simple. Given the fine margin at the top between success and failure, many contracts will provide cover for a fall in form. For example, a big pay-out for a manager or CEO sacked prematurely, further reduces the incentive to keep performing well. Previous accomplishment and fame also provide a degree of protection for the slacking performer. Many, past their peak (according to certain Fan TV channels, at least) still make their way from one club disaster to another. The managerial merry-go-round is another example, where the same faces circle the bottom clubs because of their previous history of keeping teams from relegation. As a result, new talent is stifled, but continues to bang its head against the door because of the small potential for huge rewards.

It is no surprise perhaps, that some of the biggest clubs in football, despite all their wealth and prestige, often find themselves falling spectacularly from grace.

Nottingham Forest and Rangers in the UK, Parma and Fiorentina in Italy, and 1860 Munich and FC Maggdeburg in Germany, all these clubs have toppled out of their respective top divisions, and even out of their professional leagues, despite enjoying previous domestic and European glory. Even clubs with huge injections of finances do not immediately shoot to stardom. United spent almost one billion pounds on transfer fees in the seven years leading up to 2020, £375.3m on defenders alone, and yet have remained well off the pace of the League leaders. They have even fallen behind the likes of Leicester City and even Southampton at times, both of whom have invested far less money. (I very much hope ManU proves me wrong by the time you read this).

So why is high demand or sudden wealth not an automatic pathway to success? After all, in most production-based industries, high demand for a product rarely results in the firm packing up.

This problem is two-fold, the first of which is evident at Barcelona, one of the world's biggest clubs.

You'll Never Win Anything with Kids

Barcelona's problem, while far from insurmountable (they are still regular competitors for the Spanish league cup and Champions League, but currently are set to miss out on the league for the third year running, nor have they won the major European honour since the 2014/15 season), can largely be demonstrated by three teams.

In November 2012, Barcelona won 4-0 away at the Valencian club Levante. More significant than the score, was that after a substitution early in the game for an injured Dani Alves, all eleven players on the pitch were graduates of the youth academy, La Masia.

The second game of note came in April 2018, against Celta Vigo, where, of the full eleven starting players, none were graduates of the famous youth academy.

Finally, in June 2019, in the under-21 European Championship match, Spain versus Italy, the squad fielded no Barcelona player for the first time ever at this tournament. From the start of 2020 to early 2021, the number of minutes played in the team by any Barcelona players combined, was just 23 minutes.

These games show how a lack of time and investment in developing new players at Barcelona has resulted in a large fall in young home-grown talent, at the first-team level. This seems unthinkable given the huge number of quality players seen there over the past decades. However, this lack of local talent has resulted in less competition in the squad and a greater demand for players from other clubs. This in turn has caused other clubs to place a premium price on their players, given the lack of alternatives at Barcelona. The club has, therefore, spent huge sums on players that, it can be argued, the stats reveal were not worth the price. Over 400 million euros were spent on just three attacking players from other teams between 2017 and 2019. The first, sadly, has been racked with injury since he joined, the second has failed to reach double figures for goals in the league (something he managed regularly at his previous club), and the third was sent out on loan to European rival Bayern Munich, after less than two years at the Club. Wages have skyrocketed, with 63% of the club's revenues going on wages in 2019. Once losses from the Coronavirus are toted up this could grow to 80%, even with the announced pay cuts. This makes it more difficult to move on underperforming players, as few clubs will pay their wages, leaving even less wriggle room for transfer fees.

Barcelona is not an isolated incident. Manchester United suffered the same issue after its last title-winning season. With few young players rising through the ranks, overly expensive deals were made, but good value failed to materialise.

Leeds's Leverage

A far worse fate and the second major issue suffered by other clubs making the first issue look small, can be seen in the story of Leeds United's 2004 relegation from the premier league. I promise I have not picked Leeds solely because they are a ManU rival!

In 1998 Leeds changed managers, promoting former assistant manager David O'Leary. He quickly brought several players through the youth academy. These future stars, who included names like Jonathan Woodgate and Alan Smith, rapidly made their way into the first team. Their numbers were bolstered by young players from outside the club, paid for by the sale of talismanic striker Hasslebaink. European football followed quickly after Leeds qualified with a third-place position in the 1999/00 season. New players and famous wins against Lazio and AC Milan had Leeds's fans dreaming. Sadly, however the reality was soon to hit hard.

Despite their successes in Europe, Leeds eventually went out to Valencia and finished outside the European spaces in the League in 2000/01. It was at this point that the $60m loan against the club's earnings, predicated on the continuation of the European dream, started to bite. Most of this money had gone on players (£18m for Rio Ferdinand was the then-record amount for a defender), meaning that any trouble on the pitch could lead to a sudden fall in value and therefore loss of collateral against loans.

Despite this, the owner at the time, continued making additions to the squad, with more household names coming through the club's doors for a combined £28m. This made qualification for Europe the following year all the more imperative. Once again, however, Leeds finished outside those crucial top (three at the time) spots. O'Leary was sacked at the end of the 2001/02 season and replaced by Terry Venables. At this point the rotten foundations of Leeds's spending were evident. Despite the sale of Rio Ferdinand for £30m to Manchester United (haha), it emerged during the 2002/03 season that Leeds had a debt of approximately £80 million. This led to an exodus of players to prop up the club's finances. Venables went too in March, followed closely by the club owner. The ensuing panic meant the sale of three more players, followed by yet more at the end of the season, and even the ownership of their stadium and training ground, realised far less than they would have just a year before. This loss of talent finally told in 2004 when Leeds was relegated from the topflight and would eventually slip into administration.

Fortunately, Leeds have recovered magnificently under Marcelo Bielsa and continue to play the attacking-at-all-costs football that was characteristic of their previous topflight team. However, this provides a good warning to football clubs and other institutions of the dangers of over leveraging.

Playing Football Manager

The plights of these two clubs are remarkably similar to those of major financial institutions, which led in part to the collapse of credit in 2008, as well as more recent instability in markets. (sorry, we are back to economics!)

In the run up to 2008, banks saw the amount of money that could be earnt from volatile assets would rise if enough of them were packaged together to diversify risk. The only issue was that these assets, things like mortgages, were finite. In the case of mortgages, there are only so many houses being bought at one time. Therefore, they quickly found ways of making more money from the same stock of assets. Instead of selling the mortgage, they sold a bet on the mortgage being repaid

(Credit Default Swaps in finance lingo). Quickly these bets grew into a tower, built on the same foundations of assets. This meant it would only take a slight miscalculation of the strength of the assets for the foundations to go, and the whole tower to come crashing down. It transpired, not only were these assets riskier than the rating they were given by independent ratings agencies, but that the sellers knew this. They were happy to keep selling these default swaps, as once sold, if the value went down or even started costing the buyer money, the seller was not on the hook for those losses.

If this doesn't sound risky enough for you, mortgages which were too risky to be bought by other banks, pension funds, etc, where repackaged together into a Credit Debt Obligation (CDO), which were even riskier than the original assets. Bets on these were also made (synthetic CDOs), creating more towers of even dodgier assets. This reliance on a lack of new products causing inflated prices and high volatility is a serious risk to all involved, whether it's financial markets or football clubs.

How can we solve the problem of too many bets on the same set of goods? While this question looks obscure in a financial sense, there are certainly plenty of people who would have a go at the football problem, Football Manager is full of them! Looking at the troubles of clubs overpaying for new foreign talent, it is easy to see an answer - invest in your youth squad. If money and time is spent on developing home grown talent early on, competition will avoid you spending lots more on foreign imports. We only have to look at the likes of Southampton and Borussia Dortmund to see the quality that can be produced with surprising regularity, even if some of their best players are routinely snapped up by larger clubs.

But suppose we aren't in charge of the club? Another manager comes in and acts on a short-term basis, bringing in ageing talent to win quickly, before leaving for the next club rather than building a squad for the future. Many might characterise a certain Portuguese manager as this sort of pantomime villain. We can make our feelings felt through demonstrations, banners or social media in the hope of influencing the club and its manager's decision-making. We might be able to convince club owners to mandate their clubs to invest in enough youth players to ensure, not only that local talent shines through, but that the absurd prices we currently see for players are depressed. This might sound feasible. However, watching a certain fan TV channel more than I care to admit, it looks like bringing together enough of a fanbase in order to change a board's decisions is somewhere between difficult and farcical. Perhaps now, the parallel problem in financial markets of placing too many bets on the same pile of assets looks more surmountable?

Some will jump into the trenches with the free marketeers and argue that banks should be left to their own devices (but, somehow, drop this line once a bailout is required), while others will call for an end to the City altogether. Can we not find a more positive way of making the banks act to benefit both themselves and the wider economy for the long term, instead of simply until the next shareholder meeting?

Restricting how many bets are made on the same pile of assets would be a start. So too would be requiring banks to set aside reserves for nothing but a rainy day, thereby reducing the risk of total collapse if one set of investments goes awry. These limitations would hopefully stimulate greater diversity in the types of loans and investment financial institutions make. With the right policy incentives focussed on new businesses, particularly those that produce tangible goods, we may slow the profits of these institutions in the short term, but we will also reduce the instability in the financial markets that have caused them (and us taxpayers!) so much grief. Some of these innovations have already been successfully imposed on banks following the 2008 global recession. Banks are now regulated to keep a specific % of their assets in cash and liquid investments, rather than being allowed to speculate with all their money, not to mention borrowing other people's, in order to spend their company's value several times over.

This has been crucial during the Coronavirus Crisis. The 15 largest US banks had to set aside $76 billion to cover projected bad debts, while €56 billion euros were ear-marked by the 32 biggest European banks, the highest estimated losses since 2009. In March 2020, as the Coronavirus ravaged the global economy, credit appeared to be drying up, causing real panic that there might be massive bankruptcies in the financial sector again. Fortunately, the loss-absorbing buffers put in place by regulators prevented, or at least postponed, the bank collapses that characterised the last crisis.

There has been some criticism that the leverage ratio, (the amount banks can borrow as a percentage of their total value), simply incentivised banks to take on the riskiest assets as they could only borrow a certain amount, but the risk of this borrowing was not measured. However, the overall resilience of the financial system has improved and to date has met the challenge of the Pandemic. The reason for this can be explained if we simplify this to a micro level, such as an individual's finances.

Imagine a bank which must decide between two strategies for loaning out money. It can either limit the riskiness of what the loans are to be spent on, (for example authorising car loans but not expeditions to the moon,) or it can limit loans to a % of the applicant's savings (i.e. forcing the applicant to have some collateral). The latter may seem to incentivise the loanee to spend the money on riskier assets than the former and this is true. However, the more collateral the applicant is forced to provide, the more they will lose if it all goes wrong. Therefore, regardless of how risky the investment, the individual and the bank's incentives are aligned, as both are set to lose from a bad loan. Meanwhile, an applicant who has only to limit the riskiness of the use of his money, is not incentivised to make sure that money is well spent, because he is not on the hook for any losses. They are in fact incentivised to take out as many loans as possible and even perhaps hide the true riskiness of their plans. Finally, unexpected shocks can mean that even a loan which looks safe can actually be toxic, as seen in the aftermath of 2008. In the real world, anyone who has asked for a loan or a mortgage will know that we are often subjected to both tests, but that the overall income or wealth question is far more important to the bank than the former. We can see, therefore, that on a micro scale, limits on an individual's leverage when taking on loans, is key. On a macro level it is arguably even more important as central banks will ultimately foot the bill for any losses, once the collateral runs out (too big to fail and all that!)

Data from the Bank of England supports the view that while a limit on bank borrowing does increase the riskiness of individual asset purchases, the overall leverage of banks is reduced and of the two, the latter effect dominates and financial stability increases.

One can liken this type of regulation to a speed limit. Bad driving is still perfectly possible below 70 miles per hour and setting a limit may make people blasé about driving all the time they stay below the limit. However, keeping a ceiling on the speed cars can go lessens the damage caused when bad driving results in an accident, both for those directly involved, and those who are left to pick up the pieces.

So, we have solved the problem of the big clubs; we have more home-grown talent and therefore reduced pricing bubbles, but what about those clubs who's funding dries up overnight?

Liberating financial markets in the 1980s allowed for greater movement of funding to the best and most lucrative sources of income. However, it has resulted in a disparity in speed and therefore a growing funding gap between finance and the rest of the economy; between Wall Street and the High Street. This has led to greater instability coupled with a lack of patient investment for non-financial industries, particularly manufacturing. These industries require patient funding, rather than sudden riches, which can be just as quickly taken away, as was the case with Leeds United.

My father has recently been absorbed with the idea of 'dabbling', as he calls it, in different funds and other investments. This has led to a number of interesting discussions, not least because this is his and my mother's pension, not some pile of extra cash we have lying around (I wish). One recent question is whether it is worth moving into tech stocks following a rise in Coronavirus cases and the latest lockdown being imposed, or into a gaming stock, following the release of a new game or piece of software. The trouble with such comments is that it is easy to forget that not only are there thousands of other people thinking exactly the same, but there are also thousands more experts whose job is to predict these changes having spent decades in the industry. There are also scores of people who will have had insider knowledge of these announcements before they even happened. As a result, many of the price changes my Dad and so many others hope to take advantage of, have already occurred. Hence the common expression that 'if you hear about it in the news it's too late!' As a result, often before such events even become public, their impact is often encompassed into the value of assets. Much like match betting, previous results and any relevant information are included in the odds. You are unlikely to make money by using public information, except in areas where people have guessed the impact or probability of a result incorrectly.

To give an idea of how quickly financial markets move, know that the reaction time of an Olympic sprinter is 0.0150 Seconds. In high frequency trading, the reaction time is less than a microsecond or 0.0000001 seconds.

This demonstrates the speed of the financial markets right now and how detached they are from the more mundane speeds of the high street. Experts who have more time and experience to make correct estimates of where to invest than my father (who sticks to simply reading the papers on Sunday mornings) is not just acceptable, but to be encouraged. If those with only a casual interest in, and burgeoning knowledge of, financial markets start making investment decisions for us, we'll all be in trouble! What is less desirable however, is the sudden movements in funding that leave productive companies, which require long-term investment, in jeopardy.

It may grate heavily with my personal and economic values, but less efficiency in the financial markets would lead to better outcomes in the rest of the economy.

The big reduction in financial regulation in the 80s and 90s led to booms in economic growth in many western countries, from the UK, to the unexpected financial miracle story of Iceland, which became the fifth richest country in the world, by 2005. This is understandable, given that financial services have, since the 1980s, overtaken non-financial services in terms of annual profits. Unfortunately, the same countries that relied most on financial services suffered most during the great recession, from Iceland, to Ireland to Dubai. The first two suffered falls in GDP by over 7% in 2009. As mentioned previously, as the importance of financial services grew, the number of CDOs (bets) grew relative to the comparatively slower growing number of assets (races). This meant that if anything unexpected happened to these 'races' there would be a much bigger loss for those placing 'bets', than if they had spread their money more widely.

Financial management is important for development, but potentially dangerous for macro stability, as it is much more liquid than industrial capital. This means business owners who can access funding from the financial sector are able to bring in capital, even when their business is yet to manufacture a single item. They can sell part of their business (in stock) to allow for faster expansion, rather than having to wait for the existing goods to be sold. Essentially, illiquid goods can be transferred to liquid assets, and therefore increase efficiency. The trouble is, while factories take years to build, funding can be granted and retracted within minutes. This speed means long term investments are not made, as short-termism, has led to only quick profits being sought. This lack of consideration for the future has resulted in overall growth in the developed and more financially-driven countries falling, following the initial boom of the deregulation in the 80s.

As a result, policy decisions like a Tobin tax, where costs are imposed on financial transfers to reduce these short-term actions, should be considered. They also restrict the ability of firms to merge, particularly through hostile takeover, which inspire speculation rather than considered investment. Speculators will jump in and out of investments in the hope they go public or are bought, raising their value massively, and then exiting immediately after, causing massive undue stress on these companies, just look at WeWork.

Despite losing $1.9 billion in 2018, WeWork reached a peak valuation of $47 billion by Christmas Eve of the same year. BBC research of WeWork's rivals earlier in the year show just how ridiculous this valuation was, with one peer earning almost twice the annual revenue but being worth less than a tenth of the value of WeWork.

The remarkable valuation was thanks to investments of over $10 billion by Vision Fund, the world's largest technology-focused venture capital fund. The first of these investments, $4 billion, was agreed in the back of a car, following a mere 12-minute tour of the company's headquarters. By the end of its botched IPO saga, the company was valued at less than $10 billion. These seismic shifts in valuation are what happen when investment can be given and taken away in such short time periods. Only with greater scrutiny before such deals are made can we protect the industry from dangerous fluctuations that cost us all in the long run. Before you rush to discard this as fat cats getting what they deserve, its these people that manage most of our pensions and savings!

"Our valuation and size today are much more based on our energy and spirituality than it is on a multiple of revenue."

- Adam Neumann, former WeWork CEO

"People were high. There's not a human being in America who doesn't look at the number forty-seven billion dollars" —

WeWork's valuation in January — "and not get goosebumps. It seems insane now, but at the time it made so much sense."

> - Scott Galloway, New York University Business School

Internationally, slowing global capital transfers would also prevent this turbulence at a national level. The sudden rush for safe currencies, caused by uncertainty wrought by the Coronavirus Pandemic left developing countries with a sudden depreciation in their currencies and a lack of much needed investment in their industries.

The financial system has been a huge part of what has catapulted countries into modern levels of development and living standards, but if they continue to be allowed to fluctuate at the speed they currently operate, the ensuing uncertainty and volatility will cost us far more. For example, taxes and regulation may cost us something in efficiencies and incentives, but they are unlikely to cost as much as the £70bn of UK taxpayers' money that was paid to Lloyds and the Royal Bank of Scotland alone to keep them afloat during the Credit Crunch.

We Just Don't Produce Anything Anymore!

One of the most common comments to be sent flying across the dinner table and a popular one in political discourse as a reason for the UK's decline, is the claim that we are now a post-industrial society where nothing is produced. While the answer that we have transcended manufacturing and rely on services for incomes is usually the response, this view has dangerous consequences for our economy. Domestically, overreliance on the service sector can lead to slow wage growth, as productivity stagnates. The main reason for this is that unlike production of goods, the production of services cannot easily be sped up to make it more productive. For example, watching the latest blockbuster at the cinema could not be improved by playing it at double speed, even if it did mean more people could see it every day. While the quality of some services can be improved, by say having better directing or more accomplished actors, the pay benefits of these are felt by very few, whereas high-paying jobs in manufacturing are far more plentiful.

On the international stage it can be even more damaging, as while it is easy to import German cars and French wine, it is more difficult to export haircuts and other services. This can culminate, as has occurred in the UK, with high trade deficits with the rest of the world, funded largely by borrowing from other countries.

In the long term, this will eventually lead to a depreciation in the sovereign currency, pushing down prices and so increase the quantity of our exports. This will also lead to inflation, driven by a weaker currency, resulting in more expensive imports, forcing us to consume less from overseas and produce more simplistic, homegrown goods. Less access to inputs from overseas will limit the range of goods we can produce, depressing incomes and living standards. Borrowing from overseas, which is known as Foreign Direct Investment (when you think about it - if I borrow something from you, you are effectively investing in my future repayment), has historically kept this at bay, but Brexit shows the fragility of this. A UCL study this year estimated a fall of 37% in FDI following the completion of Brexit. Further, The London School of Economics found in 2021, that following the referendum result, there was roughly a 10% depreciation of sterling in the immediate aftermath, which increased consumer prices by 2.9% and led to a measurable decline in living standards. This because there had been no increase in incomes over the same time period, resulting in a £870 per year rise in the cost of living for the average household.

Therefore, if we want to guard our living standards against future falls, we must balance reducing our overreliance on financial services, while maintaining our international advantage in this area. Also important, is that the well-documented riches made by members of 'The City' remind us that this might have propped up our trade figures and currency with other countries, but it has not solved our income inequality problems, which as mentioned before, are likely the cause of the anger that stimulated decisions like Brexit in the first place.

As before, encouraging investment in productive areas rather than short returns will help in this regard, but as tempting as this is, we cannot blame the banks for all of this.

Financial services have in fact sheltered our other industries for too long and Covid has shown our need to diversify. It has also exposed weaknesses in some industries that need repurposing.

Some may argue that governments are not the answer to reinvigorating old industries, or picking new industry leaders for tomorrow. They point to creations like the O2 arena in the UK, and the Concorde project as evidence of the government's inability to create profitable enterprises. Yet, we should focus on overall past performance, and not just concentrate on the examples dredged up by, predictably, established interests in industry that are set to lose most from such intervention. After all, I know that if I were in their position, I would put everything I could into preventing competition from the public sector.

South Korea's now world-beating steel manufacturers began in a country that produces neither of the two ingredients essential for making steel. No private company would support this project and funding had to come from Japanese war reparations. By 2010 South Korea had become the 4th largest steel producer in the world and by 2019 it was the 3rd largest exporter.

Other government-backed success stories include, LG and Hundai Shipbuilding in South Korea, and the internet and Apple in the US.

The reason so many private companies that receive financial and strategic support from governments succeed, is often because, the insider knowledge of the private sector alone can be a blocker to long term success, as much as a catalyst. For example, shareholders might prefer short-term rewards to their money, like dividends, over investing back into the company. However, this does not mean that such a decision is the best thing for the country, or indeed the company, in the long run.

Mistakes in the private sector are also widespread. Many of us will have heard of some of these catastrophic failures, but here are a few of my favourites:

Excite refusing to buy Google in 1999 for $750,000, when it was the 2nd most used search engine, and Google was just starting out. Excite was bought by Ask.com, which by 2015 was just 2% of the search market, while Google was now worth $130 billion, 173,333 times what Excite would have paid for it.

Kodak patented one of the first digital cameras in 1977 but didn't start supplying it to the public, as the company was making so much from film cameras. When it was finally dragged into the digital market it was unable to wrestle market share from the new leaders, even when it started selling cameras at a loss.

London publishers rejecting Harry Potter, Decca Records rejecting the Beatles, Blockbuster rejecting the chance to buy Netflix, the list is endless!

The best way to maximise the chances of success is to have close working relationships between business and government. The truth is that winners and losers are being picked all the time by both sectors. By combining the knowledge from both sides we can increase our chances of picking winners. Doing so, combined with governments limiting the current focus on Wall St and fleeting investments, to the benefit of Main St and productive companies, that require consistent, patient funding, we can ensure both our long-term prosperity and equality.

11
Magic Money Trees

I can imagine my father, and many others, making it to this point in the book and beginning to recite well coined phrases such as, "Yes, but where is this money going to come from?", and "We can't just keep borrowing." This argument has always been a popular one on both sides of the political aisle, with even liberal thinkers admitting that spending more than we earn, is not something we can do forever.

My first introduction to this idea of fiscal responsibility was pocket money. I was given a regular allowance, not for any meaningful work, usually just for not being a pain and keeping my room tidy. As one might expect this did not warrant much recompense. This coupled with my failure to avoid spending regularly on sweets, meant I was often unable to buy the things I really wanted. For a child, and probably for many of us, this is a useful lesson. If we want to buy the things that are really important to us, we must cut back on other spending, or increase our income. This is why, historically, how governments should fund themselves boils down to whether we should cut public services or pay more tax. Borrowing is seen only as a temporary solution. When I finally started saving enough to maintain a full piggy bank, my parents would use the box as petty cash, replacing it with an IOU.

While my 'hard earned' money was a useful source of spare change, it was not free, but something they promised to repay.

Since The Great Recession in 2008, the ability of the country to live within its means has been a key focus of debate. The succeeding period of austerity is the obvious example, but even in more recent elections the arguments have not evolved much. For example, the Theresa May government talked about there being no 'Magic Money Tree', before promptly finding £1bn to give to the Democratic Unionist Party in order to create a coalition and maintain power.

Looking back, however, the UK government has actually been in debt since the beginning of the 1900s. Don't worry, I will not be claiming this means debt has no repercussions, but it does show that viewing the country in the same way as a child with its pocket money, or even an individual household is oversimplified. I can't imagine my parents allowing me to continue borrowing from them for the next 100 years!

Firstly, it is useful to put government borrowing into perspective, by drawing on our misleading statistics chapter reading:

The UK government debt stood at 104.7% of GDP in October 2020, a jump from 84.6% in March, which was almost entirely driven by Coronavirus spending. At the same time however, the average debt as a % of earnings for UK citizens was 109.1%. Incredibly, this was down from over 111% from the year before. For those complaining about the government's need to balance its books, it might be worth a few more of us looking at our own borrowing habits too!

Of course, GDP is not the same as government earnings. Only by having a tax rate of 100% would we achieve this. However, the UK government has far from the highest level of debt to earnings compared with other countries. We stood at 29th in the overall rankings of debt to GDP, below not just countries like Japan, Italy, and Greece, but also Spain, France, the US and Belgium. The UK also pays a far lower rate of interest on its debt than many other countries, or indeed, the average taxpayer. For example, in 2020 the debt interest payments as a % of GDP were just 2.2% in March and 1% in November of the same year, while for the average UK citizen they were 2.9%.

Another advantage the government can usually rely on, that few of us can, is a consistently rising income. The economy may still be recovering from downturn at the time of writing, but it is worth remembering that before Coronavirus, the UK and US were enjoying the longest ever periods of sustained stock market growth (bull runs). As a result, overall output was rising and so were tax revenues. This is the equivalent of a typical UK worker, on a monthly income of £2,500 and with a monthly mortgage payment of £700, receiving a 20% pay rise over ten years. The result being their proportion of monthly income taken by mortgage repayment drops from 28% to just 23%

This increasing growth, contributing to tax revenue (effectively income) is why government debt must be seen in context. If revenue growth is faster than the interest on the borrowing, then overtime the size of the national debt relative to GDP will fall. This can occur even if the country borrows throughout. So, if you hear that the government is in debt, or that we remain in deficit for another year, make sure to look behind the headlines and check what this really means. Despite what some newspapers might say, the government debt should not be seen in the same way as a child's pocket money, even if those using it are made to look like children.

Vindication!?

While this might be a boon to fiscal doves (fancy term for people who want the government to spend/borrow more to stimulate growth), the scale of the recent increase in the public debt cannot be totally hidden, and the hawks (the opposing side to the doves) are already arguing that we have already blown whatever spare cash we had lying around. The UK is expected to have a net debt to GDP ratio of between 80 – 109% in 2023/24, up from just 34% in 2007/08.

So, does this possible trebling of net debt to GDP since the last economic crisis prove that government debt has spun out of control? Well this view is still oversimplified (you're in the final chapters now, we're going to have to work a little harder for straight answers!)

While increasing income puts a limit on how damaging debt can be for government, the real difference between you, me and it, is that sovereign governments can be propped up by their central banks. While in most functioning democracies the government cannot tell the central bank when to give it money, the central bank will often buy and sell government bonds to affect interest rates, and in extreme circumstances, will create money to buy these gilts. This effectively gives the government, through private sector banks, as much funding as the Bank wants. Therefore, theoretically a government can borrow as much as it likes as the central bank can always print or, in reality, simply create money electronically to fund the debts.

Before those socialist champagne corks start flying and we give everyone a Ferrari, we must consider the impacts such money creation can have. Printing money has the rather obvious effect of meaning there are more pounds in the economy, and so the wider world, than there were before. Firstly, this means that if we go away and buy foreign goods, then the number of pounds available in France, Germany and further a-field will become more widespread. If we do not recover these pounds by convincing foreigners to buy our goods, then the greater supply of pounds in the international market will mean the value of each one will fall. The key to understanding this, is that on a global stage, currency has innate value, as it allows you to purchase another country's goods. A UK car manufacturer does not have a use for euros beyond buying in more goods from overseas, so eventually foreign buyers will have to purchase pounds to buy cars. If there are only a small number of pounds out there in the market, it may start bidding wars between fans of British cars (the thought of demand for British cars signals that this analogy is creaking heavily but stay with me). If the central bank prints money and more pounds flood overseas, suddenly there is less need for competition and so the number of euros for one pound drops, known as depreciation. Ultimately this means that the price we pay for foreign goods rises, meaning more expensive holidays and difficulty producing goods that rely on raw material from overseas.

But who cares, just print more money to pay for foreign goods! While this might sound feasible, it does show how dangerous printing can be. A small push can stimulate a need for more and more, and more printing until the cost of foreign products and experiences becomes extreme.

So, we won't be going on many Spanish holidays, but it could be a small price to pay for not having to worry about debt again I suppose.

Unfortunately, there is another issue with printing money, and it's every critic's favourite - inflation. In the same way as we saw internationally, giving the same number of people more money to purchase the same amount of goods, causes bidding wars and inflated prices. As a result, printing money with no increase in goods, will result in a country facing an increase in the overall price of goods. This in turn means that while you might hold more money in your pocket, you will be unable to buy any more goods than you did before and so, living standards, which is what we ultimately care about, remain the same.

If businesses can invest this money and increase the size of their output so the bidding process is calmed, and prices fall, profits will rise, and the government will recoup the spending back in receipts and everyone is happy. Unfortunately, things are rarely that simple, businesses can't just increase table numbers because there are a few more customers. If they are cramped into a small space, expansion might be difficult, so they may stick the extra revenue in the bank instead. This means little has come of the printing accept a rise in prices and more government debt. Even worse, is when spending achieves no increase in earnings. Unemployment benefit, however beneficial, is essentially a payment to a person who was productive but is no longer. As a result, no growth, no repayment in tax and greater borrowing.

We can see quickly how printing can do nothing except necessitate more printing. The central bank can remedy inflation by raising interest rates, but this can just lower the growth you were looking to achieve with the printing. This is because people and businesses bank their money, rather than spending it, to take advantage of the higher interest rates. As a result, central banks try to balance providing money in times of need, with higher interest rates which incentivise us to save for a rainy day during the good times, as well as keeping prices under control.

In this way, borrowing money is much like a comedic sketch of a sinking ship, where as fast as sailors plug one hole in a leaking hull, another opens in another spot. Spending more than you receive in tax revenue, results in borrowing. Preventing further borrowing with central bank money printing, will result in inflation. Inflation can only be tamed by increasing output (often a slow process which limits the amount you can print at one time), or by reducing the money supply and increasing interest rates. Increasing interest rates reduces the rate of economic growth, the very thing you were looking to achieve in the first place. Ignoring this simple logic can have disastrous results.

In October 2019, the IMF estimated that Venezuela's annual inflation had risen to 200,000%, well in excess of the widely accepted definition of hyperinflation (over 50% monthly inflation.) This seemingly damning judgement of a sovereign's monetary control describes a country that was previously flying high. Its rapid degradation has largely been driven by successive falls in the global price of oil, resulting in one of the country's most valuable exports suddenly becoming far less so. In order to maintain the level of social security brought in by their socialist predecessors, the government turned to printing money to support the falling oil revenues. This resulted in the devaluation of the currency as outlined above, leaving the country with shortages of food and medical supplies. Incredibly this is not the most extreme case of hyperinflation, even in recent history.

Zimbabwe achieved monthly inflation of 80 billion percent, equivalent to a doubling of prices every 25 hours. Again, this was stimulated when the government began to print money, in response to dwindling public support. Poor implementation of land reform and protests against higher taxes meant that the need for more printing increased between 1997 and 2000. The government moved to increase interest rates in an attempt to stem the fall in the value of the currency. However, this simply reduced output and so further increased inflation, as spending continued, but the stock of goods for people to fight over, fell. Eventually the currency was officially suspended by the government due to the insurmountable levels of inflation.

A final, more positive case study is of Hungary between 1945 and 1946, where the daily inflation rate stood at 207%. While previous examples of hyperinflation are generally put down to government ineptitude, this was apparently planned by Hungarian policy makers. Hyperinflation was able to solve the dual problems of weak economic activity and the vast war reparations imposed on the country by Soviet Russia. It provided intense incentives to businesses to invest and spend, rather than watch their savings be eaten away by inflation. Government debt was also reduced as wages fell up to 80% in real terms, making inflation a severe and abnormal type of tax. As a result, Hungary's industrial capacity had recovered by the time prices stabilised.

So why did I bother going through all this just to say there is no magic money tree?

Well, while printing with no thought for effect may be wrong, it doesn't mean borrowing is never an option. While certain types of spending do not stimulate the economy, others do.

Spending on investment, such as infrastructure can increase output (by providing jobs in construction, public services and technology) thereby reducing overall debt as a % of GDP, and therefore, interest repayments. It will also facilitate greater productivity in the future. At the same time, current spending, e.g. on welfare will have a far smaller impact on future output.

Looking back at the previous chapter, we see how governments, especially when working closely and transparently with the private sector, can spend money in areas that see extraordinary growth, as a result of this support.

So, some borrowing can be effective.

Inflation, That's So 1970s

The UK inflation rate has not risen beyond 3%, excluding external crises, since 1992. This is far from the 1970s spikes, when inflation rose to over 24%, at its peak, in 1975. The scars from these periods of high inflation, together with the horror stories I have mentioned from overseas, have kept us from discussing a different target for inflation, that could benefit our economies.

Spending more during periods of low interest rates is cheap. In recent years, the real interest rate on borrowing for the Bank of England has been negative, and recent Federal Reserve and Bank of England announcements have suggested that they won't be raising them anytime soon.

"We think that the economy's going to need low interest rates, which support economic activity, for an extended period of time,"
"It will be measured in years."
- *Jerome Powell, Chairman of the Federal Reserve*

Inflation would reduce the size of debt to GDP, as was the case for the UK in the 1970s and in the Hungarian case study set out above. Therefore, developed economies with productivity problems should look to continue spending to reinforce their recovery from Coronavirus. Controlled and sensible investment will stimulate the economy for the long term at a historically low cost. A controlled rise in inflation will help to reduce debt, encourage more productive investment, and rebalance our economies in a far more sustainable way than simply cutting spending, which would slow growth and so tax receipts.

For the people on the street, higher rates of inflation will have a redistributive effect. Those who hold more in savings will see a reduction in their value in the short term, while those with less, or who are borrowing to support themselves will benefit. More than four in every ten UK working-age adults used at least one form of borrowing to cover everyday living costs during the Pandemic as of September 2020, so this is far from a tiny minority. Moreover, successfully increasing productivity in the future would stimulate stronger wage growth which will mitigate the costs of inflation for all workers.

While the Hungarian example gives some glimpse of the positives of not obsessing over inflation, I am not suggesting we aim for a level of high inflation, let alone hyperinflation. The Zimbabwe example gives us two warnings on going overboard with a laissez-faire monetary policy. Firstly, faith in the government is extremely important. Japan has the highest debt to GDP level in the world, and yet many other countries have defaulted while Japan stays standing. This shows how faith in national governments to manage debt levels, interest payments, and interest rates is crucial, if countries are to avoid inflation rates spiralling, as debt racks up. Also, we see how once control is lost, even making moves to mitigate the impacts can have limited effects.

Government must have a strong relationship with an independent central bank, as both have to work in tandem for a calm and considered shift in inflation expectations to occur. In February 2021, Andy Haldane, Chief Economist at the Bank of England, argued that even without a step change in the Bank's attitude to interest rates, inflation could still pose a major problem to economic recovery, as lockdowns are lifted. He pointed to UK households saving an extra £100bn as a result of the Pandemic-induced lockdowns and government support as the likely source of a rapid increase in spending in the future, and so rising prices. All that pent-up boredom and money has to go somewhere. It appears that, as people start to leave their homes, hospitality and leisure industries have seen demand spike. As a result, those industries may be forced to raise prices, if they cannot grow their businesses from the deep freeze of the last 12 months, to meet this demand.

I (and fortunately some others in this policy area) feel these fears are unlikely to materialise in the long-term. For one, while on average, savings have increased, those at the bottom of the pay distribution saw their savings fall in 2020. Lower earners have the highest propensity to consume (spending the highest proportion of their incomes, rather than saving it). Therefore, the very people who would normally drive consumption, and so inflation fastest once allowed to spend on meals out and package holidays, are in fact in no position to do so. Meanwhile those at the higher end are limited, simply in their physical ability to consume. Whereas someone who has been unable to afford nice meals out and book foreign holidays might increase this consumption, those already earning enough to support this lifestyle will find it harder to increase it. The average Brit went on 3.9 holidays in 2019, which given that average annual leave (including privilege days) is just 33.5 days, suggests many of us were already maximising our time away from work. There is an obvious limit too, on how many meals out someone can have in a week. This doesn't even consider the fear of future tax rises, that might encourage people to squirrel away money today, for fear of earning less tomorrow.

Even if there is an initial rise in inflation, this will be temporary, unless wages rise, meaning the total spending power will have permanently increased. Given the high levels of unemployment caused by the Pandemic and the resulting global slowdown, I feel confident, if loathed, to say that businesses will find it suitably easy to hire workers on the same rate of pay as before Covid, if not lower.

That said, it would take a brave (or foolish) individual to ignore the Bank of England's most senior economist out of hand and there will no doubt be some fluctuation in inflation at least in the short term.

Therefore, I believe we must untether ourselves from the fear of hyperinflation, and understand we are not limited by our ability to borrow, but by our pain threshold for inflation and interest rates. However, at the same time, we must tread carefully to ensure we do not allow inflation to run away from us, or thereby lose the confidence of our international partners. Fortunately, as I write the US and UK appear to be reversing their initially poor response to the Pandemic, by rolling out successful vaccination programmes. The UK has also finally managed to come to a deal to withdraw from the European Union. While still in their infancy, these policy successes should offer a greater level of certainty for business and the population in these countries, thereby preventing animal spirits from converting a small rise in prices to the madness of hyperinflation.

Will I Ever Buy my Own House?

If we are able to stabilise interest rates and inflation at a higher rate than the historical lows we see currently, we may also solve another major problem facing our economy and which most agree needs to be solved, the cost of housing in the developed world.

"We need to build more homes!"

Opposition parties, of all stripes, bring this forward on a regular basis. The financial crisis in 2007-08 was, in no small part, driven by the push from the US government for Americans to purchase their own homes. A combination of low interest rates, which enabled cheap borrowing, and subsidies for state run mortgage programmes Freddie Mac and Fanny Mae, led to a ballooning of household debt from 104 to 144% between 2000 and 2007. As a result, house prices rose 50% in this period, further pushing Americans to drop into debt, in order to climb onto the housing ladder and benefit from the booming housing market. As those most indebted began to fall behind on mortgage payments and foreclosures ticked up, the reality of the situation eventually dawned, and prices plummeted.

Evidence from the Bank of England suggests that the continued low level of interest rates since the crash, has continued to inflate asset prices, including housing.

But why are house prices so sensitive to interest rates?

I Shamelessly copy an excellent explanation from the Bank, which draws parallels with the Dutch Tulip Mania:

"Economic theory says asset prices should be determined by the value of future income flows. So how much is a bulb that produces £100 of tulips annually worth? If real interest rates on other assets are say 10%, then people would be willing to pay £1,000 for the bulb to get the same return. If they fall to 5%, the value of that same stream of flowers doubles to £2,000. Supply hasn't changed, the price of tulips hasn't changed either, but bulb prices have doubled."

While interest rates have been a factor in the rising price of housing across the world, the classic story of house building as the root of the problem does hold some water, but not for the reason you might think. Rather than ineffective governments failing to be able to build houses quickly, we find that for all the talk of people needing more housing, it is local opposition to development that has stalled a lot of housing in the rich world. This is understandable, given that between the 1940s and 2000, home ownership has skyrocketed, from 30 to 70% in the UK. This means that the majority of people own their own home and therefore are not particularly keen on a huge block of flats going up next door. This 'NIMBYism', combined with the view of the green belt system as a ring of woodlands and fields around cities (when in fact buildings as inelegant as a car wash can be built on them), has led to private and public attempts at housebuilding being weakened and often stopped completely.

"Across just five big cities in England there are over 47,000 hectares (about 116,000 acres) of similar land, which is not

particularly green, is close to train stations with a good service to their centres, and yet cannot be built on."

- *The Economist*

This unresponsiveness of housebuilding to a rise in prices means there is nothing to stop house values spiralling. The story is similar in the US. In Pine Bluff, the area where housing supply increases quickest when prices rise, the average house price is low, at only $90,000, compared to the least responsive part of the US to price changes, California, where the average is $725,000.

A simple way of improving this situation, in the western world, can be seen in the central European countries of Germany and Switzerland. Here there are ruled-based planning systems, where if developers meet all the regulation standards, development is approved, regardless of local objections. Taxes from developments also go directly to the local government of the area in these countries, incentivising them to allow development. Meanwhile in the UK, the money is hoovered up by central government, removing a good incentive for local government to work with house builders. These nations also have a lower proportion of the population as homeowners. In Germany the number is just 44%, in Switzerland it is 40%. This, coupled with more stable house prices, means that renting is a longer-term and more enjoyable experience in these countries. The average tenancy in Germany is 11-12 years, compared with just 2-3 in the UK. As a result, tenants and landlords alike are incentivised to look after their living spaces and build positive relationships. Slower growing house prices also mean that landlords rely less on the price of their asset increasing and so earn less from an empty building. As a result, renters have more power, as moving out holds a higher cost in earnings for the landlord, resulting in lower prices and greater support.

Higher house prices and homelessness in some of the most developed cities in the world (homelessness is up 60% in New York, 2009-2019) shows how failing to get this right can lead to serious consequences. Housing benefits that have put money in the pockets of the destitute instead of housing them has simply added to the problem by inflating prices further. A study from France in 2006 found that, for every euro added to housing benefit, 80 cents was added to rent. Higher asset prices brought on by low interest rates has concentrated housing wealth at the top, leaving many younger people unable to step on the housing ladder. This is breeding discontent in younger age groups and disdain for their elders, further polarising the populations of the Western nations that have failed in this area. Much like a greater policy focus on income inequality post-2008 might have avoided the wave of populism in recent years, we might avoid a similar, understandably motivated, but ultimately knee-jerk reaction to the question of housing, which is unlikely to bring about efficient and equal change. As homeownership becomes less widespread and more renters are exposed to horror landlords who refuse to aid renters with the most basic of problems (a friend of mine at University was told paying for the cooker, washing machine and even broken pipes was his responsibility during his 12-month rent), the pressure on politicians for a quick fix over preparing properly for the long-term will only grow.

The reality is that unlike most goods, land is finite and so the normal rules of supply and demand do not apply. As land in an area becomes scarce, the option to increase supply as the price rises becomes impossible. As a result, landowners have sat on land as prices have risen. Low interest rates have supercharged this since 2008 as other investment opportunities have become less attractive. Low inflation has meant the cost of tying your money in brick and mortar has fallen too. By aiming for a greater level of inflation, we can incentivise movement away from stagnant things like land and property and into faster growing sources of wealth that are more productive.

The Power of Car Parks

My hometown of Eastbourne cannot be described as a trading hub, more often it is referred to as 'God's waiting room' due to the high average age in the town. Despite this there is still a high demand for parking in and around the town centre and beach. As a result, one source of income for the town, to the annoyance of many of its occupants, is the charge for a parking space. In nearby Brighton, however, a rather more popular, if louder, seaside spot, the demand is even higher and so the price of parking is at times extortionate, previously making its way to the fourth most expensive city for parking after London, Cambridge and Edinburgh.

Unlike a car parking spot at your house where a lump sum for the property has given you permanent access to the plot, with a car parking space you are effectively being taxed for your use of the plot while you visit the shops. This is a relief, as if car park places were a permanent transaction, prices would surely rocket making even Brighton's cost per hour seem small. What's more, only one household could use one space, while with the current system, multiple people can use the same piece of land. This makes for greater access for all and greater efficient use of the spaces. Anyone who has, as a young child or even uninterested teen, been pulled around the shops by their parents because 'we must be back within the hour or we'll have to pay for another!' will know how even a small tax on people's use of a car park inspires greater productivity of those using the space.

In the same way, a land value tax would incentivise development over holding onto land. Owners would not benefit simply from holding on to land, but instead need to develop it and sell it on to make a profit, increasing house building and reducing buying to invest. Thus, more of those with a true interest in living on the land will want to hold on to it, making the use of the land more optimal.

The debate on interest rates is far from over. Analysis from the Bank of England's macro-financial risks division suggests that other factors in addition to housing supply, such as the availability of credit, how house prices differ across different regions, and growth expectations, can also impact prices.

Despite this, housing provides an example of how good policy, whether monetary or on stimulating greater housebuilding with taxation, is an option for lawmakers. Rather than replacing the private market entirely, or continuing to let it drift into purely rent-seeking, a pro-development and growth set of policies should encourage a greater level of bipartisan support. Property wealth is one of the leading causes of inequality in our societies. By reinvigorating the capitalist system that underpins it, we can level the playing field for those yet to join the property ladder while also reviving the companies and industries which are currently no longer incentivised to build. The alternative is sinking back to a pre-capitalist society, where wealth is earned, not by the work of the individual, but by the land he stands on.

But What About Current Spending?

Inflation in the short run may not be as risky as first thought and borrowing to invest can lead to not less, but greater wages and growth. Not all spending, however, in fact the majority of spending in the UK and US, does not go on long term investments. The right may blame handouts, the left defence and cronyism, but the reality for most wealthy countries is that spending on pensions makes up the single largest amount of spending by government. In the US, almost 25% of all spending goes on social security (old-age, survivors and disability insurance). In the UK, around 52% of cash transfers through the welfare system (c.£128bn in 2020-21) are paid to pensioners. Here we see again how policy decisions can divide the nation, this time old against young.

It hasn't just been pensioners cashing in. Social security, including unemployment, pension and health benefits has grown spectacularly since the Second World War, with such high levels of popular support that it has been political suicide to oppose its onward march.

In the US, between 1965 and 2013 the average annual increase in social benefits was 9.3%, far ahead of average overall output growth, resulting in social benefits rising from 4.6% to 14.3% of GDP during this period. Remarkably, post 1965, Democrats in the US presided over an average increase of 7.9%, (4.5% for the Clinton administration), while the number for Republicans, the supposed anti-spenders, was 10.5% (7.3% for Reagan). The reason for these seemingly anomalous results seems largely due to the political power that increasing social benefit spending wields. I suppose conservatives must feel that if they do not take advantage of such benefits, liberals most certainly will. As a result, current spending over investment, in infrastructure, and research and development, outlined earlier as beneficial areas for borrowing, has been the norm for 60 years and counting.

In the immediate aftermath of the Great Depression, Keynesian economics proved successful in stimulating demand and recovering economies, by increasing government spending to bolster growth and employment. By the 1960s growth had returned, and the economy was in a very different state to the one for which Keynes had been creating policy prescriptions over 30 years before. As he had died in the 40s, he was not in a position to adjust his views. However, his policy responses to a once in a lifetime slow-down continued to be used in an era of far stronger growth, resulting in the wage and commodity bubbles of the late 70s, that ushered in 80s Thatcherism. Despite this, and the popular narrative around Thatcherism, by the last year of that Conservative Government (1996-97), spending on welfare as a % of GDP had remained as high as under the Labour governments of twenty years before. The story of the death of the welfare state 'by a thousand cuts' was instead a reallocation of spending from housing and education, to health and social security. So even during the periods of Conservative dominance in the western world, current spending on welfare has continued to increase, irrespective of the economic conditions.

As spending has mounted, savings both in government and amongst households have declined. Since 2009, annual US government savings have been negative (deficits) at on average 6% of GDP. Domestic savings have been falling since 1963, from 24.6% to 18% by 2013. According to the US Department of Commerce, this has been taken up, almost pound for pound, by the rise in social benefit spending. What makes this so troubling is that since humanity moved from hunter gatherers to more organised civilisations, saving a proportion of our income (at that time food from farming) has been crucial to our advancement as a race. Having a storage of grain gave the population time to work on producing aids to production (tools) which improved the harvest in future years.

Interestingly, government policy can have a large impact on the public's saving rate. Whether it is providing support in our later years reducing the need to save, or through increased taxation, as a way of forcing increased savings on a national scale. For example, rationing during the second world war, was not just a matter of distributing the limited supply of some goods more evenly across the population, but also a way of reducing total consumption across the country. This also increased savings, as consumption was limited, which provided banks with a greater set of reserves for the government to tap to finance the war effort. Aside from these extreme cases however, governments have not been able to encourage their civilians to save above 20% of their incomes without draconian measures such as rationing. As a result, while Keynes' inspired spending to help an economy recover from recession can be impactful in the short term, eventually government borrowing will have to settle back into line with domestic savings. Failure to do so will result in trade deficits and ultimately a decision for policy makers between high inflation and high interest rates. Large government borrowing also leaves less for the private sector, pulling funding away from small and new businesses that, especially following recessions and lockdowns, will need it the most. Even if taxes do rise to cover the higher level of current spending on welfare, if money is not saved for more than spending money today, there will be none left for investing for tomorrow. This will result in the stagnation of technological advancement and productivity that currently plagues much of the rich world, known in political and economist circles, as the Productivity Puzzle. For example, since the benefits surge of 1965, US business productivity (excluding farming) has been 0.2% lower per annum. While this sounds small, it amounted to $1.2trillion by 2012, effectively halving the benefits of the welfare increase of $2.3trillion over the same period. As the theory on borrowing and net exports above predicted, US trade deficits have also grown, rising consistently to 6% of GDP between 1992 to 2006. Had it not been for a steady reduction in defence spending over the same period, these impacts would have been even more keenly felt.

"Unless the upward momentum of entitlement spending is contained and turned around, the erosion of our gross domestic savings rate will almost surely continue to suppress capital spending, productivity and growth in standards of living."
-       *Alan Greenspan*

While one might discount this as the ramblings of a conservative, anti-establishment firebrand, it is in fact the thoughts of a previous chair of the Federal Reserve, arguably as institutionalised an establishment viewpoint as you can get!

Prolonged borrowing on long-term aids to productivity during slowdowns is one thing, continuous borrowing on short-term day-to-day spending at the expense of savings for tomorrow is another altogether.

The truth is therefore, that we, in many of the rich countries, face a choice, do we want low government intervention and the low tax rates that come with it, or high provision of welfare at the cost of our take-home pay?

The trouble for the UK particularly, is that for the past two decades, we have attempted to run a country with the tax system of the US but the welfare state of the Scandinavian countries. We are not the first in this endeavour. Sweden's welfare provision ran into crisis in the 1990s and was forced to significantly reduce the size of the state between 1993 to 2013. Earnings-related benefits became more tightly linked to contributions, as with the German model outlined earlier. Many programmes are means-tested, and a wider range of qualification rules have been added to ensure support goes to those in most need. Some services, particularly for the elderly have been privatised, but with state regulation and financing kept in place to maintain standards. This provides a blueprint for many countries to follow, allowing for greater private sector competition, while maintaining the state's position as a regulator and referee on markets, which prevent the turmoil of laissez-faire capitalism abundant in the build-up to 2008.

> *"The world will be studying the Nordic model for years to come."*
> -   *The Economist*

For my part, I hope the UK follows the lead of the Nordic countries, ensuring that welfare is efficiently implemented and well financed by tax. This does not necessitate big government but the efficient provision of support from the most productive available provider. Borrowing should not be seen in such negative terms as was the case during austerity but should focus on long-term investments in productivity and living standards, rather than on short-term spending. Provision of public goods and services should be overseen by government, but the state should also act as a market maker. It should facilitate the private sector, rather than replacing it, wherever possible, on everything from climate change to housebuilding. Reducing the size of the state on a purely cost-cutting basis, while continuing to grow social security to maintain political popularity, will only result in the continued stagnation of our economies.

12
Now What?

"It will always be easier to sell tickets to the Ghost Train than to the Speak Your Weight Machine."

-       *James O'Brien*

Gordon Ramsay's various television exploits are popular both in the US, the UK and in my kitchen when I'm doing the dinner. Perhaps it's the comfort that however bad my food is, there will always be someone in the background getting far more abuse from the fiery chef. One series documents Ramsay's attempt to save failing restaurants, although most of the episodes mainly cover him swearing heavily at the owners and chefs. While we visit a seemingly endless stream of restaurants, only a handful are revisited, with even fewer managing to stay open despite Ramsay's best efforts. The winning formula is evidently more about getting Gordon into a verbal war with the owners, as well as the exposés of terrible kitchen practices, such as serving produce that has fallen on the floor or is far past is sell by date, than worrying about the results of his work. The truth is that fighting, drama and the fear of food poisoning are far more popular than the real business lessons behind such a show. The same can be seen with a popular US business show led by a certain former president. The most popular scenes online are not made up of glittering business plans or flawless pitches, but by silly mistakes.

The news is the same and has often been accused of sensationalism. Whether it's covering the overthrow of a dictator, but not what life is like in the country six months later, or the coverage of a flood, but not the attempts to prevent future disasters, the media will always offer more screen time to exciting, anxiety-driving, scary features. Controversy is also important for selling stories, which is why opposing views are often brought together, with the biggest bust-ups most likely to go viral.

The problem with this, is that there will always be someone who tries to create non-existent scandal, (football transfer rumours being a classic example). Also, constant exposure to extremes can be damaging for consumers, especially if we stick to views that only affirm our own.

The US currently leads the West in the polarization of its media.

"Over the past several weeks, top hosts and personalities on the conservative cable news network downplayed concerns about the virus, baselessly accusing credible news organizations of overhyping the crisis to hurt Trump politically."

- *CNN*

"The national left-wing media have been playing up fears of the Coronavirus!

- *Lou Dobbs, Fox News*

Polarization has been further pushed by those in power, with stories from the media regularly being deemed fake news by politicians, all the way up to the White House. The number of people emulating this, claiming that any story they don't like is fake, has unsurprisingly grown.

Studies by Oxford University have found that polarization of the media is lower in Europe. However, many fear that the move to social media by so many as their main source of news, risks creating online echo chambers, where unsavoury or extremist views can become the norm.

The concern is that when given the choice of their media consumption, people will only seek out, and agree with, views that align with their pre-existing beliefs. Lab experiments have confirmed that people are more likely to take advice from people with familiar political views. This is regardless of the adviser's knowledge on the question or task in hand. What is even more worrying, is that evidence from Duke University showed that exposure to opposing views on social media (often held up as the antidote to polarisation), actually enhanced pre-existing opinions rather than diversifying them.

This divergence of opinions in Europe links back to the ghost train analogy. Social media has become more important to politicians and other influencers, and evidence suggests that more combative, emotive language achieves more retweets. This has encouraged more extreme views on social media and wider news coverage, because this is likely to reach more voters and potential customers. Perhaps I should try writing sabre-rattling rhetoric on my bread-making blog to see if it attracts more views.

This language means that what readers might think are standard viewpoints are in fact aggressive, over-the-top caricatures, rather than the much milder set of views that people often hold.

One reason for starting this book (that went alongside the fact that I had 5 weeks of leave from work and prevented from going on holiday - First World problems), was my intention to remind myself, and others, that opinions in the news may feel poles apart, but rarely are things that simple or extreme. No matter how many arguments I have with my family across the dinner table, we always happily talk to each other again – eventually! My fear is that many of the issues we face today are because of our failure to discuss issues with each other calmly and factually. If we could, the result would be, if not agreement, then at least a true understanding of why our opinions differ. If we know what drives the wedge between us, then we should be able to find compromise. Believing that the other side is simply 'a basket of deplorables' will not only destroy any chance of negotiation, but also create bad blood for the next time our opinions diverge.

How to Drive a Wedge

"An imbalance between rich and poor is the oldest and most fatal ailment of all republics."

- *Plutarch*

As discussed at the beginning, inequality rose to historically high levels in the 1980s. Despite the increase in wages at the bottom of the pay distribution, this inequality was maintained in the 21st century, as those at the top of the income distribution widened the gap with those in the middle. As a result, those in the middle of the distribution have felt left behind for decades. This feeling is shared with those in the bottom half who have not benefited from equal pay and political representation of the now protected characteristics such as sexuality and race. While the growth in output and wages prior to the 07/08 recession papered over these cracks, the succeeding slump in wages and productivity has uncovered this frustration people feel at being held back and forgotten. People across the Western world, particularly those in the UK and the US who saw inequality spike most, were looking for an opportunity, a scapegoat, to explain why their lives and opportunities had stagnated. For the UK, this became Brussels, for the US, it was the whole political class.

Only 27% of British respondents in the run up to the 2016 referendum could answer three basic true or false questions on the EU correctly:

1. The EU currently consists of 28 member states.
2. The members of the European parliament are directly elected by the citizens of each member state.
3. Switzerland is a member state of the EU.

These results were among the lowest of the 28 countries at the time. The competitive amongst you, the answers are: True, True, False.

This has historically benefited politicians in Westminster, as it has produced a faceless regulator that is to blame for all our ills. The success of the 1990s non-inflationary growth, the devolution of Scotland and Wales and liberalism of gay rights were harked as Westminster triumphs, while the eastern expansion of the EU and the free movement of labour, despite there being little argument from UK policymakers at the time, have become firmly Brussels' mistakes. Policies on capping banker bonuses and block-wide taxes on financial transactions have also been blocked by UK MEPs but blamed squarely on the EU. Many prominent Leave voters blamed everything from fishing rights to the infamous 'bendy bananas' on Brussels, despite the British government voting against proposed EU law only 2% of the time since 1999.

By the time the referendum was held in 2016, we had a motive and a target on which the UK population could vent its frustration. This was summarised brilliantly in the 2019 historical drama, Brexit: The Uncivil War.

Many of the claims made about the EU, at this time, were inaccurate, with the majority of the most famous coming from the Leave side. There was concern about Turkey's entrance into the Union (now looking less likely than ever, given the Country's actions in the Mediterranean in 2020 may result in it being the subject of sanctions by the Bloc). Also, a belief in the ease with which we could do a trade deal (since 2016, this has not aged well). It was suggested by different Leave groups, that there were a wide range of deals possible, akin to the agreements enjoyed by Norway to Canada. These deals were always unlikely given the UK's unique position of encompassing Northern Ireland, which Remainers raised as a major stumbling block, and Leavers discarded as 'Project Fear'. Others will claim comments from the Remain side about the economy were equally disingenuous. However, following the vote, the actions by the then-Bank of England governor, Mark Carney and other policy makers to reduce the impacts on the economy dampened much of the damage forecast. For example, the reduction in the interest rate to historic lows. The claim will come that this should have been factored into the doomsday wording of pro-Remainers. However, as mentioned before, for every lever you pull in economics, another is let go. In this case by reducing interest rates to keep economic growth going, the pound plummeted, leading to higher costs of living for the UK as a net importer.

The focus on policy decision losers, as mentioned in chapter 9, is another common mistake made over the EU's impact on our lives. The UK has suffered at the hands of the EU agricultural policy for example, benefitting large farms and fisheries over the UK's less concentrated industry with a greater number of smaller operators. However, this has more than been made up by the ability of the UK's trading in comparatively more important sectors. For example, financial services make up 100 times more of the UK's GDP, than fishing. Again, it has been the failure of this country's previous leaders to redistribute these gains that has prevented the improvement of competitiveness in its other industries. As mentioned previously, governments can pick winners. Investment in the retraining of workers and subsidies for new, rather than zombie firms should have been the policy. The break from the EU will offer an opportunity for the UK government to correct this issue, but it will still need to negotiate hard, or face retaliatory tariffs for government-backed aid.

Another of the common biases and errors we make in everyday life, outlined in this book, came to a head during the vote, was the misuse of statistics. The cost of EU membership was estimated by the Leave side at £18.2 billion a year (or as some would have it, £350 million a week). The equivalent figure for 2018/19 had risen to £20.2 billion However, this did not include the immediate rebate of around £4.6bn, the £7.3bn in structural funds for deprived areas, payments for farms and research grants the government now has to cover, or the slew of other benefits, such as our share of the Block's tariff revenues (£0.7bn). This reduced the cost to just £7.6bn a year, which has been eaten up by the Office for Budget Responsibility's forecast of GDP falling as a result of the vote (forecast in 2016 to be 2.4% lower by 2020, along with an increase in the deficit of over £15bn).It is worth noting this estimate of falling GDP as a result of Brexit, back in 2016, was off by less than 0.4% compared to outturn figures published at the start of 2020. Perhaps forecasting is not a completely dead art! While negotiations are ongoing over the final details of the deal, and tensions continue to heat up over the Northern Ireland Protocol, it is difficult to estimate what the long run impact of leaving will be. The OBR have estimated a fall in long-run productivity of 4%, but until the dust settles and we can see the full extent of Brexit's impacts the result on living standards and wages will be hard to gauge. One thing is for certain however, this level of nuance and reason failed to make its way into the newspaper headlines and TV debates in the run-up to the Referendum. This should be a cause for concern, regardless of which way you voted.

Immigration and Sovereignty

Whatever your feelings on immigration, one cannot pretend that this has not been a defining theme of the past decade, if not century, in the UK and the West. Everything from the health service, to the latest crime figures, to the disappearance of 'good old manners,' has been used as a battleground over immigration.

Despite all this debate, as a nation, we have little knowledge of immigration.

Studies from King's College London and the UK government's Migration Advisory Committee (MAC) found that Britons misunderstand the impact of immigration on almost every aspect of their lives.

ON EU immigrants' contribution to public finances:

"Only 29% of the public correctly think that immigrants from European countries pay £4.7bn more in taxes than they receive in welfare benefits and services. Leave supporters are least likely to correctly identify that this is the case (16%) and most likely to wrongly think that European immigrants contribute less than they take out (42%)."

On Crime:

"56% of the public and 75% of Leave supporters think that European immigration has increased crime levels, when evidence from the MAC report finds no link."

On Healthcare:

"39% of the public and 53% of Leave supporters think that European immigration has led to a decline in the quality of healthcare services in the UK, when evidence from the MAC report shows this isn't the case."

On 'that' £350m claim:

"Two-thirds of the public (67%) have heard of the claim that the UK sends £350m a week to the EU, and 42% of these believe it is true, despite it being labelled a misuse of statistics by the UK Statistics Authority."

On Unemployment:

"Half of the public (47%) and 61% of Leave supporters believe that unemployment among lower-skilled workers has increased as a result of European immigration, despite the MAC report concluding there is little or no impact."

On Immigration levels:

"People overestimate the proportion of the UK population that is from an EU country by a factor of almost three, thinking it's 16% when it's only 6%."

-     *King's College London, October 2018*

Another common misconception is that migration has depressed wages. While there has been a small reduction in low-income wages as a result of rising EU immigration this century, this change has been dwarfed by the rise in the minimum wage, showing once again how public policy is far more important to determining the impacts of migration than the EU ever was.

While few would argue that immigration should be limitless, the idea that developed countries and particularly the EU have permitted any amount of immigration, is inaccurate. The fact that people are paid far less for doing the same job in developing countries prove that migration controls are far from dead. Cleaners in Belgium are paid six times what they are in India, while Flemish cooks are paid five times their Brazilian counterparts and a qualified nurse in the US is paid over ten times for the same job as a nurse in Indonesia. If we lived in a society without immigration barriers, surely these individuals would all move to take advantage of higher wages until the glut in supply would reduce wages in the developed countries and end the differences between countries. This shows barriers to immigration, be they policy, or simply geographical, prevent much of the feared uncontrollable tide of immigration, that was of concern in the run up to the Brexit vote. As for immigration from the EU, pay disparities remain. Anyone thinking barriers cannot be put up between European countries should probably ask themselves why so few people were able to go on holiday to the Mediterranean in 2020.

Some argue that the focus on immigration is misplaced, and that sovereignty was the true goal of those looking to leave the European Union. This too is misjudged, as the ability of member states to make unilateral policy actions has been brought into sharp relief by the Coronavirus Pandemic. On everything from lockdowns to vaccines, European parliaments have had the ability to create their own strategy. When France decides on its latest local lockdown, or Germany allows hairdressers to open, this is done independently and does not require the Commission's consent. Of all the recent examples, the actions by member states to block the use of the AstraZeneca vaccine is perhaps the most pertinent, as these actions were done independently of the EU regulatory body.

Moreover, whether we like it or not, leaving the European Union does not end the conversation over sovereignty. Whenever a country agrees a trade agreement with another, sovereignty is shared. For example, when we reach a free trade agreement with another country, we give up our right to put tariffs on their exports to us. Borders and sovereignty are always a two-way street. Whether we are in the EU or out, we will still need to negotiate with Europe. The balance between influence and direct control is always a fine one.

While this may seem like gloating from a sad Remoaner, the real failure has been from those on the Remain side of the argument. All these disputes over sovereignty, the economy and immigration were actually symptoms of a much wider issue, namely that the current system was not working for many people. Instead of engaging in mudslinging over the EU, people and policymakers that wanted to stay in should instead have focussed on alternative solutions to the problems of stagnating productivity, wages and livelihoods.

Sadly, for over a decade it was easier to let others take the hit for difficult policy decisions and allow the electorate to blame the enemies put before them, be they immigrants or 'unelected bureaucrats'. Thus, the systemic underinvestment in our economies, slow response to technological advancement and unambitious monetary/fiscal policy were forgotten. This is the true failure of Brexit.

Bigger Fish to Fry

The argument over Brexit has been fought and won, so why am I harping on about it?

Misallocation of blame is unlikely to result in the right policy remedies being put forward, in the same way a misdiagnosis and prescription can be more harmful for the patient than the original disease. In the case of Brexit, if we believe that the UK had become unproductive and wages at the bottom were being pushed down by globalisation, could we not have come up with a better policy than leaving the EU, seeing the pound depreciate, a relative rise in prices by 2.9% and increasing the cost of the average household you are trying help £870 a year?

Brexit might be yesterday's problem but many people, particularly those on the pro-EU side, are yet to recognise the true driving force of the decision. Remainers can smirk all they like as evidence continues to shrink the reasons why Brexit was a good idea. The reality, however, is much like walking out in front of a speeding lorry on a zebra crossing. We can scream we are right all day long, but we will definitely be worse off than the lorry. Raising awareness about the true nature of these populist topics, a greater understanding of the real issues driving division, and coming up with answers to these deeper challenges which eat away at societal cohesion, will reduce the likelihood of knee-jerk reactions to future issues.

While I am keen to move on from Brexit, and believe there are at least a few in the US that feel the same way about Trump, Coronavirus has taught us that polarisation of the electorate and Populism at the expense of informed opinion are not one-offs, nor are their impacts.

As of March 2021, the UK had the sixth highest number of deaths to Coronavirus per 100,000 of the population and the highest in the G7. In the second quarter of 2020, peak first wave, the UK ranked third for greatest economic decline (21.7% down vs. 2019 Q2 data). All this, despite public sector support (including central bank support) being the fifth highest in the world.

The fact that countries with similar levels of polarisation and populist influences have fared equally poorly in the face of the Pandemic is telling. The hallmarks of populism, such as undermining institutions, questioning informed opinions and pushing for greater individual responsibility over direct intervention from the state, have all been woeful policy responses to the Pandemic. The most obvious example of this was the delay to the UK's first lockdown during a period when cases were doubling every few days, making any procrastination very damaging.

The slow policy response was magnified by the mixed response from the media which, rather than following the evidence from countries that had responded well to the disease, compared masks to muzzles, and described the lethality of Covid as less than flu. One particular argument, that broke through during the first lockdown and remained for much of 2020, was that there was a trade-off between deaths and the economy. The implication was that a more damaged economy, as a result of lockdown, would cause as many, if not more deaths and destruction to people's lives, as staying open. Analysis from LSE, however, uncovered that this was never the case, and that if there was a correlation between deaths and economic damage, it was in the other direction, with countries who locked down earlier and saved more lives also fared better on the economic front too.

Despite the UK's poor performance during the first wave of the Pandemic, in the months leading up to Christmas, media pressure for the government to open up the economy and allow families and friends to meet for Christmas lead to another spike in cases and deaths, peaking at over 1,300 deaths in one day.

"The number of people dying today is the same as it would be in any other year in total."

-       UK Mainstream Radio, November 2020

"The latest figures from the Office for National Statistics (ONS) show the number of deaths registered in England and Wales in the week ending 6 November 2020 was 14.3% higher than the five-year average."

-       Full Fact, November 2020

"There's essentially no substantial connection between lockdown and outcomes of ICU and mortality. That's a reality."

-       UK Mainstream Radio

"This is simply untrue. A research paper published in June in Nature, one of the most prestigious scientific journals in the world, concludes: "Our results show that major non-pharmaceutical interventions—and lockdowns in particular—have had a large effect on reducing transmission."

-       Full Fact

One can also add the claim that the UK had reached herd immunity before the second wave hit, which promptly proved the country had not, to the pile of anti-establishment claims that have been so damaging to government efforts, to keep their populations safe.

Therefore, Coronavirus presents another case study to the long list of evidence that making a country more polarised and populist does not result in long-term benefits for its citizens. A recent study by the Centre for Economic Policy Research found, by looking at over 50 populist leaders from 1900-2018 that having one such person in control reduces GDP on average by 1% a year. A good example of how populism can trigger this slowdown in growth is the recent US-China trade war. Tariffs between the two countries have risen by 15 percentage points between 2018 and 2020, reducing global trade flows and spending by households and businesses. For the US specifically, analysis from the Bank of England found that the level of trade-related uncertainty increased, meaning business-related investment in the States was 5-7% lower than it would otherwise have been.

Sadly, despite the relative failure of populists in Brazil and the US, Coronavirus is not likely to spell the end of populism and divisive rhetoric. The full economic damage of Coronavirus is still yet to settle. When governments and electorates have to face this, I have no doubt, there will be plenty of easy answers, and scapegoats, made available for people, at the expense of difficult and necessary decision-making. Moreover, recovering from the Pandemic will not be the only challenge we face in the coming years.

Climate change poses another very serious challenge to the World. However, my real fear is that the present undercurrent of anger in the West, driven by inequality and the fall of dynamic and meritocratic capitalism will result in more knee-jerk, inaccurate responses to the, as yet invisible, challenges of tomorrow.

"There are known knowns. There are things we know that we know. There are known unknowns. That is to say there are things that we now know we don't know. But there are also unknown unknowns. There are things we do not know we don't know."

- Donald Rumsfeld

I cannot hope to guess the new challenges of tomorrow. Instead, the chapters of this book focus on the everyday questions and challenges life throws at us, from how to lose weight to how to read a bar chart. My hope is that by recognising the value of understanding and exploring different opinions, rather than immediately jumping to defend 'your team's' position, we are likely to come to the consensus and compromises key to overcoming the far greater challenges of the latter chapters.

Bibliography

Introduction – Parents and Populism

Stephen Bush

Divided Britain. How the EU referendum exposed a new culture war

The New Statesman

https://www.newstatesman.com/politics/uk/2016/06/divided-britain-how-referendum-exposed-britains-culture-war

4/10/2020

Luke May

Ever get the feeling you've been cheated?

Mail Online

https://www.dailymail.co.uk/news/article-8353977/British-Press-divided-response-Dominic-Cummings-scandal.html

4/10/2020

The Express

Dominic Cummings should stay – he just acted as any good father would

https://www.express.co.uk/comment/expresscomment/1286780/dominic-cummings-lockdown-coronavirus

4/10/2020

Sherelle Jacobs

Marxist-chic BLM is a disturbing threat to racial progress

Daily Telegraph

https://www.telegraph.co.uk/news/2020/08/13/marxist-chic-blm-disturbing-threat-racial-progress/

4/10/2020

Blake Welton

Premier League's Black Lives Matter support cannot be fleeting

Sky Sports

https://www.skysports.com/football/news/11661/12011135/eni-aluko-premier-leagues-black-lives-matter-support-cannot-be-fleeting

4/10/2020

Bobby Duffy et al.

'Divided Britain'

King's College London

https://www.kcl.ac.uk/policy-institute/research-analysis/divided-britain

4/10/2020

J Curtice

'The emotional legacy of Brexit',

NatCen Mixed Mode Random Probability Panel, June 2018

https://whatukthinks.org/eu/wp-content/uploads/2018/10/WUKT-EU-Briefing-Paper-15-Oct-18-Emotional-legacy-paper-final.pdf

4/10/2020

Lukas Audickas et al.

'UK Election Statistics: 1918-2019 - A century of elections'

House of Commons Library

https://commonslibrary.parliament.uk/research-briefings/cbp-7529/

4/10/2020

Dominic Weber

'Household income inequality, UK: financial year ending 2020;

ONS

https://www.ons.gov.uk/peoplepopulationandcommunity/personalandhouseholdfinances/incomeandwealth/bulletins/householdincomeinequalityfinancial/financialyearending2020provisional#:~:text=Income%20inequality%20has%20been%20broadly,the%20late%201990s%20and%202000s.

4/10/2020

Facundo Alvaredo et al.

'World Inequality Report, 2018'

World Inequality Lab

https://wir2018.wid.world/

4/10/2020

Max Roser

'Income Inequality'

Our World In Data

https://ourworldindata.org/income-inequality

4/10/2020

OECD

'Income Inequality'

https://data.oecd.org/inequality/income-inequality.htm

4/10/2020

FT

'Richest 10% enjoy biggest gains in household wealth'

https://www.ft.com/content/1dbb9820-175c-11ea-8d73-6303645ac406

4/10/2020

Piketty, Thomas, and Arthur Goldhammer.

Capital in the Twenty-first Century.

Cambridge Massachusetts: The Belknap Press of Harvard University Press, 2014.

4/10/2020

Adam Corlett et al.

'Who Gains? The importance of accounting for capital gains'

Resolution Foundation

https://www.resolutionfoundation.org/publications/who-gains/

4/10/2020

FT

'England in 2019: Split by wealth but united by Brexit'

https://www.ft.com/content/b398d284-11dc-11ea-a225-db2f231cfeae

4/10/2020

The Economist

Populism and polarisation threaten Latin America

https://www.economist.com/briefing/2019/05/09/populism-and-polarisation-threaten-latin-america

01/01/2021

Giles, C

UK's high Covid spending delivers worse outcomes than peers

FT

https://www.ft.com/content/1f52fd2b-7daf-418e-be8b-acc38f819b8d

01/01/2020

Making a Circle of a Horseshoe

Mokyr, Joel

The Industrial Revolution and the Netherlands:

Why did it not happen?

Northwestern University

https://faculty.wcas.northwestern.edu/~jmokyr/amsterdam.pdf

11/10/2020

Mokyr, Joel

'Progress isn't natural'

The Atlantic

https://www.theatlantic.com/business/archive/2016/11/progres
s-isnt-natural-mokyr/507740/

11/10/2020

Luiten van Riel, Jan

'The Strictures of Inheritance: The Dutch Economy in the
Nineteenth Century'

Economic History Association

https://press.princeton.edu/books/hardcover/9780691114385/th
e-strictures-of-inheritance

11/10/2020

The History of Economic Thought

'The Mercantilists'

Institute for New Economic Thinking

11/10/2020

O'Brien, Patrick

'Political Components of the Industrial Revolution: Parliament
and the English Cotton Textile Industry, 1660-1774'

The Economic History Review

https://www.jstor.org/stable/2597536

11/10/2020

University of Wisconsin-Madison

'British History, Government in the 18th Century'

UWM Legal Studies Program

https://www.english-heritage.org.uk/learn/story-of-england/georgians/power-and-politics/#:~:text=The%2018th%20century%20was%20a,Commons%2C%20emerged%20in%20this%20period.

11/10/2020

J. G. C. Blacker

Social ambitions of the bourgeoisie in 18th century France, and their relation to family limitation

Taylor & Francis

https://www.tandfonline.com/doi/abs/10.1080/00324728.1957.10413230

11/10/2020

Marie-Louise Stig Sorensen et al.

History of Europe

Encyclopedia Britannica

https://www.britannica.com/topic/history-of-Europe

11/10/2020

Washing up, Going to the Gym and Other Things I'll do Tomorrow

Tim Bale et al.

'Mind the Values Gap'

The UK in a Changing Europe

June 2020

https://ukandeu.ac.uk/wp-content/uploads/2020/06/Mind-the-values-gap.pdf

11/10/2020

    Kahneman, Daniel

Thinking, Fast and Slow

New York: Farrar, Straus and Giroux

2011

    Vigna, Stefano et al.

'Paying not to go to the gym'

American Economic Review

https://www.aeaweb.org/articles?id=10.1257/aer.96.3.694

18/10/2020

    Burkeman, Oliver

'why you feel busy all the time (when you're really not')

BBC

https://www.bbc.com/future/article/20160909-why-you-feel-busy-all-the-time-when-youre-actually-not

18/10/2020

    Kahneman et al.

Anomalies: The endowment effect, loss aversion and status quo bias

Journal of Economic Perspectives

https://scholar.princeton.edu/sites/default/files/kahneman/files/anomalies_dk_jlk_rht_1991.pdf

09/01/2020

    Bond, C

6 ways to capture the magic of hyperbolic discounting

The WordStream Blog

https://www.wordstream.com/blog/ws/2018/11/28/hyperbolic-discounting

09/01/2020

Stafford, T

Why we love to hoard… and how you can overcome it

BBC

https://www.bbc.com/future/article/20120717-why-we-love-to-hoard

09/01/2020

BBC Reality Check

Is Boris Johnson right about the rules on Kippers?

https://www.bbc.co.uk/news/uk-49030873

09/01/2020

Lies, Damn lies and misread statistics

Harford, Tim

'How to make the world add up'

The bridge street press

2020

Huff, Darrell

'How to lie with statistics'

W.W.Norton & Company Inc.

1954

Hall Suzanne

'Numerate Nations? What the UK thinks about numbers'

Ipsos Mori

https://www.ipsos.com/ipsos-mori/en-uk/numerate-nation-what-uk-thinks-about-numbers

18/10/2020

Morris, H

Why do airlines have such large gender pay gaps? And whose is the biggest?

The Telegraph

https://www.telegraph.co.uk/travel/news/airline-gender-pay-gaps-female-pilots/

16/01/2021

John Hopkins University

Mortality Analyses

https://coronavirus.jhu.edu/data/mortality

16/01/2021

Forbes

Exactly How Much Has the Earth Warmed? And Does It Matter?

https://www.forbes.com/sites/uhenergy/2018/09/07/exactly-how-much-has-the-earth-warmed-and-does-it-matter/?sh=161344975c22

16/01/2021

Wikimedia

2000 Year Temperature Comparison

https://commons.wikimedia.org/wiki/File:2000_Year_Temperature_Comparison.png

17/01/2021

Real GDP growth

International Monetary Fund

https://www.imf.org/external/datamapper/NGDP_RPCH@WEO/OEMDC/ADVEC/WEOWORLD/SSD

17/01/2021

PRINCE HARRY AND MEGHAN MARKLE'S AFRICA TOUR COST TAXPAYERS £245,000, ACCOUNTS SHOW

The Independent

https://www.independent.co.uk/life-style/royal-family/meghan-markle-prince-harry-southern-africa-tour-cost-taxpayers-royals-b575609.html

17/01/2020

Milberger, S et al.

Tobacco manufacturers' defence against plaintiffs' claims of cancer causation: throwing mud at the wall and hoping some of it will stick

NCBI

https://www.ncbi.nlm.nih.gov/pmc/articles/PMC2563590/

17/01/2020

I'll start dieting Next Week!

HealthLinkBC

Finding reliable healthy eating information on the internet

https://www.healthlinkbc.ca/healthy-eating/reliable-information

23/01/21

A, Naveen

Do product reviews really produce search costs

Taylor & Francis Online

https://www.tandfonline.com/doi/abs/10.1080/10919392.2017.1332142?journalCode=hoce20

23/01/21

University of Minnesota

Examples of ever-changing data from nutritional research

https://www.takingcharge.csh.umn.edu/explore-healing-practices/food-medicine/why-does-nutrition-advice-change/examples-ever-changing-data

23/01/21

Y, Bakos

Reducing buyer search costs: implications for electronic marketplaces

http://people.stern.nyu.edu/bakos/emkts.pdf

23/01/21

E, Waddell

What are Britain's favourite breakfast habits

Public Sector Catering

https://www.publicsectorcatering.co.uk/in-depth/what-are-britains-favourite-breakfast-habits#:~:text=As%20many%20as%2020%25%20of,be%20detrimental%20to%20your%20health

23/01/21

A, Fleming

Flying high: kids in the UK are wild about energy drinks - but how harmful are they?

The Guardian

https://www.theguardian.com/lifeandstyle/2018/jul/09/flying-high-kids-in-the-uk-are-wild-about-energy-drinks-but-how-harmful-are-they

23/01/21

British Nutrition Foundation

A quarter of UK secondary school children have no breakfast

https://www.nutrition.org.uk/press-office/pressreleases/a-quarter-of-uk-secondary-school-children-have-no-breakfast.html

23/01/21

G, Lowenstein

Out of Control: Viscera; Influences on Behaviour

Carnegie Mellon University

https://www.cmu.edu/dietrich/sds/docs/loewenstein/Outofcon trol.PDF

23/01/21

H, Critchley

Visceral influences on brain and behaviour

Neuron

https://www.cell.com/neuron/comments/S0896-6273(13)00140-2

23/01/21

Statista

Advertising spending in the United Kingdom (UK) 2017, by industry sector

Statista Research Department

https://www.statista.com/statistics/452411/advertising-expenditure-by-industry-sector-in-uk/

23/01/21

Freeriding on the Planet

Berghoff, H

Green Capitalism?

University of Pennsylvania Press

23/01/21

HM Government

'Delivering UK Energy Investment: Low Carbon Energy'

https://assets.publishing.service.gov.uk/government/uploads/system/uploads/attachment_data/file/419024/DECC_LowCarbonEnergyReport.pdf

25/10/20

Simon Evans

UK's CO2 emissions have fallen 29% over the past decade'

Carbon Brief

https://www.carbonbrief.org/analysis-uks-co2-emissions-have-fallen-29-per-cent-over-the-past-decade#:~:text=The%20UK's%20CO2%20emissions%20fell,according%20to%20Carbon%20Brief%20analysis.&text=Another%2029%25%20reduction%20in%20coal,and%20gas%20use%20largely%20unchanged.

25/10/20

C, Coyne

Can capitalism be 'green'

Institute of Economic Affairs

08/11/20

Michael A. McPherson and Michael L. Nieswiadomy.

"African elephants: The effect of property rights and political stability,"

Contemporary Economic Policy

08/11/20

T, Nathalie

'How Britain ended its coal addiction'

The Financial Times

8/11/20

Wilson, T

Extremism Rebellion

Policy Exchange

https://policyexchange.org.uk/wp-content/uploads/2019/07/Extremism-Rebellion.pdf

31/01/21

Taylor, M

The Evolution of Extinction Rebellion

The Guardian

https://www.theguardian.com/environment/2020/aug/04/evolu
tion-of-extinction-rebellion-climate-emergency-protest-
coronavirus-pandemic

31/10/21

   Montegriffo, M

Yes, "Socialism or Extinction" Is Exactly the Choice We Face

Jacobin

https://www.jacobinmag.com/2020/09/extinction-rebellion-
socialism-capitalism

31/01/21

   Bergenas, J

Public-Private Partnerships Essential to Combat Poaching

World Politics Review

https://www.worldpoliticsreview.com/articles/12907/public-
private-partnerships-essential-to-combat-poaching

31/01/21

   Gov.UK

GES Fast Stream Scheme Guidance

https://www.gov.uk/government/publications/2017-
government-economic-fast-stream-scheme

31/01/21

   McKie, R

Is this the end for 'king coal' in Britain?

The Guardian

https://www.theguardian.com/environment/2020/aug/09/is-
this-the-end-for-king-coal-in-britain

31/01/21

   Petit et al.

Climate and atmospheric history of the past 420,000 years from the Vostok ice core, Antarctica

E Scholarship

https://escholarship.org/uc/item/7rx4413n

31/01/21

    Freeman, A

The Last Time CO2 Was This High, Humans Didn't Exist

Climate Central

https://www.climatecentral.org/news/the-last-time-co2-was-this-high-humans-didnt-exist-15938

31/01/21

    Leahy, S

Europe has had five 500-year summers in 15 years. And now this

National Geographic

https://www.nationalgeographic.com/environment/2019/06/europe-has-had-five-500-year-summers-in-15-years/

31/01/21

    Little, A

John Kerry's Climate Plan, in His Own Words

Bloomberg Opinion

https://www.bloomberg.com/opinion/articles/2021-01-28/kerry-aoc-and-bernie-find-a-new-path-in-climate-change-fight?cmpid=BBD013021_WKND&utm_medium=email&utm_source=newsletter&utm_term=210130&utm_campaign=weekendreading

31/01/21

    Carbon Brief

Mapped: How climate change affects extreme weather around the world https://www.carbonbrief.org/mapped-how-climate-change-affects-extreme-weather-around-the-world

31/01/21

Peterson, T

Explaining Extreme Events of 2011 from a Climate Perspective

Bulletin of the American Meteorological Society

https://journals.ametsoc.org/view/journals/bams/93/7/bams-d-12-00021.1.xml?tab_body=fulltext-display

31/01/21

Gneezy, U

A fine is a Price

Journal of Legal Studies

https://rady.ucsd.edu/faculty/directory/gneezy/pub/docs/fine.pdf

31/01/21

Lau, T

Criminal Justice Fees and Fines Don't Work

Brennan Centre for Justice

https://www.brennancenter.org/our-work/analysis-opinion/criminal-justice-fees-and-fines-dont-work

31/01/21

Crew, I

What Did I Agree To? Contracts in our Everyday Lives

Queen's University

https://certificate.queenslaw.ca/blog/what-did-i-agree-to-contracts-in-our-everyday-lives

31/01/21

Gregory, A

GP appointments missed by 20,000 patients each day

The Sunday Times

https://www.thetimes.co.uk/article/gp-appointments-missed-by-20-000-patients-each-day-w5lsq0dx8

31/01/21

Smithers, R

Use of plastic bags in England drops by 59% in a year

The Guardian

https://www.theguardian.com/environment/2020/jul/30/use-of-plastic-bags-in-england-drops-by-59-in-a-year

31/01/21

Gabbatiss, J

'Shocking' failure to cut emissions from biggest-polluting sector in UK as others improve

The Independent

https://www.independent.co.uk/news/uk/politics/transport-pollution-greenhouse-gas-emissions-cars-climate-change-global-warming-a8763961.html

31/01/21

Institute for Government

The Common Agricultural Policy

https://www.instituteforgovernment.org.uk/explainers/common-agricultural-policy

31/01/21

Economics Cliché no.1 – A Chapter on China

Hu, Zuliu

Why is China growing so fast?

International Monetary Fund

https://www.imf.org/external/pubs/ft/issues8/index.htm

15/11/2020

Rickter, F

Statistica

https://www.statista.com/chart/20858/top-10-countries-by-share-of-global-manufacturing-output/

21/11/2020

Bajpai, P

Investopedia

https://www.investopedia.com/articles/investing/102214/why-china-worlds-factory.asp#:~:text=One%20of%20the%20reasons%20companies,workers%20available%20in%20the%20country.&text=China%20has%20been%20accused%20of,those%20produced%20by%20U.S.%20competitors.

21/11/2020

Taylor, T

China's vanishing trade surplus

Milken Review

https://www.milkenreview.org/articles/chinas-vanishing-trade-surplus

21/11/2020

Palmer, D

China trade deficit shrinks as deficit with EU hits record high

Politico

https://www.politico.com/news/2020/02/05/trump-cuts-china-trade-deficit-as-us-buys-more-from-other-nations-110810

21/11/2020

Hammer, A

Exporting US innovative capacity to China

Centre for Strategic and International studies

21/11/2020

Paul Krugman

The Accidental Theorist

New York: Norton

1998

Satyajit, D

$3 Trillion Can't Buy China Out of Virus Trouble

https://www.bloomberg.com/opinion/articles/2020-02-11/coronavirus-china-s-foreign-reserves-won-t-help-recovery

21/11/2020

Huizhong, Z

China's September forex reserves fall to $3.092 trillion

https://www.reuters.com/article/us-china-economy-forex-reserves/chinas-september-forex-reserves-fall-to-3-092-trillion-idUSKCN1WL07P

21/11/2020

Gough, N

China Devalues Its Currency As Worries Grow About Economic Slowdown

https://www.nytimes.com/2015/08/11/business/international/china-lowers-value-of-its-currency-as-economic-slowdown-raises-concerns.html

21/11/2020

Guilford, G

China has now spent $1 trillion defending its currency

https://qz.com/904718/china-now-has-less-than-3-trillion-in-foreign-reserves-as-it-spends-dollars-to-defend-the-value-of-its-currency-the-yuan/

21/11/2020

Huang, T

As China recovers from the pandemic, will zombie firms return?

https://www.piie.com/blogs/china-economic-watch/china-recovers-pandemic-will-zombie-firms-return

21/11/2020

Zhong, N et al.

Chinese corporate debt and credit misallocation, the Chinese Economic Transformation

Australian National University

22/11/2020

Abrami, R

Why China Can't innovate

Harvard Business Review

https://hbr.org/2018/03/is-lack-of-competition-strangling-the-u-s-economy

https://www.ey.com/en_uk/news/2020/05/uk-misses-out-on-top-spot-for-fdi-in-2019-but-surged-ahead-in-digital-as-economy-transforms-new-ey-report

https://www.theguardian.com/society/2020/jan/21/social-mobility-decline-britain-official-survey-finds

22/11/2020

Harford, T

The Undercover Economist

Abacus

15/11/2020

You can do whatever you like, as long as its maths

Berezow, A

Humanities Enrolment Is In Free Fall

American Council on Science and Health

https://www.acsh.org/news/2018/07/31/humanities-enrollment-free-fall-13243

14/02/2021

Belfield, C

The relative labour market returns to different degrees

IFS

https://www.ifs.org.uk/publications/13036

14/02/21

Britton, J

The degrees that make you rich... and the ones that don't

BBC News

https://www.bbc.co.uk/news/education-41693230

14/02/21

Schmidt, B

Mea culpa: there *is* a crisis in the humanities

Blogger

http://sappingattention.blogspot.com/2018/07/mea-culpa-there-is-crisis-in-humanities.html

14/02/21

Ruggeri, A

Why 'worthless' humanities degrees may set you up for life

BBC Worklife

https://www.bbc.com/worklife/article/20190401-why-worthless-humanities-degrees-may-set-you-up-for-life

14/02/21

Rsopigliosi, A

Human capital or signalling – Unpacking the graduate premium

EconPapers

https://econpapers.repec.org/article/emeijsepp/v_3a41_3ay_3a2
014_3ai_3a5_3ap_3a420-432.htm

14/02/21

Horn, B

Do colleges truly understand what students want from them?

Harvard Business review

https://hbr.org/2019/10/do-colleges-truly-understand-what-
students-want-from-them

14/02/21

Belfield, C

Using graduate earnings to assess universities

IFS

https://www.ifs.org.uk/publications/13059

14/02/21

Schmidt, B

The Humanities are in Crisis

The Atlantic

https://www.theatlantic.com/ideas/archive/2018/08/the-
humanities-face-a-crisisof-confidence/567565/

14/02/21

McKinsey Centre for Government

Education to Employment

https://www.mckinsey.com/~/media/mckinsey/industries/publ
ic%20and%20social%20sector/our%20insights/converting%20e
ducation%20to%20employment%20in%20europe/education%2
0to%20employment%20getting%20europes%20youth%20into
%20work%20full%20report.pdf

14/02/21

Tuckett, S

Popularity of vocational training in UK not reflected in
funding

FeWeek

https://feweek.co.uk/2020/03/07/popularity-of-vocational-training-in-uk-not-reflected-in-funding/

14/02/21

Garner, R

Teachers in England work longer hours than the rest of the world - but not in the classroom

The Independent

https://www.independent.co.uk/news/education/education-news/teachers-england-work-longer-hours-rest-world-not-classroom-9562812.html

14/02/21

Dickinson, K

How does Finland's top-ranking education system work?

World Economic Forum

https://www.weforum.org/agenda/2019/02/how-does-finland-s-top-ranking-education-system-work

14/02/21

Morgan, K

'Degree inflation': How the four-year degree became required

BBC Worklife

https://www.bbc.com/worklife/article/20210126-degree-inflation-how-the-four-year-degree-became-required

14/02/21

Rise of the Machines

Adam Corlett

Robot Wars, automation and the labour market

Resolution Foundation

https://www.resolutionfoundation.org/app/uploads/2016/07/R
obot-
wars.pdf?utm_source=RF+Mailing+List&utm_campaign=3108e
65b75-
EMAIL_CAMPAIGN_2020_11_20_01_50_COPY_01&utm_med
ium=email&utm_term=0_c0e8a99f92-3108e65b75-
313082042&mc_cid=3108e65b75&mc_eid=bbf26b33d7#page=11

05/12/20

Hillary Vipond

Technological Unemployment in Victorian Britain

Economic History Society

https://ehs.org.uk/technological-unemployment-in-victorian-
britain/?utm_source=RF+Mailing+List&utm_campaign=3108e6
5b75-
EMAIL_CAMPAIGN_2020_11_20_01_50_COPY_01&utm_med
ium=email&utm_term=0_c0e8a99f92-3108e65b75-
313082042&mc_cid=3108e65b75&mc_eid=bbf26b33d7

05/12/2020

Nakamura, H

Automation and unemployment: Help is on the way

Vox EU

https://voxeu.org/article/automation-and-unemployment-help-
way#:~:text=Its%20main%20message%20is%20that,reduces%20
the%20rate%20of%20unemployment.

05/12/2020

ONS

Which occupations are at highest risk of being automated?

https://www.ons.gov.uk/employmentandlabourmarket/people
inwork/employmentandemployeetypes/articles/whichoccupati
onsareathighestriskofbeingautomated/2019-03-25

05/12/2020

Nedelkoska, L

OECD social, employment and migration working papers

OECD

https://www.oecd-ilibrary.org/docserver/2e2f4eea-en.pdf?expires=1607159454&id=id&accname=guest&checksum=83E882597BECC9F553F0C08A124CC69F

5/12/2020

    Munbodh, E

Many supermarket prices soaring during lockdown - but some goods are now cheaper

The Mirror

https://www.mirror.co.uk/money/coronavirus-supermarket-items-soared-price-21882452

28/02/21

    Feigenbaum, J

Automation and the fate of young workers

National Bureau of Economic Research

https://www.nber.org/system/files/working_papers/w28061/w28061.pdf?utm_source=PANTHEON_STRIPPED&amp%3Butm_campaign=PANTHEON_STRIPPED&amp%3Butm_mediu m=PANTHEON_STRIPPED&amp%3Butm_term=PANTHEON_STRIPPED&amp%3Bmc_cid=a7395118e1&amp%3Bmc_eid=bbf26b33d7

30/11/2020

    Daron Acemoglu (MIT), Andrea Manera (MIT), and Pascual Restrepo (BU)

Taxes, Automation and the future of labor

MIT

https://workofthefuture.mit.edu/wp-content/uploads/2020/10/2020-Research-Brief-Acemoglu-Manera-Restrepo.pdf

28/02/21

    Noah Smith

No, Pandmeic UI didn't kill jobs

Substack

https://noahpinion.substack.com/p/no-pandemic-ui-didnt-kill-jobs?utm_source=RF+Mailing+List&utm_campaign=b91cfb7922-EMAIL_CAMPAIGN_2020_12_11_12_39&utm_medium=email&utm_term=0_c0e8a99f92-b91cfb7922-313082042&mc_cid=b91cfb7922&mc_eid=bbf26b33d7

12/12/2020

   McKinsey Global Institute

Retraining and reskilling workers in the age of automation

https://www.mckinsey.com/featured-insights/future-of-work/retraining-and-reskilling-workers-in-the-age-of-automation

13/12/2020

   Urmi, S

The Life and Death of Zombies – Evidence from Government Subsidies of Firms

LSE

https://papers.ssrn.com/sol3/papers.cfm?abstract_id=3601386

13/12/2020

   Iddekinge, C

A meta-analysis of the criterion-related validity of pre-hire work experience

https://onlinelibrary.wiley.com/doi/10.1111/peps.12335

13/12/2020

   Acemoglu, D

OutSide: In, Open Innovation Team

HM Government

20/02/21

Whites, Women and Wokeness

Frijters, P

The Colour of a Free Ride

The Economic Journal

https://academic.oup.com/ej/advance-article-abstract/doi/10.1093/ej/ueaa090/5898389?redirectedFrom=fulltext

07/03/2021

Booth, R

Racism rising since Brexit vote, nationwide study reveals

The Guardian

https://www.theguardian.com/world/2019/may/20/racism-on-the-rise-since-brexit-vote-nationwide-study-reveals

13/12/2020

ONS

Ethnicity Pay Gaps

https://www.ons.gov.uk/employmentandlabourmarket/peopleinwork/earningsandworkinghours/articles/ethnicitypaygapsingreatbritain/2019

07/03/2021

ONS

Research report on population estimates by characteristics

https://www.ons.gov.uk/peoplepopulationandcommunity/populationandmigration/populationestimates/methodologies/researchreportonpopulationestimatesbycharacteristics#outputs

07/03/21

Sandhu, S

Black Britons

BBC

http://www.bbc.co.uk/history/british/empire_seapower/black_
britons_01.shtml

07/03/2021

Historic England

Black Lives in England

https://historicengland.org.uk/research/inclusive-heritage/the-
slave-trade-and-abolition/sites-of-memory/black-lives-in-
england/

07/03/2021

Creighton, T

Coverage of Black versus White Males in Local Television
News Lead

Stories

Journal of Mass Communication & Journalism

https://www.hilarispublisher.com/open-access/coverage-of-
black-versus-white-males-in-local-television-news-lead-stories-
2165-7912.1000216.pdf

07/03/21

Matiluko, S

Early 20th-century black British history is as important as
Windrush. These are the three lessons whitewashing has
denied us

The Independent

https://www.independent.co.uk/voices/black-history-month-
lcp-harold-moody-una-marson-windrush-b572875.html

07/03/2021

Sky History

Black Britons Who Shaped History

https://www.history.co.uk/articles/black-britons-who-shaped-
history

07/03/2021

Wingfield, A

Color-Blindness Is Counterproductive

The Atlantic

https://www.theatlantic.com/politics/archive/2015/09/color-blindness-is-counterproductive/405037/

07/03/2021

Coy, P

Trickle-Down Economics Fails a Sophisticated Statistical Test

Bloomberg

https://www.bloomberg.com/news/articles/2020-12-21/trickle-down-economics-fails-a-sophisticated-statistical-test

07/03/2021

Diamond, Jared M.

Guns, Germs, and Steel: The Fates of Human Societies

New York Norton

07/03/2021

McWhorter, J

Racism in America is over

Forbes

https://www.forbes.com/2008/12/30/end-of-racism-oped-cx_jm_1230mcwhorter.html?sh=59db389349f8

07/03/2021

Price, J

Racial Discrimination among NBA Referees

Quarterly Journal of Economics

http://users.nber.org/~jwolfers/papers/NBARace(QJE).pdf

15/12/2020

Sean Coughlan

Unconscious Bias training to be scrapped by ministers

BBC NEWS

https://www.bbc.co.uk/news/education-55309923

15/12/2020

OECD

A family affair: intergenerational social mobility across OECD countries

OECD, Economic Policy Reforms

https://www.oecd.org/centrodemexico/medios/44582910.pdf

15/12/2020

Kocher, S

These are the most popular jobs kids dream of doing when they grow up

SWNS digital

https://www.swnsdigital.com/2019/12/these-are-the-most-popular-jobs-kids-dream-of-doing-when-they-grow-up/

15/12/2020

Luscombe, B

Kids Believe Gender Stereotypes by Age 10, Global Study Finds

TIME

https://time.com/4948607/gender-stereotypes-roles/

08/03/2021

Fawcett Equality

FAWCETT RESEARCH SHOWS EXPOSURE TO GENDER STEREOTYPES AS A CHILD CAUSES HARM IN LATER LIFE

https://www.fawcettsociety.org.uk/news/fawcett-research-exposure-gender-stereotypes-child-causes-harm-later-life

07/03/2021

BBC

Brexit 'major influence' in racism and hate crime rise

https://www.bbc.co.uk/news/uk-wales-48692863

07/03/2021

Financial Fair Play – What do Football Clubs and Investment Clubs Have in Common?

Morris, S

Banks braced as pandemic poses biggest test since financial crisis

Financial Times

https://www.ft.com/content/b0b241d9-7c94-4b91-b727-d39245005d07

19/12/2020

Smith, J

The leverage ratio: a balance between risk and safety

Bank Underground

https://bankunderground.co.uk/2020/10/06/the-leverage-ratio-a-balance-between-risk-and-safety/#more-7231

19/12/2020

Breinlich, H

The Brexit Vote, Inflation and UK Living Standards

LSE

https://personal.lse.ac.uk/sampsont/XRatePrices.pdf

20/12/2020

Campos, N

Foreign investment expected to fall 37% post-Brexit

UCL

https://www.ucl.ac.uk/news/headlines/2020/oct/foreign-investment-expected-fall-37-post-brexit

20/12/2020

Chu, B

How does this coronavirus fiscal package compare to the bank bailouts of 2008?

The Independent

https://www.independent.co.uk/news/business/analysis-and-features/coronavirus-bailout-business-banks-rishi-sunak-financial-crisis-covid-19-a9407691.html

13/03/21

Gough, O

The ten biggest business blunders you can learn from

Growth Business.co.uk

https://www.growthbusiness.co.uk/ten-biggest-business-blunders-learn-2552940/

13/03/21

Widdicombe, L

The rise and fall of WeWork

The New yorker

https://www.newyorker.com/culture/culture-desk/the-rise-and-fall-of-wework

13/03/2021

BBC

WeWork: The rise and fall of co-founder Adam Neumann

September 2019

https://www.bbc.co.uk/news/business-49817037

13/03/2021

Magic money trees

United Nations

NationalAccounts – Analysis of Main Aggregates

https://unstats.un.org/UNSD/snaama/Index

https://worldpopulationreview.com/countries/countries-by-national-debt

27/12/2020

    The Money Charity

The Money Statistics December 2020

https://themoneycharity.org.uk/money-statistics/#:~:text=UK%20Personal%20Debt&text=This%20is%20up%20by%20%C2%A3,around%20109.1%25%20of%20average%20earnings.

27/12/2020

    Matthew Keep

Government borrowing, debt and debt interest: statistics

Commons Library

https://commonslibrary.parliament.uk/research-briefings/sn05745/

27/12/2020

    Martin Wolf

Restoring UK growth is more urgent than cutting public debt

Financial Times

https://www.ft.com/content/50394d54-1b2e-417b-ba6d-2204a4b05f24

27/12/2020

    Matthew Johnston

Worst Cases of Hyperinflation in History

Investopedia

https://www.investopedia.com/articles/personal-finance/122915/worst-hyperinflations-history.asp

27/12/2020

    Alan Greenspan

The Map and the Territory 2.0

Penguin Books

27/12/2020

    The Economist

The Horrible Housing Blunder

January 2020

27/12/2020

    Lewis, J

Houses are assets not goods: What the difference between bulbs and flowers tells us about the housing market

Bank Underground Blog

https://bankunderground.co.uk/2019/09/05/houses-are-assets-not-goods:-what-the-difference-between-bulbs-and-flowers-tells-us-about-the-housing-market/

27/12/2020

    Panigrahi, L

There's more to house prices than interest rates

Bank Underground Blog

https://bankunderground.co.uk/2020/06/03/theres-more-to-house-prices-than-interest-rates/

27/12/2020

    Amadeo, K

U.S. Federal Budget Breakdown

The Balance

https://www.thebalance.com/u-s-federal-budget-breakdown-3305789

21/05/21

    Hills, J

Thatcherism, New Labour and the Welfare State

LSE

http://eprints.lse.ac.uk/5553/1/Thatcherism_New_Labour_and_the_Welfare_State.pdf

21/05/21

   OBR

A Brief Guide to the Public Finances

https://obr.uk/forecasts-in-depth/brief-guides-and-explainers/public-finances/

21/05/21

   Fulya, F

AN INTRODUCTION TO THE SWEDISH WELFARE STATE

https://ticaret.edu.tr/uploads/kutuphane/dergi/s7/M00094.pdf

21/05/21

   Statista

Average number of holidays taken abroad or domestically per person in the United Kingdom (UK) from 2011 to 2019

https://www.statista.com/statistics/480188/average-number-of-holidays-per-person-in-the-uk/#:~:text=In%20the%20United%20Kingdom%20people,vacations%20at%20home%20and%20abroad.

21/05/21

   Handscombe, K

Caught in a (Covid) trap

Resolution Foundation

https://www.resolutionfoundation.org/app/uploads/2020/11/Caught-in-a-Covid-trap.pdf

21/05/21

Now what?

European Parliamentary Research Service

Polarisation and the news media in Europe

https://reutersinstitute.politics.ox.ac.uk/our-research/polarisation-and-news-media-europe

28/12/2020

De-Wit, L

Are social media driving political polarization?

Greater Good Magazine

https://greatergood.berkeley.edu/article/item/is_social_media_driving_political_polarization

28/12/2020

Hagemann, S

Government Decision records from the Council of the European Union 1999-2016, dataset v. March 2016.

LSE

28/12/2020

Hix, S

Britons among least knowledgeable about European Union

UK in a changing Europe

https://ukandeu.ac.uk/britons-among-least-knowledgeable-about-european-union/

28/12/2020

Institute for Government

Brexit Dividend

https://www.instituteforgovernment.org.uk/explainers/brexit-dividend

31/12/2020

ONS

Gross Domestic Product, Q3 2020

https://www.ons.gov.uk/economy/grossdomesticproductgdp

31/12/2020

King's College London

Public wrong on key facts around Brexit and impact of EU membership

https://www.kcl.ac.uk/news/public-wrong-on-key-facts-around-brexit-and-impact-of-eu-membership

31/12/2020

Reality Check

Reality Check: Has immigration held down wages?

BBC

https://www.bbc.co.uk/news/business-46918729

31/12/2020

Breinlich, H

The Brexit Vote, Inflation and UK Living Standards

LSE

https://personal.lse.ac.uk/sampsont/XRatePrices.pdf

31/12/2020

John Hopkins University

MORTALITY ANALYSES

https://coronavirus.jhu.edu/data/mortality

31/12/2020

FT

Coronavirus could kill off populism

https://www.ft.com/content/3bcf2b5e-e5f1-48e4-bb15-cd29615a9198

31/12/20

Sehran, J

The Pandemic Isn't a Death Knell for Populism

The Atlantic

https://www.theatlantic.com/international/archive/2020/08/populism-will-survive-the-pandemic/615358/

Bibliography

31/12/20820

Casey, B

Covid-19: Is there a trade-off between economic damage and loss of life?

LSE

https://blogs.lse.ac.uk/europpblog/2020/12/18/covid-19-is-there-a-trade-off-between-economic-damage-and-loss-of-life/

31/12/2020

VoxEU

VoxEU & CEPR Coverage of the Covid-19 Global Pandemic

https://voxeu.org/

31/12/2020

FullFact

The number of people dying right now is not the same as in any other year

https://fullfact.org/health/coronavirus-figures-talk-radio/

31/12/2020

Manuel, E

Cloudy with a chance of tariffs: the impact of policy uncertainty on the global economy

Bank Underground

https://bankunderground.co.uk

31/12/2020

Printed in Great Britain
by Amazon

70085488R00168